D1709810

Morandi's Last Prophecy and the End of Renaissance Politics

Morandi's Last Prophecy and the End of Renaissance Politics

Brendan Dooley

PRINCETON UNIVERSITY PRESS

PRINCETON AND OXFORD

COPYRIGHT © 2002 BY PRINCETON UNIVERSITY PRESS

PUBLISHED BY PRINCETON UNIVERSITY PRESS, 41 WILLIAM STREET,
PRINCETON, NEW JERSEY 08540
IN THE UNITED KINGDOM: PRINCETON UNIVERSITY PRESS,
3 MARKET PLACE, WOODSTOCK, OXFORDSHIRE OX20 1SY

ALL RIGHTS RESERVED

LIBRARY OF CONGRESS CATALOGING-IN-PUBLICATION DATA

DOOLEY, BRENDAN MAURICE, 1953–
MORANDI'S LAST PROPHECY AND THE END OF RENAISSANCE
POLITICS / BRENDAN DOOLEY.
P. CM.
INCLUDES BIBLIOGRAPHICAL REFERENCES AND INDEX.
ISBN 0-691-04864-9 (CLOTH : ALK. PAPER)
1. MORANDI, ORAZIO, D. 1630. 2. ASTROLOGERS—ITALY—BIOGRAPHY.
3. ASTROLOGY—HISTORY—17TH CENTURY. 4. EUROPE—INTELLECTUAL
LIFE—17TH CENTURY. I. TITLE.
BF1679.8.M59 D66 2002
133.5′0945′63209032—DC21 2001045848

THIS BOOK HAS BEEN COMPOSED IN SABON

PRINTED ON ACID-FREE PAPER. ∞

WWW.PUP.PRINCETON.EDU

PRINTED IN THE UNITED STATES OF AMERICA

1 3 5 7 9 10 8 6 4 2

"Me, poor man, my library was dukedom large enough."
—Shakespeare, *The Tempest*, I, ii, 109–10

"Nihil utilius in vita comperiet quisquam quam noscere ordinem et finem sui status."
—Barthélmy de Chassoneux, *Catalogus gloriae mundi* (1529)

CONTENTS

ILLUSTRATIONS

PROLOGUE

IT WAS THE AGE of Galileo. Pioneers of knowledge sought out new shores of thought. Turning their backs on much that had been said before about nature and humanity, they prepared themselves for what could be discovered. In going about their investigations, they promised to pay particular attention to evidence the eye could see and the hand could feel. And among the tools of their intellectual trade they included a formidable array of new instruments along with the traditional books, paper, and quill pens. The thinker's study was beginning to look more like an artisan's shop than a diplomat's quarters, the smoke of a furnace dulling the finish of the gleaming marble and the stench of live specimens overcoming the odor of polished wood. In the first decades of the seventeenth century, the voices proclaiming the new knowledge became a chorus. They belonged to figures whose names are now enshrined in the history of philosophy and science. Galileo in Italy was joined elsewhere by Francis Bacon and William Harvey. As far as existing patterns of thought were concerned, their innovations all added up to the same thing: an attack on the intellectual establishment.

No wonder the new knowledge encountered fierce resistance. Those who did not abide by its precepts or accept its methods could only regard it as a threat. Those with the greatest investment in traditional ways fought to keep it in check. Galileo himself said schools stood to lose their enrollments, professors stood to lose their jobs. And the history of this century-long "revolution" in thought is marked as much by defeats as by victories, by checks as by advances. Indeed, the implications of the attack on the intellectual establishment went far beyond the scientific ideas that have become its most memorable features. More was at issue than just questions about the movement of the earth or the circulation of the blood. There was also the problem of the relation between knowledge and religious faith. In certain quarters, philosophers who dared to debate any points where faith was concerned might suffer the fate of Giordano Bruno, burned at the stake in 1600.

The consequences of the battle between the old knowledge and the new affected ideas about power as well as ideas about nature; states as well as schools. Tommaso Campanella developed his theories about nature into a compelling vision of a democratic society. At the opposite end of Europe decades later, Thomas Hobbes sought to refound government according to the precepts of natural law. Patrons in conspicuous positions of authority could not help but take notice of the dangers, as well as the uses, of such thinking.

However, the new knowledge of the seventeenth century had more to contend with than the culture of the schools and the suspicions of governments and the Church. An equally insidious challenge came from deep within its own ranks. Many of those who shared its precepts also followed other ways of thought regarded as no less dangerous in official circles. Its own adepts, along with many educated people of the time, continued to pay heed to the powerful allure of Renaissance occult philosophy. A few of them still regarded alchemy, cabala, and astrology as legitimate ways of exploring the fundamental connections between the earthly and the heavenly, between the microcosm of human experience and the macrocosm of the celestial spheres. When they undertook investigations into the realms of the occult, especially astrology, they did so with the same seriousness as when they investigated any other realm.

What is more, no knowledge, however specialized, however innovative, exists in a vacuum. The Age of Galileo coincided with the Thirty Years War and the rise of modern states. And the new ideas of the seventeenth century were immersed in the context of the violent power struggles of a society battling against itself, crisscrossed by political as well as status differences. Nor were the persons whom we are about to meet merely disembodied minds. They were made of flesh and blood. Like their contemporaries in other walks of life, they too were driven by hunger for esteem, desire for control, and fear of failure. They too bartered their ideas in return for the social capital they desired, in order to lead the lives they thought they deserved.

In Italy, the fortunes of the new knowledge hung on the ambitions of one man, whom the spectacular episode of Galileo's trial and condemnation has almost erased from memory. That man was Orazio Morandi. This is his story.

Morandi's Last Prophecy and the End of Renaissance Politics

INTRODUCTION

OF MEDIUM HEIGHT, perhaps fifty-five years old. Nut-brown beard, with flecks of white. Dressed in a simple monk's robe with a black hood over the head." The corpse that lay across a straw mat in a small cell of the Tor di Nona prison in Rome was nothing special. Nor was the manner of death, if we are to trust in the candor of the physician writing the death certificate. "I do not suspect nor do I see signs of poisoning," he protested, perhaps too emphatically.[1] No, he continued, Orazio Morandi died of a simple malignant fever of unknown origin, which began twelve days before. Fra Michelangelo Soderini confirmed the doctor's opinion. "I know he died a natural death," he specifies, "because I always assisted him while he was in solitary confinement and during the whole time of his illness, of which he died at around twelve hours of the clock today"—November 7, 1630.

The Roman rumor mill was not quite so prudent. "It is believed without a doubt that [Morandi] was killed by poison administered through his food," Giacinto Gigli, a historian, wrote in his diary.[2] At least among those who paid attention to city gossip, Orazio Morandi, the abbot of Santa Prassede, one-time general of the Vallombrosa Order, was a victim of foul play. A quick dispatch of the suspect had obviously been ordered to protect the honor of the high officials in Rome, more and more of whose names had begun to come up during the trial proceedings because of their connections with what went on at the monastery. It was not the first time a judicious cover-up had taken the form of a murder. Nor, in the violent world of seventeenth-century Italian politics, would it be the last.

For Morandi's fellow Romans, once the initial suspicions about papal mischief hardened into convictions, the moral of the story had to do with the ignominious end of one who had risen so high. And indeed, only four months before, Morandi was the most honored astrologer in town. Galileo Galilei and members of the Roman aristocracy attended his elegant soirées. Among the visitors to his library were the greatest cultural figures in Rome, from Gian Lorenzo Bernini to Cassiano Dal Pozzo, and the highest prelates in the ecclesiastical hierarchy—including the cardinals sitting on the Congregation of the Index of Forbidden Books. To many of these Morandi offered advice on astrology and other aspects of the occult, which they gratefully acknowledged in the form of protection and favors. And his renown reached outside of Rome to wherever his vast correspondence carried his counsels and opinions to legions of admirers. If anyone in Rome was safe from the vicissitudes of fortune, it should have been Morandi.

Then in May 1630, Morandi delivered what he evidently intended to be his masterstroke, the gesture that would win him a place in modern history: a prediction about Pope Urban VIII's imminent death due to the nefarious influence of a solar eclipse on the pope's horoscope. But the effect was far different from Morandi's intention. In the rumor-saturated world of early modern Europe, the prediction rapidly slid out of its author's control. It was quickly taken up by the writers of the clandestine manuscript newsletters, who peddled their malicious gossip throughout the Roman streets and squares. News of it reached as far as Spain, urging the Spanish cardinals to rush to Rome to be on hand for what they and everyone else believed would be the next conclave. In France, it excited the curiosity of none other than Cardinal Richelieu. All for nothing. The prescribed date passed; the pope lived on. No conclave was held, and speculation about Urban's successor, at least for now, ground to a halt.

Urban VIII's reaction was predictable. Political astrology has always been risky, even in ages when astrology was a dominant intellectual category. The Roman emperors in antiquity forbade predictions about themselves. In Morandi's time, so did most rulers. The popes, concerned as much with their own vulnerability as with the theological implications, condemned all sorts of judicial astrology without exception. So Urban was fully within the law when he personally ordered Morandi to be brought into custody. When evidence of other activities at the monastery came to light, these were merely added to a list that was to include astrology along with the circulation of prohibited books and political chicanery among the heinous crimes for which the pope ordered the governor of Rome to seek a condemnation.

The consequences of the case were enormous. Astrology itself was hurt by the growing impression that predictions were mere merchandise in the game of political and social favors. Soon after the trial, Urban VIII came out with some of the severest anti-astrology legislation ever written. And this legislation, as well as Morandi's crimes, deeply affected the outcome of the Galileo affair, which began the following year. For this alone, Morandi deserves more than an antiquary's footnote in the annals of scientific curiosities. But his real importance lies elsewhere.

For contemporaries, the death and the definitive official explanation effectively put an end to the story, at least so far as it regarded Morandi himself. For us, the story has just begun. Why would a man of Morandi's intelligence put at risk the distinguished position he had striven for a lifetime to attain? What in the Roman environment convinced him he could get away with it? And how, in the end, could he have been so tragically deceived? The mystery of Morandi concerns the basic compulsions of advancement in a status-drenched society, and the very nature of knowledge at the origins of science.

Part of the answer lies buried in the documents before us. We are in the State Archives in Rome, along bustling Corso del Rinascimento in the center of the city, where government records are kept, as distinguished from the ecclesiastical records across the river at the Vatican. By a stroke of luck, or, we might say, an exceptional moment of premodern bureaucratic efficiency, Morandi's trial record, all 2,800 pages of it, has been preserved here. Urban took the unusual step of ordering all the imputations in the trial, political and criminal as well as theological, to be tried under a single trial judge rather than divided between the governor's court and the Inquisition. For this reason, at the time of writing, the records that are the basis of this book were in the public archive instead of hidden away, along with many other equally interesting documents, behind ecclesiastical discretion.

Surprisingly informative about some aspects of his life, the documents seem strangely mute about others. We know what Morandi read, who his friends were, how he spent much of his time. But what were his thoughts, his desires, his passions—who, indeed, was Morandi? This book responds by recounting the story of one man's search for esteem, revealing the dark secret concealed behind the monastery walls.

Several months in Morandi's life stand out in sharp relief: those leading up to the trial and during the trial itself. The rest of the months, years, decades, fade off into more or less obscurity. How far back must we go to discover the springs of his desire? How much information can we urge forth without asking leading questions, without organizing the inquiry so as to produce a spurious result, without torturing the subject into giving up a false confession? Simplicity is the enemy of accuracy, we can imagine the Baroque lawyers whispering in our ears. While we must surely take care to separate fact from opinion, we are as much concerned with what the principals in our case said and thought as with what actually happened.[3]

Our attentions as modern-day investigators are focused less on a physical person than on a tiny sampling of material from Morandi's life. A probate inventory, a library catalogue, a book of secrets, a collection of horoscopes, a scrap of poetry, a suspect's defense. These are the elements from which Morandi's accusers sought to build their case. From the same elements we must build our own. Each one leads out in new directions, beyond the courtroom, beyond the criminal, beyond the crime. Possessions accumulated during a lifetime shed light on a person's behavior. They also illuminate a time when objects tied individuals to their reality in a way no longer possible in our own commodity-filled, disposable environment. Books, about which notices are scattered thickly through our evidence, tell much about the bibliophile; they also tell about a world in which books were points of contact between one person and another, between societies and their cultures. And secrets, sharing the heart of our story along with prophecies, express the wishes of the seeker; they also express the longings, the aspirations, and at times the fears and loathings of an entire neighborhood, an entire community. The resonance of Morandi's story reaches the farthest corners of the civilization of his time, and our own.

As the story ventures out along these forgotten byways, the period and place seem more and more remote. Astrology here is not simply an intellectual curiosity; it is present in varying degrees nearly everywhere we look.[4] It is only one of many traditional cultural patterns that seem to exist side by side with revolutionary ones. Thinkers of every sort—innovative and not—partake of an atmosphere of libertinism and free thinking that is impossible to dispel. And if the monarchs of Rome, or anywhere else, with all their new mechanisms of surveillance and control, never manage either to destroy the old culture or hasten the advent of the new, perhaps their authority is not as absolute as we once thought.[5]

And yet, some aspects of Morandi's world seem uncomfortably familiar. We should not be too surprised that even Galileo, the precursor of modern science, occasionally believed what he could not prove—and not just concerning the influence of the planets, the corpuscular theory of matter, and the origin of meteors. Nor should we be too surprised that many of his followers accepted his postulates on faith alone. After all, modern researchers on complex projects involving, say, cosmology and nuclear physics, or even history and anthropology, occasionally accept the affirmations of their colleagues in other specializations without testing for reliability.[6] Perhaps blind belief and reasonable persuasion can occasionally coexist. Whether science be science or pseudoscience surely makes a difference, especially in matters of life and death. But the attitude of mind of those who put their faith in a scientific discipline beyond their comprehension might not always be so far removed as we would like to think from that of those who believe in forms of knowledge unapproved by the laboratory or by academe. We must imagine that the physicians who abandon the postulates of their training to recommend homeopathy or acupuncture or Zen meditation are just the more newsworthy examples. Our protagonist is not the only one whose mentality is attuned to myth in an age more and more preoccupied with facts.[7]

Real or imaginary, the natural knowledge bought and sold by our astrologers contributed to a market, a new set of commodities, that was to have a decisive influence on science. Astrology, along with the other branches of the occult, not only contributed to science a fascination for nature.[8] It also contributed an entrepreneurial point of view.[9] In the new environment, preeminence in astrology belonged to the successful bearer of a spectacular prediction. Similarly, natural philosophers competed for the attention of powerful patrons and their reading audiences by spectacular performances, like Galileo's discovery of the moons of Jupiter for the Medici dukes.[10] However, the transformation of astrology into an exclusively commercial enterprise eventually had the opposite effect. The competition of disciplines that could deliver more certainty, perhaps for less expense, helped finally to resolve the centuries-long debate about its credibility. By then, the marginalization of astrological knowledge from the mainstream of intellectual life was only a matter of time. Morandi, relentless in his search for new experiences and new advancement strategies, was the last great Roman astrologer of a dying age.

ONE

CRIME AND MEMORY

INTERROGATOR: Have you anything to add to your previous testimony?
BENIGNO BRACCIOLINI: Having considered the question put to me at other times, I now remember, indeed, I have resolved to tell Your Lordships the truth about everything I know happened in the monastery after the incarceration of our Father Abbot. (*Morandi Trial*, fol. 409r, October 1, 1630)

THE COVER-UP WAS over. There was no choice but to give in. Urged into a penitent frame of mind by the offer of immunity from prosecution, Benigno Bracciolini, sacristan at the convent of Santa Prassede, began his richly detailed narrative of the desperate last-minute measures taken by the monks at around ten P.M. on July 13, 1630, some eight weeks before, to save the monastery from an indictment ordered personally by Urban VIII.[1]

"On the evening when our Father Abbot was led off to prison," Bracciolini went on, "Alessandro, his servant, having returned to the convent at around three hours of the night, Padre Leonardo and I met with the Prior General in the cloister. The Prior told us it would be well to remove all the books and writings that were in the armoire of the library." It was a dangerous calculation, Bracciolini knew well. But the certain consequences of breaking a police seal were less fearsome than the possible consequences of the various other forbidden activities the monks had long engaged in, should evidence ever reach the judge. For there was no telling what some legal mind close to the Church might conclude from the books and papers in Orazio Morandi's famous armoire, attesting to prohibited readings, astrological predictions, political discussion, and much else besides.

So taking care not to awaken the entire monastery, Bracciolini and the others, along with the monastery's cook, one Lupido Rossi, waited tensely in the cloister while Matteo Maiani, servant to Francesco Ripa, the prior general, dashed silently down a corridor with Alessandro Del Vicario into the rooms of Giovanni Ambrogio Maggi to retrieve the key to a secret library entrance. They found Maggi wide awake, despite the late hour, and ready to collaborate in the enterprise at least to the extent of untucking the key from the hosiery hanging on a peg by his bed. The two servants, one of them holding the key, joined the other four men in the cloister; then they all crowded into Ripa's room, unlocked and slid up the folding door, and scrambled into the library.

What followed was an amateur performance through and through. Leonardo Neri wrestled for several precious moments with the police seal on the armoire before someone finally produced a hammer and began pounding away. Meanwhile, Bracciolini went looking in Neri's room for something in which to place the incriminating material. There he located a half-filled trunk, which he promptly emptied of the linens it contained and carried back into the library. But when the monks finally broke the seal and pried open the door of the armoire, they realized that the quantity of material there was far greater than they had anticipated. So goes Bracciolini's account:

> We took printed books and manuscripts and other writings from the said armoire and put them in the said trunk. Since there were still more books and writings, I went into my room to find a needle and thread, and I sewed two corners of a bed sheet together to make a sack with an opening on one side. I took that sheet, sewn in that manner, into the library. The cook brought a grain sack, and we put the rest of the books and writings from the armoire into the said sack and sheet. Then we dragged everything into the sacristy.

Piled in a corner of the sacristy, the material was safe at least for now; and nothing more could be done that night.

Hours after his arrest, Morandi was called for the first time before the governor's court to answer questions about his activities put to him by Antonio Fido and his assistant Pietro Paolo Febeo. The court could scarcely have found a more compliant suspect—or so Morandi appeared. After expressing due ignorance about the purpose of the encounter, he sought to gratify his questioners by admitting every point. "Yes indeed," he affirmed, certain manuscripts and papers had been found among his possessions at the monastery. And yes indeed, they included nativities of Urban VIII, along with Cardinals Sant'Onofrio, Magalotti, and Francesco Barberini. "There were more," he added; and if his questioners wished, he might even recollect whose they were. Asked where he got such a wealth of astrological materials, he seemed amazed. Surely, his questioners knew that material of the sort was everywhere available—in Rome and in any other city. Urban VIII's nativity, for instance, he had found many years ago in Florence, where "it is very easy to find such things."[2] The same went for the cabalistic writings composed by Domenico the Arab. But he was perfectly content to sign each fascicle they showed him, certifying that he had seen the papers and recognized them as identical to some that had been in his possession.

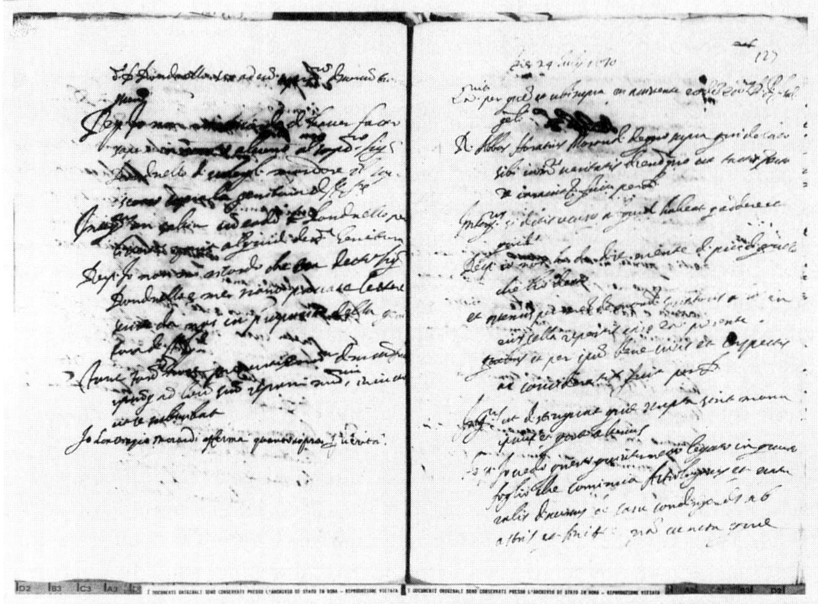

Figure 1. A page from the testimony of Orazio Morandi. (Rome, Archivio di Stato, *Governatore*, Processi, sec. XVII, b. 251.)

At this point the judge and his assistant pulled out a document they hoped would fluster the suspect into giving out an inadvertent admission of guilt: a letter, dated Lyons, February 21, 1630, ostensibly containing the incriminating prophecies about Urban VIII. To their surprise, even faced with this jarring testimony, Morandi kept his composure. In fact, he was only too ready to acknowledge the letter as his own. As he spoke, he naturally took care to make clear to his questioners that they were dealing with a man whose high connections placed him beyond reach of their accusations. The letter, he explained, originated from a discussion between himself and Raffaele Visconti, an employee of the Holy Office in Rome, concerning Urban's nativity.

Next, describing the letter's contents, Morandi not only took full responsibility for the ideas expressed. He also flaunted a little of his astrological knowledge, as though to remind his questioners that they were dealing with a man whose high expertise placed him beyond the reach of their understanding. So, he went on, when he and Visconti got around to identifying the apheta or life-giving point in the nativity, they considered Ptolemy's opinion that this point was usually in the ninth house. If such was the case here, and the sun, present in the ninth house, was the apheta, they reasoned, given the other planetary positions in the nativity, Urban could be in trouble. Yet, Morandi went on, "we began to think that the sun was not indeed the apheta," so sorely beset was it by a quadrate with the moon and with Mars. Urban was safe, they had agreed. Obviously, the prophecy they made on that occasion could not have been the one that caused so much scandal. The letter from Lyons, drafted by Visconti, who "added some of his own ideas," basically contained the substance of the conversations between the two men; and Morandi admitted to having copied the final version himself.[3] The contents of the letter as well as the elegant tiny handwriting, by now familiar to the court, backed up his claim.

Two nights in jail sufficed to jog Morandi's memory. Present at the discussions of the Lyons letter, he now recalled, were not only Visconti but also Monsignor Francesco Usimbardi, a prelate in the Apostolic Chamber, as well as a nobleman named Vitellio Malaspina and Francesco Maria Merlini, later bishop of Cervia. Six more days of reflection (and five nights in jail) brought up more details. To his earlier statement, Morandi joined the recollection that he had not just drawn up the letter with Visconti. He had read it to the other members of the Santa Prassede community, and perhaps even sent it along with other correspondence to some of his more distant friends and acquaintances. That the letter in the court's possession was the same and only one that he had allowed to circulate in this fashion, he left no doubt.

However, as interrogations continued concerning the letter from Lyons, officials of the court encountered their first contradiction. For Morandi's claim to authorship did not go uncontested. When they questioned Visconti, he too clearly recalled the discussions in Morandi's chambers. What engaged his curiosity then, Visconti said, was Ptolemy's theory that the duration of life was to be measured in terms of the degrees of longitude between the apheta and the anaretic or death-giving point. In Urban's case, the ninth house was occupied by the sun and the death-giving point appeared to be Saturn in the eighth house. As a result, he too claimed to have written a letter dated from Lyons, which had been copied in a fine hand by Morandi. "In it," he explained, "I conclude that whereas the present direction could not bring any danger to Urban's life, nonetheless there might be a danger in the year 1643 or 1644—if I recall correctly."[4] His and only his was the Lyons letter shown to him by the court. That it seemed to reply to an earlier, perhaps more dire prediction ("I am aware of Your Lordship's letter, and of your anxiety to receive my immediate response," it began) seemed to corroborate his claim.[5] The questioners were forced to conclude that either Visconti was exaggerating his role in the letter, and Morandi was innocent, or else there were two letters—of which one, still undisclosed, contained the death prediction of 1630.

Further interrogation seemed to suggest that at least among the members of the library circle, the 1630 prediction was never really taken seriously. So claimed Gherardo Gherardi, a visiting professor from Padua, in portraying himself as a steadfast proponent of the view that present circumstances gave no cause for alarm.[6] Francesco Lamponi went even further, tracing his own partisanship for the more optimistic analysis of Urban VIII's future prospects back to the last illness of the previous pope, Gregory XV. Having correctly picked Urban as Gregory's successor at that time, later, during Urban's first illness as pope, he provided Cardinal Desiderio Scaglia and the pope's auditor, Raimondi, with still more insights. To them he unhesitatingly conveyed the same happy news of the pope's longevity that he had continued to impart to his friends at Santa Prassede. There might be some cause for alarm in the year 1640, he had said; but he had always joined to such assertions, so he assured the court, the caveat that "everything is in God's hands."[7]

Without the proper evidence, the court could make an indictment and begin questioning only at the risk of invalidating its own proceedings. Such scrupulousness was essential, explained Prospero Farinacci in one of the most authoritative legal manuals of the time. Otherwise, "an evil judge might think he can go around interrogating any person without the slightest pretext."[8] Particular solicitude, moreover, was to be observed when ecclesiastics were involved, the manual warned. In such cases, "proceedings must be carefully tempered and arrests undertaken with greater deliberation than against lay persons." After all, "religious and clerics are naturally presumed to be good."[9] Fortunately in this case, the evidence accumulated at the scene of the crime was just enough to suggest that at times ecclesiastics might also be bad.

The rest was up to the interrogators to discover. And whether they were able to make some sense of the evidence thus gathered, and find enough other evidence to prove Morandi was indeed the author of the notorious predictions, with or without the collaboration of other suspects, depended on their mastery of contemporary interrogation techniques. Not that there was anything in these techniques that endless practice might not perfect. All that was required was that "the interrogation should be certain, specific and clear," noted our manual, "comprising all the qualities and circumstances of the crime."[10] But the procedures of the investigators were hedged around with so many conditions designed to preserve the dignity of the court and the rights of the suspect that one false move could spoil everything. "An obscure, general and uncertain interrogation is invalid," the manual went on. Instead, the suspect in a theft case, for instance, "must be asked, whether he committed a particular theft of a particular quantity from a particular person in a particular place." Should such precision be lacking, the suspect was unlikely to be able to prepare any sort of defense; and justice would be made a mockery.

With the case gradually unraveling before the very eyes of the judges, some observers in Rome began to think that Morandi might get off scot-free. As late as the seventeenth of August, one of Galileo's correspondents suggested that Morandi's best prospects lay in none other than "the good intentions and nature" of the pope himself, who "without very substantial reasons would not come to extraordinary resolutions against a person so qualified."[11] New information was needed to break down the witnesses, but finding persons in Rome who knew the facts and were also sufficiently detached from the case to provide dispassionate third-party accounts was not going to be easy.

The officials therefore resorted to the prisoners' fellow inmates awaiting trial on unrelated charges—an acceptable expedient, noted the author of our manual, "where the truth could not be found in any other way."[12] In one of their most important breaks in the case, on August 28, they heard from a certain Scipione Leoni, imprisoned for unnamed crimes, that Gherardo Gherardi had discussed defense strategies in the cell they shared. According to Leoni, Gherardi worried about what might happen should the court ever discover that his constant insistence on having viewed the pope as being out of danger was all a sham. In fact, he had concurred in the prophecy about Urban's imminent death. Now, only the most powerful patrons, Gherardi had said, could get him off; and so he requested Leoni, perhaps in a fit of jailhouse braggadocio, to "ask Monsignor Ciampoli," the high-level patron-bureaucrat whom Gherardi claimed as a friend, as well as the Venetian ambassador and the general of the Jesuits, "to intercede for him with Cardinal Barberini," the pope's nephew.[13] And Gherardi was not the only liar among the witnesses, at least according to a certain Francesco Valero, requested to testify in this case on September 17 while awaiting trial for falsification of documents. There was also Francesco Lamponi, a local astrologer who, Valero said, seemed "very happy" before the first interrogation but afterward seemed "all worried, and sat there two days without saying much."[14] Soon Lamponi began wondering out loud whether his letter promising the papacy to Cardinal Scaglia might eventually be discovered. "And after this, talking every day with us," that is, with Valero and two other prisoners in the cell, one on trial for breaking and entering and another for an unspecified crime, "he said that he was sure the papal see would be vacant this year and Urban VIII would die."

The circle was tightening, but nothing the officials did or said seemed sufficient to open up the black box of Morandi's guilt. Even the discovery and opening of a wooden box containing his recent correspondence at the monastery was not much help. The few letters inside from fawning admirers and minutes of his own replies, replete with the quaint salutation, "My dearest, as a brother," along with a few newsletters, seemed to attest to activities at the monastery that were as commonplace as ever, and, on the part of Morandi, conduct no different from that of dozens of other free-thinking monks in monasteries throughout Italy and abroad.[15]

In the slowly accumulating pile of documents, there was not even enough material to justify recourse to the last weapon in the arsenal of the early modern interrogator. According to contemporary practice, summarized once again by Farinacci, ecclesiastics could not be tortured unless there was evidence "beyond what is necessary" for incriminating lay persons—"weightier and more urgent" due to the extraordinary presumption of innocence that applied to them alone.[16] In order to submit Morandi's aging limbs to the tautness of rope and steel, perhaps crippling him for the rest of his life, far more convincing evidence would have to be found than was necessary to proceed against an ecclesiastic of lower rank.

In the course of interrogating another suspect on astrology-related charges, officials received their first notice of the massive cover-up operation at the monastery. On August 16, one Marco Tullio Modesti, a procurator and assessor of several taxes in the city of Rome, after having claimed that the nativities found in his house regarded only himself and his wife, remarked that he frequently browsed in the "Luna" bookstore in Piazza Pasquino and conversed with other customers. Among the many lawyers who frequented this rather specialized establishment, he recalled, was none other than the famous Fleming, Theodore Ameyden.[17] When the topic of Morandi came up during one such conversation, Ameyden had made a startling pronouncement: that the case was based on "pure vanities, because they found nothing." Explaining himself further, Ameyden had added, "The monks saw to this by burning all [Morandi's] writings." Just in case the court officials might be inclined to discount such third-party revelations, they heard a similar story the next day, in the course of interrogating the proprietor of the "Sole" bookshop in Piazza Navona. Ameyden had apparently been confabulating in that store too, and when the subject of Morandi came up, he had remarked again that "the monks had burned certain writings."[18]

Supposing Ameyden actually made such affirmations in the company of individuals with no interest in protecting either Morandi or the monastery, his motives seem somewhat difficult to assess. As the monastery's procurator, he could have been expected to extend more sympathy to the monks. But his sights evidently aimed higher than Santa Prassede and the civil causes he had taken so much time and trouble to defend for the previous twenty years. Certainly, in July 1630, his retainer from the monastery, his friendship with the monks, especially Morandi, and his association with their library must all at once have become a considerable inconvenience. Maintaining even a hint of his previous ties could damage his prospects for curial preferment just as surely as it could nullify his chances of carrying out his duties as advocate in the papal court on behalf of the Spanish monarchy. He may well have let his off-hand comment drop in a public place among educated people in a gossip-filled city in order to help the court officials drive their case to a conclusion. Perhaps he thought they could convict Morandi and the others on charges of concealing evidence, if nothing else, and put them all out of the way, at least for a time.

In any case, with verbal evidence of the cover-up now on record, the officials brought in the monks one by one. And for nearly a week, affection for Morandi combined with esprit de corps to sustain an adamant front against every accusation. At night, in the quiet of the prison, the monks conspired to make their stories agree. By day they did all they could to redirect the questioning away from astrology and toward less pertinent topics, such as the notorious venality of the jailers. What Padre Ambrogio Maggi said about never having touched any books or papers after Morandi's arrest was simply repeated, almost word for word, by fellow monks Alfredo Zuccagna and Ilario Falugi.[19] Recourse to the usual jailbird snitches would reveal nothing more.[20]

On August 19, the united front began to crumble. The monks' feverish efforts to conceal the monastery's recent past were doomed to failure anyway. Reluctant to add false testimony to the imputations already laid to their account, they accepted the court's invitation to pursue greater accuracy in their subsequent statements in return for immunity from prosecution; and Bracciolini's narrative permitted the court officials to accumulate a rich body of evidence.

The result was an indictment not just of Morandi and the monastery, and not just of the Roman society that over the years had so powerfully resisted any central ecclesiastical control. It was an indictment against a cultural and intellectual style comprising many strands that the late Renaissance had woven together, and not just in Rome, but in every cultural center on the peninsula and beyond. Now, as a result of Urban VIII's campaign to save the appearances of unity and his own reputation, all those strands of cultural and intellectual life would break apart. The narrative of how all this came about is as much a story of Morandi as it is of modern Europe as a whole. But first, let us follow the story of Morandi.

TWO

THE ROAD TO VALLOMBROSA

I, don Orazio Morandi, affirm that the present account is true.
(*Morandi Trial*, fol. 110v, July 15, 1630)

HOW COULD SUCH a man fall so precipitously? What made him commit the crime that plunged him into infamy? In some ways, the official inquiry coincides with our own. From the same evidence, we are seeking clues to the motives that could drive a seventeenth-century churchman beyond the limits of legality in pursuit of that elusive prize, esteem. And the quest begins at the monastery of Santa Prassede.

The morning after Morandi's arrest, court officials returned here to gather evidence for the case. Just past the Romanesque portal facing Via San Martino, a quiet street around the corner from Santa Maria Maggiore in the busy eastern quarters of Rome, they would have crossed the courtyard and entered the personal chambers reserved for Morandi and his closest intimates. According to the Benedictine custom, the abbot's chambers might be fitted out in a manner reflecting his own eminence and that of his special guests.[1] Attached to two or three rooms for living and studying, the rule suggested, there might be a private dining room provisioned by the main kitchen but affording a kind of privacy and discretion that the larger refectory did not.

As they surveyed the scene, officials might well have been struck by the fineness of the furnishings.[2] Circling the rooms were beautiful pieces of cabinetry: walnut sideboards, an inlaid desk with a cover framed in sapwood and another with a writing surface in ebony. Upon the latter were desk instruments of high quality: a silver ink stand and other matching implements. In the center of one of the rooms stood a stately bed with a high white lacework canopy and curtains in nine pieces. In its vicinity stood a sculpted bedwarmer, and at its foot a strongbox upholstered in leather. On the floors lay one large oriental carpet and two smaller ones. Every free space on the walls was taken up with artwork. No fewer than twenty-three paintings in various sizes—the probate inventory does not indicate of what subjects—stared out from frames carved in buffalo horn and other materials. Five terra-cotta relief busts of assorted heroes in the round imparted a classical flavor. The camelhair great-coat and leather cape draped across one of the chairs were perfectly at home in these surroundings.

What sort of man lives here? We cannot deduce much from the bold bronze crucifix that graced the bedroom wall, where there were also affixed nine small effigies of cherubs in embossed copper. In one corner stood a small portable altar. But most of the ecclesiastical effects—a rich collection of chasubles and copes for every occasion, silver chalices, a reliquary, and the like—were kept in the vestry of the chapel. Indeed, Morandi's rooms were as striking for what they did not contain as for what they did. Anyone knowing Morandi's reputation as an expert on the occult might be disappointed not to find a clutter of armillary spheres, telescopes, alembics, tubes, burners, and other paraphernalia, and perhaps a few natural specimens, partly stored on those space-saving wrap-around shelving systems positioned high up the wall in Carpaccio's drawing, now in the British Museum, of a Renaissance magus. Instead, Morandi's rooms conveyed an impression of serious this-worldly officiousness. Letters and manuscripts of various sorts overflowed from a box in a corner of the study, and in-folio volumes stood in random stacks. A mechanical clock ticked away somewhere; and a large hourglass rested on one of the pieces of furniture—an outmoded object more for decoration than for use.

Straining for clues that might reveal Morandi's guilt, court officials could hardly escape the conclusion: these were not just the rooms of an ecclesiastic. They were not even the rooms of an astrologer, at least according to the impression Morandi evidently wished to convey. Nor were they the rooms of a vulgar craftsman. These were the rooms of a man of influence, taste, and wisdom. Here indeed was a place where cardinals, papal officials, and ambassadors might come for consultation and even instruction. And on one wall of the study there hung the reminders of Morandi's high connections: four large bronze medallions depicting members of the Medici family.

Let us beware. No doubt, the path that led to these rooms and to the life they contained was far less deliberately planned than might have been suggested by the carefully cultivated elegance of the accoutrements. It began with ambitions for social advancement and a successful career, and it ended with a long ascent up the ecclesiastical hierarchy. Morandi the abbot of Santa Prassede, one-time general of the Vallombrosa order, was once Morandi the novice Benedictine, Morandi the scholar, and, still earlier, Morandi the callow youth. The discovery of how all these various versions of himself evolved forms the obligatory prelude for understanding why he came to be what he was. The youth possesses the indispensable key for unlocking the secrets of the adult and revealing the reasons for what became of him in the end.[3]

But tracing Morandi the callow youth to somewhere among the minor ranks of the Roman patriciate where he originated is no easy task.[4] Before

Orazio, or, to pronounce his name before religious orders, Bernardino, the family's presence in Rome was distinctly low in profile. There is no way of telling even whether the Alessandro Morandi, born in 1580, who died at age seventeen on the verge of marrying a Neapolitan woman, was Morandi's brother, or if the Marcantonio Morandi, born in 1585, who served as notary to the Holy See and personal auditor of Cardinal Alessandro Orsini, was Morandi's cousin.[5] Of his father Ludovico, in all likelihood a secretary or courtier in the retinue of one or another of the many cardinals and Roman patricians' houses, not a single trace has remained. Apparently, after Morandi arrived to prominence from relatively obscure origins, the family once more sank into oblivion. The only later Morandi recorded among the inscriptions of Rome was a certain poor priest, one Gelasius, who placed a stone in the church of Saints Vincenzo and Anastasio at Trevi in 1694, a few years before death.[6]

What is known is that like many Roman families with roots in ecclesiastical bureaucracy, the Morandi came from elsewhere. And in 1616, the Bergamo branch of the family, headed by one Giovanni Maria, still possessed a considerable enough property in this part of the Venetian subject territories for Orazio to extend a welcome there to his then patron, Giovanni de' Medici.[7] Indeed, to this branch of the family may have belonged a certain Morando Morandi of the Vallombrosa monastery of Astino in Bergamasque territory, who was briefly imprisoned during the Interdict controversy of 1607 between Rome and Venice. Morando had become part of the controversy itself when he helped attach Pope Paul V's bull against Venice to the doors of the monastery, prohibiting the exercise of the sacraments all over the Republic.[8] So Orazio's penchant for defiant gestures had deep roots. And if Orazio's father belonged to the poorer branch of an aristocratic family whose grandiose palazzo still graces the central square of Bergamo, he may well have traveled to Rome from the family seat to gain preferment. The poet Torquato Tasso, of a Bergamasque family transferred to Sorrento and then to Rome, had done the same thing many years later.

For Morandi, as for many others of his station, the entrance to university signaled the final adieu to childhood innocence. Now came worldly experience and the demands and responsibilities of an elite role in this power-driven society. We must beware of reading too much into a documentary record that merely attests to his attainment of a degree. We must also beware of finding too much coherence in personal episodes that may have been lived as single disconnected facts. Not every event in a life makes sense—except in the deceptive light of hindsight; and we cannot assume Morandi was any more single-minded than he seemed to be in the pursuit of his yet ill-formed goals.

What turns the meager materials at hand into a story is our knowledge of Morandi's character. A compulsive drive to gain the admiration of his fellow men marked everything he did. To achieve this, he chose the rocky road of social improvement.

This was not a man likely to suffer the inconveniences of bureaucratic and organizational stagnation without complaint. Such, however, was the result of well-intentioned efforts by generations of reformers seeking to superimpose more modern structures over an essentially medieval framework at the University of Rome. He may have been just in time to enjoy at least a few of the first fruits of the changes introduced by Sixtus V, former member of the theology faculty and now pope, in what turned out to have been one of the most momentous periods in the university's history since its founding in the fourteenth century.[9]

So when Morandi set about collecting bits of useful knowledge as well as useful acquaintances, his task was more pleasant than it might have been ten years before. Among the most useful acquaintances for an ambitious student in this as in any period were those who imparted the knowledge necessary to pass exams. With this in mind, Morandi could scarcely help coming under the influence of Marc-Antoine Muret, star of the legal faculty and one of Europe's greatest scholars,[10] or Girolamo Parisetti, Muret's colleague, who was so well regarded that Pius IV recruited him to help establish an authoritative text of Gratian's Decretals, the basic document of canon law.[11] Both were representatives of the humanist jurisprudence pioneered by Andrea Alciato, and known as the "French Manner" because its founder supposedly introduced it at Bourges before going on to propagate it at the University of Ferrara where Parisetti picked it up. Thanks to a gradual self-reform in legal teaching, Morandi was able to gain the expertise he needed without losing touch with the general education that would serve him so well later on. Under Parisetti and Muret, ancient laws were being analyzed more and more in their original contexts and as the products of a historical development. Gone was the heyday of the so-called "Italian Manner," when professors would recite the texts of the Roman Corpus Juris Civilis, followed by a dull litany of opinions from the late medieval emulators of the scholastic jurist Bartolus, attempting to extract absolute truths good for all times.[12] They now sought to unlock a law's real significance by a close reading of the text itself, applying all the methods of humanist philology, linguistics, and chronology, perfected from the time of Lorenzo Valla onward.[13]

Useful as this education was, especially compared to the earlier one imparted by the teachers of the "Italian Manner," Morandi knew as well as any other student that official courses alone were not sufficient for passing the doctoral exam. We cannot tell whether he belonged to one of the many student study clubs that had sprung up spontaneously among those interested in polishing their techniques of argumentation and putting their knowledge to use. But the Morandi we are coming to know would have leapt at the opportunity to expound the legal texts in public speeches or even in formal disputations with chosen opponents, as long as local ecclesiastical and secular dignitaries were there to admire and applaud.

So by the end of his university career, around 1590, Morandi had the opportunity to acquire what he needed. Not only was he ready to pass the exam. He was ready to set himself up in a lucrative practice in one of the richest cities in the West, and among one of the most litigious populations—including dozens of representatives of foreign courts in need of counsel to guide them in the labyrinthine networks of the Roman bureaucracy. And he was well-poised eventually to rise from legal practice into one or another of the higher offices of Church or state. Why did he not do this?

Morandi had before him a notable example of success, if he only cared to observe the career of Prospero Farinacci, one of the most famous jurists of his time.[14]

Farinacci, like Morandi, came from relatively obscure origins. The son of a notary, he was possibly even less advantaged when he came to study civil and canon law at the University of Rome a few years before the younger man. His fortunes rapidly improved. Immediately after graduation he received successive appointments to manage the small, semi-independent state of Bracciano for the Orsini family and to help Pierdonato Cesi manage the state of Civitavecchia for the papacy. In spite of a scandalous and violent style of life that landed him in jail more than once, Farinacci aspired to still higher things. In 1585 he completed the first installments of the masterwork on criminal practice that we excerpted in the last chapter. This and his activity as a counsel and territorial governor for the powerful Altemps family provided leverage for securing a prestigious judgeship in the Apostolic Chamber. More was to come in later years. By the turn of the seventeenth century, having obtained a provincial governorship all for himself and ingratiated Pope Clement VIII by a deliberately flimsy legal defense in the notorious parricide trial of Beatrice Cenci, permitting the Aldobrandini pope to confiscate the fortune of the rival Cenci family, he could set his sights on the highest magistracy in papal government: the governorship of Rome.[15]

But Morandi was not to take Farinacci as his model. Trafficking in pardons and convictions was not for him; nor was judging suits, managing property, nor even writing erudite treatises. What he sought was admiration—not only from his intimates, but from society at large. There must be, he thought, better ways to find this.

Although the inner wellsprings of Morandi's religious vocation will be forever closed to us, his eventual choice to take the tonsure immediately after graduation may well have been accompanied by a series of calculations of the following kind. He certainly recognized that for preferment to the very highest offices in Rome a prelacy was an absolute prerequisite—as Farinacci was eventually to discover when offering his own credentials to Paul V for the governorship of Rome (an office, the pope responded, meant for "an old prelate").[16] Except in the case of extraordinarily powerful sponsorship, such as a relative in the papacy or in the curia, a law degree was not enough to secure a prelacy. Only a very long career within the Church could do that.

Even if Morandi did not have this ultimate goal in view, he sought a position from which to launch his appeal for greater esteem. The Church may seem to us to have been an odd place to go. Yet, in the early modern period, a religious order could provide the ideal kind of family that no biological family could hope to be. And within that gigantic international community known as the religious, a life of leadership among like-minded companions and associates, separated from the ordinary secular struggle for survival, protected from scrutiny by too-curious politicians, could be glorious and full.

If it was to be a religious order, then, which one?[17] Among the many possibilities, the Vallombrosa order offered several advantages that anyone with Morandi's astuteness could hardly fail to perceive.[18] First of all, it was small, containing no more than 250 monks in nineteen monasteries, so the hierarchy was easier to climb than in larger orders such as the Benedictines, of which it was a branch. Moreover, the order had resisted the efforts of the Counter Reformation papacy to make it more amenable to central control. Perhaps no branch of any order was so closely tied to a single ruling family. Since the time of Cosimo I, the Medici had sought to maintain good relations with the heads of all the monastic establishments in Tuscan territory, and, where possible, to urge the appointment of their own candidates to abbacies. As their territory expanded, they were not above utilizing monasteries in outlying districts as extensions of their own power, such as the hermitage at Camaldoli on the border with Romagna. Furthermore, they recognized the usefulness of the monasteries as employment agencies for the younger sons of the Florentine patriciate whose interests they purported to protect. The Medici viewed the papacy's efforts to centralize the larger orders as just another strategy for draining money out of their state. With the Vallombrosa order, and its assets, almost entirely concentrated within Tuscany, they found them an ideal object of their policies of resistance. They therefore took the unusual step of constituting the officials of the monastery as veritable public officials in Florence.

Figure 2. Anonymous, drawing of the Monastery of Santa Prassede, Rome. (Florence, Archivio di Stato, Conventi soppressi dal governo francese, 260.)

Thus, eminence in the Vallombrosa order called not for a climb through the elaborate hierarchy of the Benedictines, but for an introduction to the patronage networks of the Medici family. Morandi may well have had opportunities to secure such an introduction already while at the University of Rome. Cardinal Alessandro de' Medici, known as the reigning "Cardinale Fiorentino," served as the Medici's regular representative in Rome since Ferdinand I gave up his cardinal's hat to become the grand duke. A distant relative of the ruling family, he became archbishop of Florence after having served first as bishop of Pistoia. He remained a dependable ally even after he was promoted to a cardinalship in 1583 and elected as pope, taking the name of Leo XI, twelve years later. But for the most sensitive assignments, the Medici confided in a more direct relation of the family, namely, Giovanni de' Medici, the grand duke's half-brother and Cosimo I's natural son by Eleonora degli Albizzi. By the late 1580s, he was Florence's most reliable soldier-diplomat.[19] In September 1590, following his return to Florence from Flanders, where he fought on behalf of the Spanish king Philip II, he went down to Rome to bring the grand duke's greetings to the newly elected pope, Urban VII. No sooner did he return to Florence from this mission than the pope died, after only twelve days in office, and Giovanni had to hurry back to Rome with precious information to be distributed to the pro-Medici party within the new conclave that was to elect Gregory XIV. Morandi could have met Giovanni or Alessando de' Medici in one of the public exercises where students invited local dignitaries to admire their prowess in legal debate, or even at his doctoral exam, where they might have been among the highly placed sponsors who customarily supported the most promising candidates—in the case of Giovanni, initiating a friendship that was to last for many years.

Whatever may have been the precise circumstances of his choice of order, Morandi embarked upon his novitiate in 1590. How starkly the peaceful provincial setting of the mother house in Vallombrosa, where he now took up residence, contrasted with the bustling activity of Rome, he must have thought. Shining like a mirage some twenty kilometers to the west of the monastery, a trip of nearly a full day, stood the dynamic state capital, Florence, almost a provocation to the homesick Roman. Could it provide a suitable stage for displaying his developing talents?

THREE

AD ASTRA PER ASPERA

> INTERROGATOR: Do you know a person by the name of Simon Carlo Rondinelli?
> MORANDI: I have known Signor Rondinelli for twenty years, from the time I was in Florence. I met him often there in the house of Alessandro de' Neri. The said Rondinelli is very well versed in astrology. (*Morandi Trial*, fol. 118, July 21, 1630)

MORANDI'S LIFE COULD NOT help being deeply affected by the new surroundings. The little settlement at Vallombrosa stood deep within Tuscan territory, some fifty kilometers north of Arezzo, on a side road leading off the main highway between Bibbiena and Pontassieve. Its present-day aspect is more or less the same as it was in Morandi's time, and so, perhaps, is the all-pervasive aroma of moss and fungi. A short distance after the turnoff, orderly rows of olive trees begin to give way to a profusion of taller and wilder fir trees, chestnuts, and beeches, in a great forest continuing up a steep hill. At the top sits a cluster of buildings dominated by a thirteenth-century bell tower and a defense tower built some two centuries later, giving the whole complex something of the aspect of a medieval castle. Here was one of the "holy dwellings of Christ amid the sylvan recesses" to which Petrarch referred in the *Vita solitaria*.[1] And here Morandi began what was to be a twenty-three-year sojourn.

To work his way by degrees from here into Florentine high society was not going to be easy. Morandi's Medici connections were not yet strong enough to guarantee him a place at court. He would first have to prove himself by parading his accomplishments on the local literary scene. To what lengths was he was willing to pursue his desires for advancement? Into what fields of licit and illicit knowledge? Were the stars the limit? Let us find out.

Morandi knew as well as anyone else that the most convenient points of entry into literary life were the late-sixteenth-century versions of the Renaissance academies. Here Florentine intellectuals and amateurs continued to translate the notion of "usefulness and pleasure" into multipurpose cultural conviviality.[2] To emphasize the last half of this formula, they still branded their associations with a whimsical name—such as the Academy of the Crusca or "bran," or of the Alterati or "agitated ones." In regularly scheduled meetings, they discussed whatever happened to be the specific interest of the academy—the Crusca, for instance, in Florentine language; and the Fiorentina and Alterati academies, in anything regarding Florentine poetry, prose, and drama. They kept a semblance of order by electing a roster of officers made up of a head academician—a "prince" or "president"—and perhaps a treasurer and a secretary or two. Often a "censor" reviewed compositions submitted for approval. A consensus was usually required on new candidates for admission. And as equal citizens of an imaginary republic, members hid their occupations and social status in real life behind the elegant and none-too-impenetrable mask of fanciful pseudonyms.[3]

No one was fooled by the whimsical names and the pseudo-democratic titles. Nor could anyone among the Crusca forget that "the Burned One" was really Vincenzo Pitti, "the Fresh One" Ottaviano de' Medici, or "the Dry One" Filippo de' Bardi. In spite of appearances, the academies, as these imposing Florentine surnames suggest, remained deeply embedded in the power structures of a highly stratified society. And that was exactly where Morandi wanted to be. Admissions policies could be quite exclusive, especially for the three main academies, the Crusca, the Fiorentina, and the Alterati, and no wonder. Members of the Crusca were specifically chartered by the grand duke, and their first president was the rector of the university of Florence and a member of the ruling Council of Two Hundred. They could consider themselves almost as agents of government policy, inasmuch as the defense of the Florentine language was a state affair—so the Gubbio-born scholar Paolo Beni was to find out when he published a work attacking the academy, only to receive a tart response from the grand duke himself.[4] The Alterati, including some of the most distinguished sons of the Florentine patriciate, actually met in the grand ducal residence at palazzo Pitti or in the almost equally prestigious palazzo Strozzi.[5]

To guarantee a foothold in this exclusive environment, while saving himself the embarrassment of a rebuff, Morandi made his debut in the relatively newer Accademia degli Spensierati (the "Carefree Ones")—by no means the humblest of the dozen or so Florentine academies still in operation at the turn of the seventeenth century. His way was no doubt prepared by Simeone Finardi, a poet, musician, and Spensierato who also happened to be the prior of Morandi's monastery. There is no reason to believe he had any previous contacts with other known members, such as Fabrizio Mattei, a law professor at the university of Pisa, and Pedro Antonio Canonhero, a doctor in philosophy, medicine, and theology apparently of Portuguese background. After he joined, Morandi prudently gravitated toward another member, Francesco Allegri, a poet and writer with contacts in the Accademia della Crusca. Perhaps he thought Francesco's brother Alessandro, an ex-courtier connected with the Accademia Fiorentina, might lead him closer to the Medici family.[6] Apart from the regular meetings and twice-yearly symposia, to be held every carnival and in August under the auspices of the academy's elected "prince," members were to dedicate a considerable portion of their efforts to procuring for each other further recognition and public applause. Morandi, too, like the others, placed his anonymous compositions in a container appropriately dubbed "scacciapensieri" (the Italian word for "Jews' harp," meaning pastime or diversion), to be judged by the academy "censors" and published at the expense of everyone.

The Spensierati, taking their cue from the three best-accredited academies, proposed above all to promote Florentine language and literature. Naturally, so did Morandi. To demonstrate his solidarity with this purpose, Morandi helped Francesco Allegri assemble a collection of poetry by Francesco's brother, Alessandro, whose verses in the burlesque style of Francesco Berni (and hence their nickname "bernesque") had suddenly come into vogue. It was a golden opportunity to draw attention to the academy and, incidentally, to himself. The language, Morandi proclaimed, "seemed to be ever more revived and flourishing" in Allegri's work than anywhere else.[7] And there, he suggested, could be found a solution to the famous Language Question that had agitated Italian minds from Petrarch to Paolo Beni, concerning the best style in speaking and writing Italian. In an appeal calculated to ingratiate both sides, Morandi suggested that the so-called "ancients," who adhered exclusively to the "ancient decorum" of Dante and Petrarch, ought to listen more carefully to the so-called "moderns," who advocated recent writers. Allegri, he went on, had done this admirably in his poetry. Morandi, qualified by his standing as the "most curious admirer" of Allegri's works, offered the collection to readers for their enjoyment and to the country for the "utility of the pure Florentine tongue"—perhaps in the hope of attracting the attention of a worthy Florentine patron.

In keeping with the prevailing ethos and the predominantly aristocratic aspirations of the academicians, the Spensierati's activities were not all entirely serious. In celebrating what might be called the more whimsical side of academic life, Allegri expressed his longed-for affiliation with the leisure class. In a poem devoted to idleness, he listed the various occupations he preferred to forego just to be able to sit at home "and poke the fire"—namely, whoring, gambling, drinking, dancing, playing music, fencing, walking, or riding.[8] Without idleness, he claimed, there could be no love:

Petrarch, lover and companion dear,
Also from around our way,
Figured love to be from leisure
Born, that through this world does run and play.

Idleness, Allegri went on, might occasionally inspire creativity:

Those subtle thoughts
The food of art
We form by sitting down, at ease.

Indeed, he added, "All the richest and most honored careers / Mainly consist in sitting down."

How true, the already somewhat corpulent Morandi must have thought as he read these verses once more in the company of the mainly well-born Florentine academics to whom they were addressed. Taking one step further the arguments of Boccaccio and Petrarch for the superiority of the contemplative over the active life, Allegri suggested that pure idleness was pleasant and desirable in itself, apart from any usefulness.:

No less esteemed
By all is he
I'm telling you
. . .
Who good nor ill doth neither do;
Keeps cares away
And so I've heard
Avoids the fray;
Waits not for what
He next may meet
But thoughtless sits
And swings his feet.

Idle or not, the Spensierati allowed their musings to stray far beyond what Morandi ought otherwise to have experienced as a monk in a monastery. And other work by Allegri, published by the poet's brother in collaboration with Morandi, crossed the boundary between love lyric and eroticism, typifying the transgressiveness that was a chief characteristic of this exquisite and exclusive cultural milieu.

What thoughts might have been going through Morandi's mind as he transcribed the following thinly veiled allegory for sexual intercourse we will find out later:

That bean-ended spoon
Must be handled with care
And brought right to the brim

Of the pan with a push
Breaking nothing, nor spilling,
Nor splattering that oil
But the bean must go straight
To the midst of the pan
And go in all the way.[9]

Elsewhere in the poem, extending the food / sex metaphor, Allegri provides instructions for anatomical correctness ("Let not the bean / Be too small or too large") and on intimate hygiene:

The pan must be clean
Must be glazed, must be red
. . .
Let only the bean
Be permitted inside
Let it often be washed,
And then thoroughly dried.

As far as we know, Morandi's concern with such expressions was purely literary—for the moment.

In publishing this work with Morandi, Allegri's brother advised readers that they might find some items "a little licentious." This was no exaggeration, as the Florentine censors apparently took note. Turning instead to Verona, Francesco protested that to remove the saucier bits was "to take the heat out of the fire, or light from the sun." Fortunately, the censor there saw fit to strike out only a few innocuous references to "bean" and the locution "and go in all the way," as well as odd references, in other poems, to "the highest thrones," to "God," and to "cuckold"—none of which was difficult for the original owner of the copy at Harvard University's Houghton Library to fill in by himself.

Still other musings of the Spensierati strayed into various fields of the occult, which had recently gained a new lease on life among the Florentine elite—if it had ever really declined in the second half of the sixteenth century.[10] On this point, Allegri was even more coy in his allusions than he was in his erotic poetry. In one poem he compared love to an alchemical distilling operation, using an elaborate metaphor reminiscent of certain poems being written by the quintessential Baroque poet Giambattista Marino in the same period, and still later by John Donne.[11] The "practical distiller," he explained, heated his vessel so that the liquid, reduced to steam, rose high up and away from the heat. Encountering the cooler atmosphere it then fell "like lead" back down through the apparatus. Likewise, his love, boiling, ascended in a vapor, only to encounter the cold heart of his beloved. Transformed into tears, it then fell in droplets and flowed back to its source.[12] In another poem he described the movement of the heavens "in fixed circuits, necessary, and by nature." These circuits, he claimed, were "the true causes of what happens in the world."[13] But there were limits to what could be published on the subject, especially after the papal anti-astrology bull of 1586; and in his preface, Allegri's brother offered the now-customary disclaimer. Where the words "fate," "destiny," "fortune," "luck," "stars," and so forth occurred, he explained, the author did not intend to signify that life events were in some way predetermined. He only intended to signify that such were secondary causes, ministers of the will, and instruments of the omnipotent hand of God. "Because [the poet] knows that man's will is free and cannot be forced by any violence whatsoever, to do what it does not wish to consent to do."[14] Even St. Thomas Aquinas could not quarrel with that.[15]

Morandi's interest in the occult did not, of course, preclude his interest in what hindsight would later regard as major scientific achievements. The renaissance of natural philosophy in the late sixteenth century encouraged a more thorough and critical reexamination of the ancient authorities in the light of the evidence of the senses. Yet several decades had to go by before Descartes would suggest reducing all natural phenomena to mere matter and motion. Meanwhile, various holistic philosophies, well known to Morandi, attempted to rediscover an orderliness in the universe that seemed to have been lost with the discrediting of scholastic, Aristotelian, and other traditional systems. In Tuscany, the effort to revise the Ancients' accounts, before Galileo's return from Padua in 1610, was led by Andrea Cesalpino and Girolamo Mercuriale. Typically, Mercuriale based his medical cures not just on experimentation and the known effect of chemicals on the body, but also on the stars, on occult sympathies between certain natural objects and certain ailments, and on a mixed repertoire of sources combining ancient scholarship with folk wisdom.[16]

Morandi could not help recognizing that for the moment, occult interests found a particularly ready audience in the Medici household. What provoked his determination to use these interests as a path to advancement?

Don Antonio de' Medici showed where some of the opportunities lay. The natural son of Bianca Cappello and Francesco I, he grew up in the esoteric environment brilliantly represented by the iconography of the ornate Studiolo created for Francesco by Giorgio Vasari in the Palazzo Vecchio. Don Antonio himself turned his habitation at the Casino di San Marco, built by Buontalenti at a moment astrologically propitious for the Medici Family, into a studying place for the occult arts.[17] He enriched his collections of medical and scientific secrets by commissioning transcriptions and translations of important contemporary works on natural magic written by John Dee and others. He built an alchemical laboratory of such high quality that it was later moved to the Pitti Palace and made the basis of the grand duke's metal foundry. It was Don Antonio who took notice of the alchemical studies of a poor Florentine priest named Antonio Neri, only later renowned as the author of a best-selling treatise on glassmaking (1612).[18] He may have been attracted by Neri's claims to possess original manuscripts containing material not included in the printed versions of works by the Swiss-born occult philosopher and physician with the resounding name: Philippus Aureolus Theophrastus von Hohenheim, called Paracelsus. And he may well have been among the recipients of a manuscript detailing Neri's discovery of the philosopher's stone, entitled *The Gift of God* and now in the Florentine National Library, so shrouded in enigmatic jargon that it has defied all efforts to decipher it from then to now. And when Neri was forced to leave Florence, reportedly to elude a group of thugs who had gotten wind of the value of his discoveries, Don Antonio conducted the effort to make sure those discoveries did not leave Florence forever along with their discoverer.

In 1592, the occult philosopher Tommaso Campanella, to whom Morandi's destiny was to become inseparably linked, applied for asylum to Grand Duke Ferdinand I. As he passed through Florence in flight from a condemnation by his Dominican superiors in Naples for his heterodox doctrines, he must have furnished an exciting example, if not exactly a role model, to the young Morandi. In return for money and encouragement as well as introductions into Florentine cultural life, before finally proceeding to Bologna, he dedicated to Ferdinand the first version of what was to become his masterpiece, *On the Sense of Things and On Magic*.[19] There we may get some idea of the sorts of discussions that were going on almost within earshot of an increasingly attentive Morandi.

Building upon the ideas of his teacher Bernardino Telesio in Naples as well as Plato and Marsilio Ficino, with significant changes, Campanella suggested that all motion and all permanence in the universe were caused by individual sensitive souls residing in every object. God communicated his power to all things by way of a world soul radiating throughout the cosmos and centered in the sun. Reflections of this soul, in the form of sensitive powers, allowed each thing, in various degrees according to the type, to do what was necessary to survive and prosper. The earth, Campanella theorized, was like a huge animate being, having the heavens for its spirit, the soil and rocks for its body, and the sea for its blood. The human body contained portions of the world soul and was therefore influenced by celestial changes at all times.[20] The heavenly bodies at the moment of birth, according to Campanella, determined the character of the spirits that would affect persons during their lives—as he later explained in detail in his *Astrology*. In the *City of the Sun*, completed some ten years later but already sketched out in his mind at this time, he was to explain that astrological portents foretold how the newly invented compass, printing press, and arquebus would make possible "a great new monarchy, reformation of the laws and arts, new prophets, and a general renewal of the world."[21]

If Morandi nearly matched this audacity in his later predictions, he would never dare to attempt to bring them to fruition, as Campanella did, in the Calabrian uprising of 1599, not long after bidding adieu to his Florentine hosts.

The supernova of 1604 may have helped focus Morandi's attention more specifically on astrology. For many in Florence and elsewhere, this event made discussions about the relation between heavenly and earthly phenomena seem ever more concrete. While Galileo, pondering the event in Padua, used it as yet another demonstration of the weakness of Aristotle's theory of a geocentric universe, Johannes Kepler in Prague, a far from credulous observer although far more typical of the time, used it as an occasion for astrological reflections. The star, he noted, occurred at a particularly significant moment in the astrological cycle. The conjunction of Saturn with Jupiter in the triplicity of fire (consisting of the constellations Sagittarius, Aries, and Leo) had begun in the eighth degree of Sagittarius in December 1603, for the first time in 800 years, and only the eighth time since the beginning of the world and the third since the birth of Christ. What was more, in September 1604, Mars passed the tenth degree of Sagittarius, completing the great conjunction of the three superior planets. It was widely believed, Kepler commented, that such unusual celestial events would be the cause of immense prodigies and political movements in the year 1604.[22] Just when certain observers, following the Arabic tradition, predicted the apparition of a comet, sure enough, on the seventeenth or the twenty-seventh of September, depending on whether they followed the Julian or the Gregorian calendar, they saw not a comet, but a supernova in the constellation Serpentarius. If God's providence is at all effective, Kepler reasoned, such an extraordinary event could scarcely have occurred by chance. The future writer of the *Harmony of the World* (1619) never doubted for a moment that the cosmos was anything but a harmonious whole, or that celestial events had significance for events on earth. If the new star was part of an orderly cosmic process, it ought to be connected to some foreseeable earthly one—which he left up to more imaginative prognosticators to determine.

In Florence, the most zealous proponent of the new star's significance was Raffaele Gualterotti, a Florentine nobleman, poet, and virtuoso whom Morandi may well have met calculating horoscopes for the Medici family.[23] On purely astronomical matters, Gualterotti sided with innovators like Galileo. The "new" star, he argued, must have come from somewhere. Coming from somewhere, it would have had to pass straight through the supposedly impenetrable crystalline spheres in which the seven planets were fixed according to Aristotle's model.[24] If the planets were not borne around in their circular paths by the movement of the crystalline spheres, they must have some other principle of locomotion. Gualterotti posited the theory, explicated in different ways by Giovanni Pontano, Francesco Patrizi, and Campanella, that they moved, instead, of their own accord, "like fish in the sea."[25] Although he suggested that the earth might be the center of the universe, as the traditional Aristotelian and Ptolemaic models demanded, he left open the possibility, asserted more emphatically by Copernicus, that the sun might be instead.

Astronomy, however, was not Gualterotti's main concern; and in his estimation of the significance of the nova of 1604, he went even further than Kepler. Indeed, he noted, the nova had not only been accompanied by the great conjunction; it had been accompanied by a solar eclipse in Libra as well. All the classic texts on astrology, from Ptolemy to the sixteenth-century Campanian scholar Luca Gaurico, agreed that solar eclipses could be premonitions of disaster. Since the great conjunction involved the highest planets, its effects were no doubt more strongly felt by the princes and leaders of the world. It began in Sagittarius, which ruled the frontiers of the Spanish Empire, the Tyrrhenian Sea, Buda, and Jerusalem. And Libra, where the eclipse occurred, was the native territory of Rome and the rest of Italy, along with Syria and Persia. "Many provinces," Gualterotti concluded, "are threatened with evils, with war, and with death." Since celestial events determined courses that were ultimately subject to free will, according to the Thomist dictum, the best policy was to ensure that the warlike forces were directed away from the countries of Christendom and toward a common enemy. Only then might morbidity become health, wars become victories, and death become glorious life among the blessed. Therefore, let the princes join together in a crusade against the Turks, who were currently at war with the Austrians in Transylvania and trying to enlarge their share of Hungary. "Thus Europe will be freed, the Church will triumph, and the stars will have told the truth about human valor."[26]

Maybe Morandi was not yet ready for such speculations. Nonetheless, he already divided his attention between recent developments in philosophical method, in astronomy, and in astrology. At least in cultivating the first two of these, he may well have benefited from Galileo's presence in town before 1592 as a university professor, or during one of the many subsequent summers Galileo spent in Florence, including a period in 1605 as preceptor to young Prince Cosimo, the grand duke's son and heir.[27] Most certainly he enjoyed Galileo's triumphant return to Florence from Padua in 1610 not as a university professor but as the newly created ducal mathematician. He expressed his personal satisfaction to Galileo when a

Figure 3. Antonio Lorenzi, Galileo at 48 years of age. (Uffizi no. 12092.)

certain Francesco Sizzi retracted an earlier attack on the clamorous discovery of the satellites of Jupiter in 1610 that had set Galileo's career on its new footing. Finally, he exclaimed, the young Sizzi had abandoned the rustic ignorance into which popular errors had seduced him and had joined the fight for the philosophical liberty that Galileo represented. Writing to Galileo from Rome in 1613, he declaimed against those "philosophasters" who shackled their reason to the dusty texts of Aristotle and other ancient masters.[28] Instead, he proclaimed, let philosophers study the book of nature, as Galileo never tired of repeating.

But it was Morandi's interest in the occult, as well as in the Spensierati academy, that led him ever closer to the Medici family—not, if he could help it, as a courtier. He left that to others with a better tolerance for the trials of servitude, which did not always end in the relatively favorable results achieved by the poets Gabriello Chiabrera and Battista Guarini and extolled in dozens of treatises on courtiership from Castiglione's *Courtier* to Torquato Tasso's *Il Malpiglio*.[29] His friend Alessandro Allegri, for instance, found only discouragement during his brief period in the Medici retinue, and later railed: "I do not wish, just to dress so well, to live so badly / For love of someone whom I scarcely see." There was nothing so indecent, Allegri claimed, as "being chained like dogs" to a prince:

> Life at court and dread disease to me
> Are kindred states, and more alike do seem,
> Than any brothers twain could ever be.[30]

Rather than courtiership, Morandi sought mutual respect, a powerful patron who might also serve as a collaborator and perhaps even as a coconspirator in his campaign for social recognition.

Soon enough, Morandi's efforts paid off. Alessandro de' Neri, of a Florentine patrician family closely connected with the Medici (but not, interestingly enough, related to Antonio Neri, the glassmaker), got wind of Morandi's impromptu performances as a poetry critic. A few successes at Neri family soirées secured Morandi a regular place on the invitation lists. There he found a soul mate in Simon Carlo Rondinelli, a passionate amateur astrologer who soon assumed a position as Cardinal Carlo de' Medici's private librarian. For a time, Morandi circled in the orbit of Cardinal Carlo, an uncle of Grand Duke Ferdinand II, before finally moving to that of another Medici, a half-brother of the cardinal's grandfather: Giovanni de' Medici.

Whether Morandi finally achieved the desired status with Giovanni de' Medici is open to question. The relationship took time to evolve. Just a few years after Morandi presumably arrived in Florence, Giovanni left for northern Europe to take a position as Emperor Rudolph II's general of artillery.[31] And no sooner did Giovanni set foot again in Florence than he was invited by Henry IV to serve as military advisor in the French court. Only the promise of a job overseeing the improvements to fortifications at Leghorn succeeded in bringing him to Florence for some appreciable length of time after 1610. Then he surrounded himself with likeminded individuals at his palace in Via del Parione and resumed full-time the cultural activities that he had almost entirely suspended before the turn of the century. Morandi, as a member of this group and a friend of Giovanni until the latter's death in 1621, avoided the strict client-patron relationship shared by the likes of Pietro Accolti, Giovanni's secretary, and Benedetto Blanis, his librarian. Unlike these, he would never appear on Giovanni's personal payroll as the regular recipient of a Medici stipend. Even when sorely tempted, he never left the Vallombrosa order to serve Giovanni exclusively, thus keeping a modicum of independence and his options open.

In the company of Giovanni, Morandi became an expert on the occult arts. The house in Parione was furnished with a complete alchemical laboratory—including "plenty of glass vessels for distilling," Giovanni's probate inventory informs us. His library was so well stocked with prohibited books that a later purchaser of the whole lot had problems with the Inquisition on account of it. Giovanni and Morandi had easy access to works by Paracelsus and by the philosopher Bernardino Telesio, both on the Index. Reading work by Johann Reuchlin, also on the Index, they exchanged information on cabalistic enigmas.[32] Together they delved into the more obscure byways of later Renaissance astrology, sharing horoscopes of famous figures of the past. Horoscopes of their contemporaries, including relatives, friends, and acquaintances in Florence, they accompanied the "appropriate discourses"—as Morandi termed them—concerning the meaning of the signs and the probable fortunes of the persons, if living, or reasons for their deaths. In all these studies, Morandi later claimed, only Giovanni was capable of "reducing me to the state of entire perfection."[33] And perfection could guarantee his value as an advisor to princes on occult affairs and, ultimately, his success in Rome.

These years of collaboration and study were some of Morandi's happiest. But intense collaboration between the two men was to end sooner than expected. In 1613 Medici patronage yielded for Morandi its first fruit: an appointment as abbot of the monastery of Santa Prassede in Rome. At first, he regarded the change as a temporary interruption and continued his trips back and forth between Rome and Florence. How he longed for "that delicious cell" at the monastery of Vallombrosa, where the sylvan recesses invited the pilgrim into a dank paradise—especially, he wrote, in the "burning heats of summer" in Rome. Again, in his last gesture of courtiership before leaving that role behind: "It wounded me deeply to be removed from Your Excellency's presence, and to lose the occasion to serve you and be honored by your benignity, who has not disdained to impart a thousand precious teachings to me, with so much largesse."[34] When Giovanni himself left Florence yet again in 1615 for a new position as commander of Venetian forces in the Friulian war, Morandi began to regard this stage in his life as having come to an end.

But now it is time to pull together the disparate strands of this increasingly complex life. By now, Morandi had already realized several of his ambitions. He made a name for himself in the highly competitive world of Florentine literary life. He made some progress along the path to ecclesiastical honors; he was now ordained and served as representative of the Roman Inquisition within his monastery. Presenting himself successfully as a master of occult arts, he gained the confidence of powerful patrons. With a formidable baggage of coveted abilities, as well as several rooms full of furniture and books, he turned his undivided attention now to Rome—the land of power, of popes, and of preferment.

FOUR

THE ASTROLOGER'S BOOKS

INTERROGATOR: Whose were the books in the library?
AMBROGIO MAGGI: All the books in the library belonged either to the monastery or to the abbot, and I do not know whether the abbot bought books for himself or for the library.
INTERROGATOR: Were there any prohibited books in the library, for instance, by Niccolò Machiavelli?
MAGGI: No, there were no such books; particularly, not by Machiavelli. (*Morandi Trial*, 394v, August 30, 1630)

MORANDI SOON FOUND that to fulfill his high ambitions, his circle of acquaintances in 1613 was not nearly enough. In Rome, the so-called "Florentines," the pro-Medici faction in the Church, were stoutly opposed by many other factions. And there, unlike in Florence, the Medici had almost as many enemies as they had friends. How was he to turn his skill in the occult arts into social capital sufficient for launching a career of political power and influence? Morandi conceived of a unique expedient that, by the way, earned him a place in the history of European libraries.

It was Morandi's expert librarianship, in fact, that earned for him much of the renown he enjoyed before reaching the height of his career. "How often have I wept over your books" was a typical reaction, in this case, by Francesco Girondo, writing from a palace in far-away San Severino Marche. For Girondo, the profound emotions experienced while living in Rome and consulting books under the watchful eye of the abbot were memories fit to soothe a mind wearied by duties as secretary to the local bishop, Francesco Sperelli.[1] And the greater the gratitude of the secretaries, courtiers, princes, and prelates who benefited from the library at Santa Prassede, its unique collections, and its unusual policies, the greater their expectations of Morandi. "Thanks for the counsel, thanks for the assistance, thanks for the favors," effused Simon Carlo Rondinelli, librarian to Cardinal Carlo de' Medici, in terms that far exceeded the obligatory hypocrisies of baroque epistolary style. "In every sense and with all the powers of my mind, of my tongue, of my pen, I declare my indebtedness."[2] Morandi naturally hoped that the feelings experienced by the better-situated of these readers during the course of their readings would extend to the protection of their librarian. And he had good reason to believe that this was so—as long as he could conceal from curious visitors the secret springs of his desire, and the dangerous acts that might have been going on in the next room.

To be sure, the exact extent of Morandi's contribution to the monastery library is not easy to determine. For there is little reason to take at face value the library inventory compiled in 1600, the only existing record we have of what the collection might have looked like before Morandi arrived. This inventory, decreed by Pope Clement VIII during his census of libraries all over Italy, had chiefly aimed at earmarking for removal to the Inquisition's vaults those unedifying volumes that were prohibited by the Indices of Forbidden Books of 1557 and later. If the monks at Santa Prassede at that time were anything like their fellow monks in other monasteries, they regarded the inquiry as an undesirable intrusion into monastery life and took care to ensure that the papal officials left the premises empty-handed.[3] They may well have adopted the stratagems reported elsewhere, of locking up dangerous books in remote parts of the compound before the Inquisition officials could get to them or of shifting books around from one part of the buildings to another while the survey was going on. In any case, the library of Santa Prassede came up with a miraculously clean bill of health on that occasion, revealing a collection of some 200 works of the most pious theology and Catholic apologetics, along with the most innocuous classics of Renaissance humanist and ancient writings. Fortunately for the monks, papal officials missed most of the collection. And while the officials could delude themselves into thinking that a major battle of the Counter Reformation had already been won, the library's copy of Machiavelli, as well as copies of other similarly "dangerous" works, most likely lay safely buried somewhere until better times.

Nevertheless, we cannot fail to recognize Morandi's personal touch on a large nucleus of books at Santa Prassede. Of these, 550 are listed in the documents as belonging to Morandi himself; and we are as unable to discern which of these he may have inherited from his own relatives as we are to discern which he may have acquired by gifts, presents, and purchases during a lifetime spent among the well-born and in the shadow of the powerful. They bespoke a man of considerable bibliographical interests, while reinforcing the impression of exquisite tastes conveyed by his other possessions. Although the trial record carefully distinguished them, as the Benedictine rule prescribed, from the common property of the monastery, he lent them out regularly along with the other books in the collection.[4] As abbot and reigning bibliophile, we can be sure he influenced the purchase of whatever newly published books the library acquired after his arrival.

Many of Morandi's additions were of a sort that would have pleased even the chief censor for the Holy Office in Rome. What could be more innocent than the biographies of St. Filippo Neri by Antonio Gallonio, of St. Carlo Borromeo by Francesco Pena, of St. Catherine of Siena by Raymond of Capua, and of St. Ignatius of Loyola by Pedro de Ribadeneyra that he added to the existing collections of popular lives of saints? The same could be said of the anonymous lives he added of Blessed Ambrose of Siena and St. Giovanni Gualberto, the founder of his order. And in a Catholic establishment, what better complement than a Catholic martyrology, perhaps the one corrected by Gregory XIII in 1610? For devotional purposes, an extra copy of Ignatius's *Spiritual Exercises* must have been welcome, as well as Roberto Bellarmino's work on the good death, Angelo Maria Torsani's extracts from the Old and New Testaments concerning Christian living and an "Art of Spiritual Life," perhaps by Fra Cherubino da Siena. Nor did Morandi neglect ecclesiological and liturgical purposes, for which he contributed the privileges of the Friars Minor and the Magnum Bullarium of papal decrees as well as ceremonial compilations for specific bishoprics in Italy and abroad. A perfect Catholic churchman, the chief censor might have thought, at the end of an exploratory visit.

However, other contributions by Morandi helped give to the library's collections a dramatic new form more appropriate for the radical role he wished to play in Roman cultural life. Outside the strictly religious field, which made up no more than a fifth of the new additions, he ranged from natural philosophy to military architecture. He acquired books in the major modern languages as well as in Greek and Latin, even a Hebrew dictionary; and from presses all over northern Europe as well as in Italy. Some went into a special large bookcase with locking front panels, more like an armoire, traditionally reserved for the abbot's personal books and affording some security for those that might excite suspicion. But this armoire had been moved into the main library room in recent memory, as Morandi's own books became less and less distinguishable from those that he ordered to be added to the ten large bookcases that, as our records suggest, housed the main collection.

As it happened, the chief censor for the Holy Office, one Niccolò Ridolfi (whose official title was Master of the Sacred Palace), actually did visit the library shortly after Morandi began enlarging it. His original intention may well have been to snoop around. Before Morandi and the library became involved in the networks of culture and power in Rome, Ridolfi may well have wondered whether he ought to become a supporter, patron, protector, or, instead, a prosecutor, initiating a larger investigation. His choice would depend on what he found. Even he, coming to the library for the first time, could easily see that it was more than a collection of books. It was also a "theater of study," according to Francesco Frugoni's felicitous late-seventeenth-century phrase—where "there appeared on the scene" of the mind "so many illustrious men," conjured up by their words on a page.[5]

In this respect, Ridolfi might well have found that the interior, at least, looked very much like the interiors of other better-known monastery libraries on a similar scale. On peeking into the library of the Barnabites at San Carlo dei Catinari in another quarter of Rome, at least according to a late-seventeenth-century description by Giambattista Piazza, he would see everything stuffed, as at Santa Prassede, into ten large ornate walnut bookcases set against the whitewashed stone walls. The large room's eastern exposure gave morning light as well as gentle dry breezes, as though Vitruvius's prescriptions for accommodating the utility of the scholars and the conservation of the books had been dogma to the late medieval architects who built it.[6] Within each bookcase, roughly corresponding to a single field of intellectual endeavor, aesthetic and space considerations competed with organizational ones. Bound mostly in vellum, according to the Italian custom, except for the less well cared-for ones that were bound in cardboard, or, if they came from abroad, in coarser hides or even wood, the books were arranged in tidy ranks with the smaller formats closest to the top: ventiquattresimo and duodecimo, for the most part, although even further miniaturization was not uncommon for breviaries and other popular items. The next ranks served the quartos, and so on down to the massive in-folio tomes, some weighing as much as a small child. As at Santa Prassede, every book had its place, not noted in any catalogue, but preserved in the minds of the monks, a knowledge passed along as part of a set of acquired patterns, behaviors, and ceremonies.

Even more than a "theater of study," the library of Santa Prassede was a theater of the mind. Catalogues in the usual sense of the term, any visitor with Ridolfi's credentials would soon realize, were wholly futile. This was not a library to be reduced to the narrow confines of a dry listing, nor even just to be enjoyed on a leisurely stroll looking for a book. It was a library to be experienced intellectually in the company of a true intellectual—perhaps the abbot. Any actual arrangement of books might give a mistaken impression of the separateness of the subject areas. The wholeness of all knowledge was something baroque readers brought to their reading as well as away from it. Asked about the ten subject categories he had contrived, so the documents attest, Morandi would reply that knowledge is not restricted by the exclusivity of wooden containers. It is subtly situated for imaginary cross-referencing in virtual space, or better yet, in the mind, like the universal libraries evoked in the fantasies of Conrad Gesner or Anton Francesco Doni.[7]

And still more than a theater of the mind, the library was also a theater of the self—that is, a self-conscious representation of the librarian. Ridolfi would, of course, have had no way of telling with any accuracy how many of the works shown to him had actually been read by their owner or purchaser. But no one could miss the traces of Morandi's eclectic and ever-curious striving to establish affiliations both in the mainstream of European intellectual life and on the most innovative fringes. There in this living manifesto our visitor might discover how Morandi wished to appear to others.

For instance, the next bookcase after religion and theology did not just contain a good selection of the Greek and Roman classics. It revealed Morandi's yearning to establish his scholarly credentials. In accompanying Morandi along its shelves, Ridolfi would quickly begin to realize that the similarity between this library and the other monastic libraries in Rome was as superficial as the resemblance between Morandi and the other monks. His host would express satisfaction at the due attention paid over the years to the humanist inspirations behind modern literary movements. Morandi might mutter aloud, he himself enriched the library by his editions of Flavius Josephus's history of the Jewish War as well as Marcus Junianus Justinus's epitome of Trogus Pompeins. And it was he who provided the complete extant works of Epictetus, Pliny, and Appianus Alexandrinus. Italian translations by Remigio Nannini of Ovid's heroic epistles and of Horace's satires by Lodovico Dolce, completed the picture of elegant learning presented here. Need our visitor bother to ask if there was indeed a copy of Plutarch's *On Curiosity*, which seemed to symbolize everything he saw? The text was carefully listed in the inventory and there on the shelf before him.

But where, in all this scholarship, was the evidence for Morandi's much-vaunted value as a counselor to cardinals and princes? Passing by a large bookcase filled with ponderous works of literary erudition, Ridolfi might stop at the next one, featuring modern historians from every corner of the known globe. No one could deny that the best advice was based on the best information. So there was Paolo Giovio's history of the world from the late fifteenth century to the 1530s. And what Giovio left out was covered by Giovanni Tarcagnota's history of the world to 1513, perhaps (our document is not clear) with the updates by Mambrino Roseo and Dionigi da Fano to 1582 and by Cesare Campana to 1598. No account of Scandinavia surpassed that of Olaus Magnus; and of the Indies, Alfonso de Ulloa's translation of Fernão Lopes de Castanheda was at least as good as many others. So Morandi's additions included both these works.

If the impatient Ridolfi (and my reader) at this point should begin to wonder whether, amid all this scholarly ornamentation, there might be some worldly wisdom, the next bookcase, containing the collections regarding the contemporary political scene, would no doubt revive his flagging interest. Alongside the descriptions of Johanna of Austria's entry into Florence in 1566 as the first wife of Grand Duke Francesco I, he could admire Giovanni Botero's brilliant reports on every part of the world including the Indies, East and West. In between long-winded theoretical treatises by Botero, Paolo Paruta, and more concise but less interesting ones by Girolamo Frachetta, he could pick out pieces of practical advice from Jean de Cholier's thesaurus of political aphorisms. He would have known that Morandi aspired not merely to epigraphic witticism, but to the kind of political astuteness that won or lost states' reputations. For examples of what he might expect from such a man, he could turn to the Interdict controversy between Venice and the papacy, comparing tracts by Paolo Sarpi, Giovanni Marsili, and Antonio Querini in defense of the Venetian position and states' rights, with those by Roberto Bellarmino, Antonio Possevino, and others in defense of the Church, the papacy, and ecclesiastical independence.

Even science had its uses, Ridolfi might have reflected; and the best potential counselor would have to know what they were. If he decided to test Morandi's awareness of the growing rapprochement between elite intellectual trends and technology, he would not have been disappointed. Knowledge of topics like sundialing, clocks, and globe construction was no longer restricted to the less-prestigious precincts of the handicrafts, Morandi could reply, brandishing authors like Christopher Clavius and Robert Hues from yet another bookcase before the startled onlooker. Treatises on machines by the likes of Guidobaldo Del Monte were in no way inferior to quintessentially elite applications of technology in the arts of fortifications and war, he might add, pulling off the shelf a copy of Giovanni Francesco Fiorentino. Art history and practice reflected the progress a few artists had made in distancing themselves from artisanal roots and inserting themselves into the most august circles of cultural life. And to show this, apart from Giorgio Vasari's *Lives*, Morandi could point to Albrecht Dürer's work on perspective translated into Latin by Joachim Camerarius, and works on the theory and practice of architecture by Alberti, Jacopo Barozzi da Vignola, and Pietro Cattaneo.

By the time Ridolfi got around to the next bookcase, he would have begun to realize that, in Morandi's mind, natural philosophy was much more than a practical pursuit. On the way to the most sublime insights, our visitor would be hurried past Francisco de Toledo's commentary on Aristotle, a reminder about Morandi's continued commitment to the ancients; past the new experimental and anti-Aristotelian trend represented by Galileo's hard-boiled and purely empirical *Discourse on Floating Bodies*, as well as by William Gilbert's perhaps more fanciful work suggesting hypotheses about the organization of the universe arrived at by observing the attractive forces in metal. Finally, Morandi pauses before a shelf of works revealing the keys to the secrets of nature. Albertus Magnus's spurious *De mirabilibus mundi* stands next to Tommaso Garzoni's study of "monsters, prodigies, fortunes, oracles, magic tricks, sibyls, dreams, astrological curiosities, miracles, and marvels." Cornelius Gemma's work on "amazing spectacles," their causes, and their significance as prognostications for the future stands next to Martin Antoin Del Rio's work revealing the techniques of natural magic while denouncing them. Ridolfi asks how all these interests fit together. In reply, Morandi points in the direction of Heinrich Khunrath's *Ampitheatrum*, offering a "sapientia eterna," at once "Christiano-cabalistical, divino-magical" and "physico-chymical."

Yet a man who traffics in ideas cannot help, from time to time, allowing his mental exertions to stray back to the source of his original seduction. So too with Morandi.

In the bookcase devoted to medicine, Ridolfi would begin to see that, in this monastery, all roads lead to the occult—even if prohibited books are strangely (miraculously?) absent. Again, he would be hurried past works more strongly influenced by the ancient writers—such as Leonhardt Fuchs's comments on the anatomical writings of Galen and Vesalius, with remedies derived from the true words of Hippocrates, or Paolo Cigalini's comment on Hippocrates' aphorisms. Perhaps Morandi would devote a word or two to works by Baldassare Pisanelli and Castoro Durante and others offering ways to prolong life by the proper regulation of food and drink, along with cures for the symptoms of gluttony, pointing out that they were no closer to the occult than were Johann van Heurne's chemical *Institutes* or Juan Valaverde de Amusco's anatomy of the human body, which Morandi possessed in the Italian translation of Antonio Tabo.

However, with his appetite whetted for alternative medicine by Leonardo Fioravanti's and Thomas Erastus's rejections of traditional cures in favor of chemical ones, Ridolfi might turn with great curiosity to Antonio Luiz's work on the occult properties of chemical substances and their medical uses. And once he had been dazzled by Evangelista Quadremio's "true declaration" of all the metaphors, similitudes, and enigmas of the ancient alchemical writers in Chaldean, Arabic, Greek, and Latin, furnishing recipes for potable gold, the elixir of life, the Fifth Essence, and the Philosopher's Stone, along with a discourse on the generation of metals, he could look up the writings of the followers of Paracelsus. Then Morandi might show him how chemical medicine was incorporated into an elaborate new system of the universe utilizing alchemical methods and based on a Christian Neoplatonic and Hermetic philosophy. And in case he began to be persuaded by Andreas Libavius's attacks on the "weapon salve," a controversial medicine of Paracelsus that supposedly acted at a distance, on the weapon rather than on the wound, Morandi might hand him Giuseppe Micheli's defense.

By now Ridolfi would not be surprised to find that the holdings on chemistry, metallurgy, and gemology in the next bookcase revealed occult alchemical interests around every turn. His eye would be drawn rapidly past metallurgical classics by Albertus Magnus and Georg Agricola, to Anselm De Boot's recent work demonstrating the origin, nature, power, and value of gems and stones as well as the ways in which "arcane essences" might be drawn from them. Ramón Lull's spurious alchemical testament seemed just as much at home in this company as Giovanni Bracceso's sixteenth-century commentary on it. And Johann Daniel Mylius's choice to offer his chemico-mystical observations in the form of a description of an imaginary *Basilica* built for a fictional prince was just as sound as was Johannes Rhenanus's choice to offer his treatise entitled *The Sun Emerging from the Well* in alchemical jargon. In case our visitor, opening a volume at random, protested about the difficulty of deciphering such works, Morandi might reply that any library worth its salt would always have on hand Martin Ruland's alchemical dictionary, with explanations for concepts that Paracelsus and others derived from the Hermetic tradition of texts supposedly written by the pre-Christian magus Hermes Trismegistus, embodying the esoteric knowledge of the ancient Egyptians.

There is only one stop left. Ridolfi is almost convinced that Morandi has what it takes to serve as a distinguished mediator between knowledge and power. Now comes the final test. Previous excursions have plunged the depths; Ridolfi now scales the heights, in the final bookcase containing the holdings on astronomy and astrology. How to gauge the expertise of the now quite jovial Morandi? Familiarity with certain texts by Ptolemy is taken for granted; next come Aristarchus of Samos on the signs and distances of the sun and moon and Galileo's *Starry Messenger.* What more is there to say? Ridolfi asks about Johannes Kepler. Morandi points to the three books on comets as well as the *Harmony of the World*, perhaps more philosophical than astronomical, and various attempts by Kepler to sort out the relation between astrology and the occult. All solid material. But how worthy of a true sage?

The proof lies in the correct proportion between planetary motions and planetary effects. Ridolfi, like others of his time, appreciates the usefulness, for the calculation of planetary motions, of a nearly complete collection of tables of the heavenly bodies: the Alphonsine tables by Isaac ben Said and collaborators, sponsored by Alphonse X of Castile in the thirteenth century and based on the Ptolemaic geocentric model of the universe; the Prutenic tables compiled by Erasmus Reinhold and dedicated to the duke of Prussia, based on the Copernican or heliocentric model; the Rudolphine tables, compiled by Johannes Kepler for Emperor Rudolph II and based in part on observations by Tycho Brahe.

But the mark of a true sage was the ability to bring all this material to bear on practical questions. Should Ridolfi desire to know about the future chances of life, Morandi ought to refer to the tables of the starry vault by Giovanni Antonio Magini and Andrea Argoli, along with Johannes Bayer's catalogue of stars current to the year 1603, with maps of all the known constellations, including the newly discovered ones in the southern hemisphere, and notes concerning the astrological significance of each. In the volumes of ephemerides by Argoli as well as by Johann Stoffler, Morandi clearly had more than enough detailed information at his fingertips to compile anyone's horoscope. And in Alessandro degli Angeli's astrological conjectures as well as the classic works, from Ptolemy, Julius Firmicus Maternus, and Aratus Solensis to the eleventh-century Arabic writer Abenragel to more recent works by Henricus Lindhout and Henrik Rantzau, he would always have a plausible interpretation ready to hand.

At the end of this long itinerary, Ridolfi could not help but conclude: There is nothing officially dangerous here; and Morandi has put the finishing touches on an education of enviable breadth. For the future of such a man, who could imagine anything less than a career administering to the intellectual needs of the mighty? Ridolfi is ready to file his report. We, however, are unsatisfied. We have exposed the intellectual roots of Morandi's preoccupations with the occult and laid bare his strategies of cultural posturing. But have we come any closer to the mystery of Morandi's deadly desires? Let us take one more look around before leaving the library.

Books alone, of course, and the intellectual credentials they establish, in themselves are no guarantee for the cultural capital required of the individual Morandi wished to be. As Ridolfi is ushered back along the corridor to the door, from which there waft aromas from the leisurely evening repast that awaits them in Morandi's rooms, he catches glimpses of books stuffed here and there belonging to the more practical literature of Renaissance self-improvement. Here is Girolamo Muzio's work on dueling and Federico Grisone's guide to horsemanship, providing suitable models of aristocratic behavior. There is Giovanni Vittore Soderini's treatise on the cultivation of the vine, fit to prepare any aspirant for the life of a country squire. Antonio de Guevara's early-sixteenth-century treatise teaches the ways of courtiership; the work of Battista Guarini covers the related topic of the office and duties of a noble or princely secretary. More to the point, Sigismondo Sigismondi offers behavioral advice to the counselors of cardinals, which Reale Fusoritto puts into action in an imaginary interview about etiquette with Cardinal Farnese's butler.

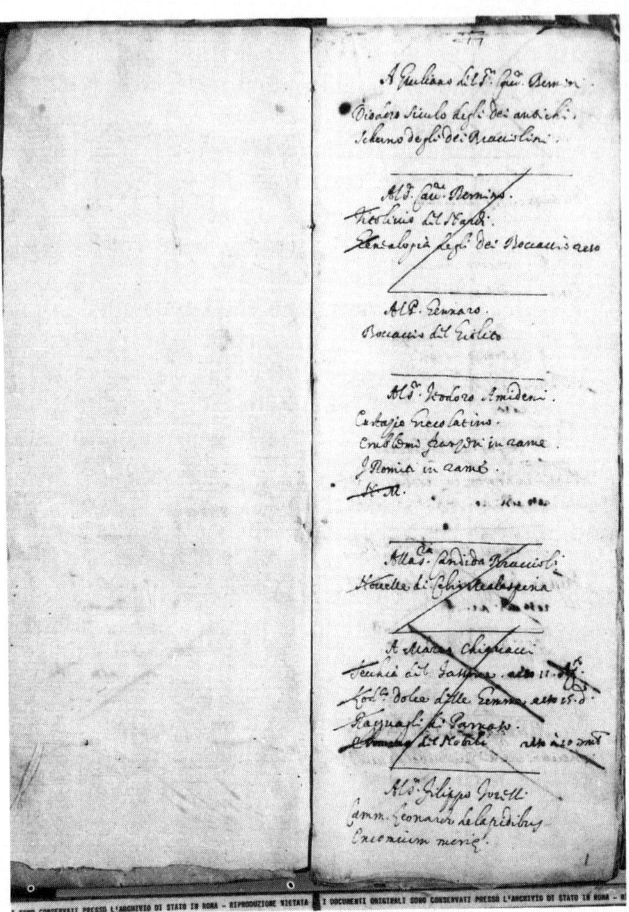

Figure 4. Library log from Morandi's trial record. (Rome, Archivio di Stato, *Governatore*, Processi, sec. XVII, b. 251.)

Finally, perhaps in some secluded corner, known to us because we have the inventory, but invisible to Ridolfi, lies the book of Morandi's dreams: Fabio Albergati's practical advice on prelacy, next to an anonymous "Manuale prelatorum," no doubt the recently published one by Antonio Pagani.[8] Even the ascent to ecclesiastical greatness can be reduced to a set of rules. As we follow in Ridolfi's footsteps, the trail to Morandi's compulsions seems to be getting warmer. The chief censor to the Holy Office does not notice.

But Ridolfi is also a reader. He is here to read books, not just see them. Soon he hears about the special advantages this library offers, besides

Morandi's prodigious bookmanship.[9] At once he is won over to Morandi's cause, and the library's. Unlike the Biblioteca Angelica recently established in the convent of Sant'Agostino by Angelo Rocca with the founder's personal collection of 40,000 books as the first truly public library in Rome, the library of Santa Prassede freely circulated its holdings among a growing selection of borrowers.[10] What better reason to cry, with Francesco Girondo, over Morandi's books—for joy!

The library thus presented a distinct novelty at a time when books were still chained to their tables at the Bodleian in Oxford, and if not actually chained were severely restricted to the premises of the Ambrosiana library in Milan and the Marciana in Venice.[11] The Biblioteca Vaticana extended borrowing privileges at least since the time of Pico della Mirandola; but it required elaborate application procedures for access. All that was required for patrons to become borrowers from Santa Prassede was some sort of connection with the wide-ranging intellectual and cultural circles of the monastery.

And as the cultural circles of the monastery began to widen, they began to intersect with some of the major cultural movements promoted by Urban VIII. For Morandi, this could only mean greater security and worldly rewards—provided he could keep playing the role set out for him.

FIVE

THE SUN POPE

List of books lent, and to whom:
Giuliano del Sig Cav. Bernini, 1627: Diodoro siculo degli dei antichi
Giuliano del Sig Cav. Bernini, 1627: Scherno degli dei, Bracciolini
Sig. Cav. Bernini, 1627: Tito Livio del Nardi
Sig. Cav. Bernini, 1627: Geneologia degli dei Boccaccio
(*Morandi Trial*, fol. Ir)

IN A TYPICAL WEEK in January 1627, visitors to the library of Santa Prassede included Gian Lorenzo Bernini and his fellow sculptor and collaborator, Giuliano Finelli. The same week, Candida Bracciolini, a relative of the Pistoiese poet Francesco now resident in Rome, stopped in; so did the famous Flemish lawyer Theodore Ameyden.[1] Their tastes varied widely. Gian Lorenzo preferred the classics, ancient and modern, though his education did not extend deeply into the scholarly languages. He therefore checked out Italian translations of Livy by Jacopo Nardi and of Boccaccio's *Genealogy of the Gods* by Giuseppe Betussi.[2] Giuliano Finelli's tastes, too, ran along classical lines: he borrowed Francesco Baldelli's translation of Diodorus Siculus's collection of ancient mythology; but he was also partial to modern poetry, and on this occasion he borrowed Francesco Bracciolini's poem *The Scorn of the Gods*, just then making the rounds of the Roman salons. Candida Bracciolini borrowed the entertaining novels of Celio Malespini, full of alchemical and astrological lore.

What all these visitors had in common, if not their tastes, were their connections to the court of Urban VIII. With any luck, some of the benefits of these high connections, shared by a considerable portion of the Santa Prassede circle, might extend to the monastery itself. So Orazio Morandi hoped, as he conceived of strategies for putting his own future on a more secure footing. At the very moment when he began reaching for the highest spheres of Roman society, however, his game became more dangerous. The more frequently the monastery circle intersected with Urban VIII's personal clientele, the more likely news about the monastery's riskier affairs was to reach the most elevated authorities in Rome. And at the moment when such news reached those with an axe to grind against Morandi, his fate was sealed.

For discovering how high Morandi's aspirations soared before the final debacle, a remarkable document has survived: namely, the library lending list. Meticulously annotated by Morandi, it is a unique document in early modern book history. Following each name is the date on which books were lent out, and occasionally that of a book's return, more frequently noted simply by a check mark. The list showed Morandi's intense interest not only in comings and goings within the monastery, but in the monastery's many contacts with the local scene. There we discover the role of a library in early modern Rome, and by implication, the role of Morandi and his monks. There we discover how Morandi used the library to catapult himself from relative obscurity within the ranks of his order to a position of preeminence and esteem.

Just ten years before, such a strategy would have been impossible. After he had squeezed the last drops of preferment from his Medici patrons in 1613, all Morandi could do, by astute maneuvering, was to bring about the conditions for his own survival. When his appointment to the generalship of his order expired four years later, in 1616, he had settled down to a permanent position as the order's procurator at the papal court.[3] Under Paul V, Pope Urban VIII's predecessor but one, his Medici ties were unlikely to take him much further. He could scarcely hope for much assistance from Cardinal Carlo de' Medici, son of Ferdinando I and the designated "Cardinale Fiorentino" (as the documents call him), who was hard pressed enough to find favor for more important Medici interests in Rome—no matter how many letters Morandi exchanged with the cardinal's librarian, Simon Carlo Rondinelli. And cultural interests alone were not enough to gain the pope's attention. For Paul V failed to emulate the great Renaissance popes only in this regard—that he cared little about the arts and sciences per se, as the Florentine ambassador complained to the secretary of state on the eve of the decree against Copernicus that was actually aimed at silencing Galileo. "This is no country for disputing about the moon," the ambassador ruefully reported, "nor, as things now stand, for sustaining or arguing new doctrines."[4]

Not being an artist or an architect, Morandi could scarcely contribute to the projects that absorbed much of Paul V's energies, aimed at expressing the outward magnificence of the papacy and of the Borghese family—from the continuing works in the basilica of St. Peter's to the construction of the palace atop the Quirinale hill and the sprawling villa and park on the outskirts of the city. Not being remotely related to the family, he could have no part in the pope's emphatically post-Tridentine plan to invest relatives with benefices, sinecures, and incomes—especially his nephew Scipione Borghese, who in this time became one of Gian Lorenzo Bernini's earliest patrons. And not being a politician or a theologian, he could contribute nothing to the pope's paranoid vendettas against any European power that seemed to oppose his controversial definition of Church-state relations—including a showdown with Venice that might have led to a dangerous armed conflict on Italian soil if not for some last-minute mediation by diplomats of King Henry IV of France.

All this changed with the arrival of Urban VIII to power in 1624. Suddenly, under the new pope, knowledge and the arts became the preeminent modes of advancement.[5] Urban VIII's administration brought together a brilliant galaxy of cultural figures, attracted to Barberini patronage, as the wits had put it, referring to the family's coat of arms, "like bees to honey." Projects at St. Peter's and Palazzo Barberini at Quattro Fontane were only the most visible effects of the program, calling upon the talents of the best painters, sculptors, and architects of the time—from Pietro da Cortona to Andrea Sacchi, from Pietro Bernini to Francesco Mochi, from Carlo Maderno to Francesco Borromini to Gian Lorenzo Bernini.

Reviewing the history of the decade ending in 1630, the papal librarian Leone Allacci enumerated no fewer than 476 scholars, writers, and naturalists who had figured among the "Barberini bees," either directly supported by the family or merely drawn to Rome during this remarkable age.[6] Morandi was not on the list, never having produced any published work. But his ties to those who were, and did, were strong and numerous. They ranged from acquaintance with a relative (Candida Bracciolini) in the case of the poet Francesco Bracciolini, who became secretary to Cardinal Antonio Barberini, to friendship with a friend (Galileo) in the case of Giovanni Ciampoli, the learned Florentine amateur who became secretary of the papal briefs. The Galileo connection may well have extended also to Benedetto Castelli, Galileo's student, hired in this period as a professor of mathematics in the university, while serving as tutor to the pope's nephew Taddeo Barberini, and as an advisor to the pope on land reclamation projects around the papal states.[7] Was there solidarity among librarians before the advent of modern library science? Then we must mention another Allacci entry, surely known to Morandi, the Hamburg-born antiquary and geographer, Lucas Holstein, custodian of the distinguished Barberini library.[8]

From Morandi's point of view, the most auspicious sign of the new epoch and of its promise for the cultivation of the kind of knowledge he intended to put to use—the kind, in other words, that strayed far from conformity to orthodox or traditional standards—was Pope Urban VIII himself. For Maffeo Barberini was in many ways, at least superficially, a Renaissance man. Before ascending to the papacy, he celebrated in verse

Figure 5. Ottavio Leoni, *The Young Bernini*. (Uffizi no. 1673.)

the accomplishments of some of his most prominent contemporaries—including Guido Reni ("you distinguish yourself as the undisputed master painter") and the poet Gabriello Chiabrera ("because of you, the Arno longs not for the swan in the crystalline streams of the songs of Ismenis"). Of Ulisse Aldrovandi, author of an ambitious system of biological classification, he said:

When your book all things specifies,
So artfully, Aldrovandi, to the wise,
Then the mind extracts and eye reveals
The many forms of things that sea and air
And ground give forth, and earth conceals.[9]

To Galileo Galilei he sent a poem saluting the discoveries of sunspots and the moons of Jupiter ("found by your glass, O wise Galileo")—the very discoveries whose heliocentric implications had provoked the condemnation of Copernicus's *On the Revolutions of the Heavenly Spheres* during the previous papacy, in 1616. His papacy, by contrast, presented what Galileo referred to as a "remarkable conjunction," likely to put Copernicus's work back into circulation.[10] Morandi, Galileo's supporter and correspondent, must have heartily agreed.

That Urban's protection might extend to the occult fields in which Morandi specialized seemed to be indicated by his relationship to Campanella, recently transferred to the prisons of the Holy Office in Rome from a jail in Naples.[11] How seriously Urban took Campanella's claim on his allegiance in the battle against Aristotle and other "pagan" philosophers is open to question. In any case, when Campanella informally conferred on him the role of the new "David," poet and leader, channel for divine inspiration among God's people on the path to salvation, he cordially accepted. When the exuberant philosopher furnished a voluminous and erudite commentary on his poetry, lauding the new revelations about God's providence that were due to come from the new knowledge about the nature of the universe obtained under his aegis, he gave him the first provisional liberty from imprisonment in twenty-seven years. Indirectly, then, Urban made possible the gift of a manuscript copy of Campanella's *Astrology* that the author now presented to the Santa Prassede library.

In smaller orbits outside the papal court in Rome were more modest patrons, such as Federico Cesi, founder of the Accademia dei Lincei, the world's first devoted specifically to science.[12] In 1616 Cesi had produced the academy's latest manifesto against contemporary culture. Was it not strange, he noted, that some of the most intelligent figures of the age remained obsessively attached to outmoded but serious philosophical traditions, while seeming to accept every frivolous popular fashion that came along? University professors, meanwhile, were so busy seeking lucrative patronage offers that, when it came to teaching, they simply gave in to students' yearnings for painless degrees and gainful employment. His answer: a far-fetched yet doubtlessly provocative appeal to the academicians to join together in small, self-financed communities. Let them dedicate their lives to investigating new realms of knowledge, engaging in collective efforts and communicating results among all the learned.[13] Some form of private funding would be found to keep them safe from the tumult of the world. How could a group of free-thinking monks situated in a nearby quarter of the city fail to agree?

Current collaborative projects of the Lincei in the late 1620s included a study of petrified trees in Acquasparta and a natural history of Mexico. A portion of Cesi's considerable inheritance would have been destined to support much more, in spite of his family's opposition, by a special bull of Urban VIII planned for publication in 1629, had not death overtaken Cesi in the following year. Some of the twenty-six members, such as Giambattista Della Porta, whom we will meet later on, and Giovanni Ciampoli, whom we have already met, had only the most tenuous of ties to Santa Prassede, chiefly by way of their friends. Other members, such as Galileo Galilei, were frequent visitors to the monastery. Cassiano dal Pozzo, a regular borrower from the library, happened to be Cardinal Francesco Barberini's right-hand man.

In this milieu, a library serving readers' shared interests in social advancement through cultural achievement could hardly fail to play a special role. Not that all borrowers were equal; but at least, at Santa Prassede, the common pursuit of protection and favors seemed to matter almost as much as any differences. Outside the library, even the most eminent women, at least before the arrival of Queen Christine of Sweden in the 1650s, were regarded with a mixture of pity and derision by an overwhelmingly male population, from Donna Anna Colonna, the wife of the pope's nephew Taddeo Barberini, to Donna Olimpia Pamphili, the notorious "papess" of Innocent X's time.[14] At Santa Prassede, Candida Bracciolini, whose gender prevented her from crossing the threshold of the many Vatican salons, was warmly welcomed. Roman polite society was also divided sharply along social lines. Most artists and architects could only barely hold their own in spite of the progress made in distancing themselves from artisanal roots.[15] At Santa Prassede, lack of scholarly pretensions did not stand in the way of Giuliano Finelli. The same welcome again extended to Gian Lorenzo Bernini, along with other members of the Bernini family, including Gian Lorenzo's brother Vincenzo, and Pietro their father.

Of course, the library integrated its borrowers into Roman society not only by its policies but by the knowledge it made available. At least in some important cases, it would be no exaggeration to say that Santa Prassede was the midwife of Urban VIII's baroque. Gian Lorenzo Bernini, for one, needed little encouragement. He did not come to the monastery just to bring to it all the prestige of a "Barberini Bee," nor simply what he derived from his association with the Borghese family or his knighthood in the Order of the Cross of Christ received from Pope Gregory XV.

He came in order to take away from it the knowledge necessary to make himself the indispensable mediator of papal glory.

Not that Bernini had any obvious use for Cesare Ripa's *Iconology*, which he took out after returning the Livy and the Boccaccio listed at the beginning of this chapter.[16] The standard depictions there of Faith and Charity, personified and equipped with a suitable array of lighted tapers and mewling babes, were too hackneyed to serve the purposes of Rome's most innovative sculptor in recent times. Far more would be required to divert a suspicious ruler's attention away from delving too deeply into the less innocuous cultural enterprises going on around Rome.

However, if the intention of Bernini was to turn Piazza di Spagna into a baroque transfiguration of Urban VIII, he no doubt found in Ripa exactly what he needed. Since he had all but taken over the so-called "Barcaccia" fountain project from his father that very year, various iconographical elements apparently had been going through his mind.[17] The choice of possible ornaments for a major crossroads in Sixtus V's urban restructuring program was limited by a technical challenge of the sort that would have delighted Bernini's artistic idol, Michelangelo Buonarroti. At that point in the city's water system, pressure from the Acqua Vergine conduit was too low to sustain a brilliant display of high-altitude spouting. Instead, Bernini settled on the image of a ship, nearly immersed in water that dribbles weakly on the inside from two large suns at either end and a central altarlike area, then flows out into the larger surrounding pool through four ornate channels and four cannonlike openings. He may well have conceived the ship at first based on the ancient history of this area at the foot of the Pincian Hill, where tradition suggested there once had been a Naumachia construction for naval battle games. Indeed, perhaps he checked out the Santa Prassede library's copy of Livy's history of Rome in order to review descriptions of the first naval games, inaugurated during the Punic Wars by Scipio Africanus to entertain troops in the anchorage at New Carthage in Spain and repeated at Syracuse.[18]

The iconographical significance of the ship image for Urban VIII's symbolic program was deep enough to occupy the pope with endless contemplation. The Church itself was often represented as a ship with the apostle Peter as the helmsman; a ship-shaped altar had recently been planned for the space over the tomb of St. Peter in the basilica. The new fountain, equipped with its cannonlike spouts, could more specifically refer to the Church Militant, at this time guided by the wise helmsman through the troubles of the Thirty Years War. In Ripa, Bernini would have found the additional connection of ship imagery to the virtue of Hope, depicted as a woman holding a ship. The suns sculpted on the inside of the ship referred, on one level, to Urban VIII by way of his horoscope, dominated by the sun, which Bernini was more likely to have

Figure 6. Bernini, Barcaccia fountain. (American Academy in Rome, no. 10228.)

known through acquaintances at the monastery than through Urban's poem, republished at that time and entitled "On the Sun and the Bee." The same image, alternated with bees, turned up on the decorations to the Baldachin columns.

The fountain hence appears to show Urban VIII filling the Ship of the Church to the brim and arming the cannons of the Church Militant—not with ammunition (Urban is careful to point out in another later poem dedicated to the fountain) but with water to extinguish the flames of war. On another level, suns, according to Ripa, represented "Benignity," "Clarity," and "Doctrine"—the qualities with which Urban would have most liked to be identified. The whole design was undoubtedly an "ingenious invention," in the words of Bernini's son and biographer, Domenico; an invention for which Morandi's books provided a learned basis. No wonder, Morandi noted, "he never returned it," on the line joining Ripa to Bernini in the library log, before finally crossing off the name.

Pietro, the other distinguished Bernini borrower, was no knight, but his credentials as a sculptor to the popes were impeccable. To Santa Prassede he brought the prestige of having worked his way up from relatively modest origins in Naples to commissions for the best patrons in Rome. He took away with him enough technical knowledge to help his son make Urban VIII as glorious a water-king as any Egyptian pharaoh.

Supposing the translation of Euclid's *Elements* and Oberto Cantone's *Arithmetic* that Pietro checked out were not destined for Gian Lorenzo's younger brother Luigi, still in school, they could have aided their borrower in his new position as architect of the Acqua Vergine aqueduct. In order to insure that the aqueduct properly serviced, among other things, his son's Barcaccia fountain, he may well have thought such readings could prepare him in a way that his previous work on fountain architecture in Naples many years before could not.[19] Restored in the 1560s under Pope Pius IV, the ancient aqueduct brought water into Rome from springs ten kilometers outside the city along the present Via Collatina. The master plan, drawn up in 1570 and still in force in Pietro's time, called for the installation of no fewer than eighteen fountains, including the one in Piazza di Spagna that was to become the Barcaccia.

And while he collaborated with his son on the construction of this fountain, Pietro, like his earliest predecessor in the aqueduct job, Giovanni Battista della Porta (not to be confused with the similarly named philosopher), was responsible for collaborating with the curial Congregation on Water and Roads to decide how pipes might be directed to this and to the other new fountains as well as to a long list of public and private buildings. A major problem was to allocate a portion of a given conduit to a given destination. If Pietro felt little inclined to delve into the highly technical discussions of such matters in Frontinus, the ancient master of hydraulic science, and, more recently, in treatises by Bernard Palissy and Benedetto Castelli, he may have thought brushing up on Euclid's discussion of the geometry of the circle in Book 3 and of the theory of proportions in Book 5 could give him some easy instruction on pipe design. Could quantities of water be translated into radii, circumferences, and eventually capacities? If so, Euclid might help bring Urban VIII's water, and by implication the currents of his influence, to its destinations around Rome.

Not Pietro nor Gian Lorenzo, but "Giuliano del Sig. Cavalier Bernini" headed the list of library borrowers in 1627. The designation was still apt, since Giuliano Finelli had little more to recommend him than his relations with the Bernini family and especially with Gian Lorenzo's shop. But his remarkable skill at manipulating marble, in such contributions as the lacelike leaf and branch work of Daphne being transformed into a tree in her flight from Apollo, now in the Borghese gallery, would soon pay off.[20] Unsatisfied with the scarce recognition of his talents, not to mention the overbearing attitude of the master, he began preparing to set up shop for himself. By the time he began to borrow books, he was the beneficiary of a commission to do a marble bust of the poet Francesco

Figure 7. Giuliano Finelli, self-portrait. (Uffizi no. 15095.)

Bracciolini. He could thus boast to Morandi of eventual endorsements that would surely come from the Barberini circles where Bracciolini's baroque tour de force of a 1,200-stanza epic poem on the election of Urban VIII had become the salon sensation of the moment.

Indeed, by borrowing Bracciolini's earlier poem, *The Scorn of the Gods*, perhaps Finelli, on that trip to the Santa Prassede library, intended more than just to gain enough of an acquaintance with Bracciolini's thoughts to be able to sculpt a compelling likeness.[21] He could not have known this poem was to become one of the bases for the ceiling fresco, depicting Urban as an agent of Divine Providence, designed by Pietro da

Cortona for the main Salon in the new Palazzo Barberini at the Quattro Fontane and executed from 1632. As in the poem, the fresco would juxtapose the triumphant pope with various pagan gods in playful though unflattering circumstances—the despondent Venus, the thoroughly drunk Bacchus, the timorous Giants, the hapless Mars, and the smelly Vulcan. Giuliano may have thought that by studying the work he could find new subjects and new treatments more in tune with the new papacy than the more traditional subjects of the mythological statues he had completed with Bernini for the Borghese family.

When Gian Lorenzo's brother Vincenzo came to the library around the same time, he brought with him little more than his clerical status, his family's papal connections, and his high hopes. He was drawn to Plutarch's moral essays, which he borrowed in Bernardo Segni's Italian translation for four months during 1627, at least as much by the prospect of picking up good sermon-writing material as by the pleasure of reading a classic. Perhaps he knew he would never equal the oratorical pyrotechnics of his contemporary, the Capuchin friar Emanuele Orchi, to whose florid and erudite style listeners in Milan flocked as to some ecclesiastical Demosthenes.[22] But he must have known how easily modern moralists as diverse as Erasmus and Montaigne had adapted Plutarch's essays to a Christian setting. Anyone with any experience could have told him that they might help the orator reach for those new variations, to accompany his exposition of the strict letter of the Scriptures, that Giulio Cesare Capaccio and other preaching methodologists seemed unanimously to recommend.[23] If he could persuade his patrons that he had other qualities besides his brother's high connections to recommend him for the canonry in San Giovanni Laterano that was soon to be offered, his new influence could hardly fail to redound to the advantage of the monastery. And drawing from Plutarch's essay on superstition, he might remind listeners who were inclined to flatter Urban VIII's predilections that a knowledge of the stars was part of good morals.

Much more to the library's benefit were the visits of Cassiano dal Pozzo, whose prestige as Cardinal Francesco Barberini's right-hand man could help Santa Prassede join the artistic culture of Rome to the city's scholarly culture. And in turn, information Cassiano received from the library could help him furnish his "paper museum," a unique tool for investigating natural and civil history, made up of images instead of actual objects.[24] Cassiano implicitly agreed with previous collectors, and members of the library circle, that observing visible reality was an essential accompaniment to reading texts, in any attempt to gain true knowledge. The mind alone, without the aid of empirical particulars, Francis Bacon had just recently reminded scholars—in passages that the monks were to take deeply to heart, as we shall see in chapter 7—could not avoid remaining buried in the same errors as the most moth-eaten traditional authorities.[25] Whereas previous collectors like Ulisse Aldrovandi in Bologna and Francesco Calzolari in Verona had emptied their pockets in order to fill their houses with natural specimens, precious architectural fragments, sculptures, and ancient coins and medals, Cassiano commissioned artists and engravers to produce drawings, according to precise specifications, of the best examples that his extensive correspondence might reveal.[26]

Yet, objects in a collection, real or on paper, were no good unless put to use. To make comparisons by kind and shape, Cassiano conceived of an ingenious system of cross-references, the forerunner to the Vatican Library's new electronic database. Although he could scarcely hope to encompass all the areas in Francis Bacon's ideal collection in the *Advancement of Learning* or in Cesi's research program for the Lincei academy, he achieved enough coverage to make some of his own original contributions to ornithological description and taxonomy. And by sharing his collection with correspondents like Giambattista Ferrari, he was able to furnish material for the latter's pioneering classification of citrus fruit, prefiguring Linnaeus.[27] Contemplating the series of ancient medals, in the light of the *Scriptores Historiae Augustae* he borrowed from Santa Prassede, he might inform his Barberini patrons about the dangers of absolute power without moral virtue, and the necessity of scholarship in books—indeed, libraries—for understanding that.

By no means the least of the library's borrowers in this period was Ferdinando Ughelli, abbot and historian, who came on a mission from Urban VIII himself. In Urban's opinion, Alfonso Chacon's late-sixteenth-century chronicle of the lives of the popes gave the best available assessment of the papacy's historic role. An annotated revision by a scholar of the caliber of an Ughelli, commissioned to work alongside the antiquary and patron Girolamo Aleandro, could lend further support to the notion of papal supremacy that Urban was committed to sustaining.[28] Ughelli availed himself of the Santa Prassede library's manuscript of the conclaves that elected the popes of the high Renaissance. The result was a subtle but powerful boost to the papal reputation. And Ughelli came away, perhaps, with some inspiration for the massive project he would publish fourteen years later, the *Italia sacra*, a treasury of baroque erudition tracing the episcopal history of all Italy from a Roman point of view.

In all the cases we have examined so far, books lay at the center of the monastery's rapport with the world of Barberini Rome. Indeed, knowledge, as well as the diversion furnished by books, was not only the library's raison d'être; it was the library's key to existence. Books reaffirmed the values cherished by the monks and bound the minds of borrowers ever closer to them. To the library, borrowers brought with them not only their minds, but also their associations. Associations, networks of powerful friends and allies, companies of like-minded patrons in their own right, determined whether Morandi and his way of life might flourish unopposed. How many acquaintances could Morandi collect, and of what sort?

SIX

THE WIDENING CIRCLE

INTERROGATOR: Do you know whether there was anything else in the said armoir?

THEODORE AMEYDEN: Inside the said bookcase, besides the writings, were also kept the prohibited books; and especially I saw a Machiavelli in octavo, as wide as it was tall, which was a very beautiful book; I do not know what other prohibited books were inside, because the Father Abbot kept the said bookcase locked. (*Morandi Trial*, fol. 261, August 18, 1630)

ONE THING SHOULD by now be clear: the library of Santa Prassede was no ordinary library. Here, in spite of the sanctimonious reports of the papal censors, works of general culture and religion shared space with notorious prohibited classics. And here readers of all sorts rubbed shoulders in a common pursuit of knowledge—even of the most secret type.

Among the most assiduous borrowers was Theodore Ameyden, a prominent Flemish-born lawyer with ties to the Spanish crown. In a given month of the year 1627, he came no fewer than five times, faithfully returning the borrowed volumes later in almost every case (indicated in the library lending list by "x"). He was also among the more adventurous readers at the monastery. Besides a book of decorative and instructive emblems illustrating the papacy of Gregory XIII, he borrowed the licentious "Drama of Hysmine and Hysminias" by the Byzantine novelist Eustathius Macrembolites, supposed to have lived in the twelfth century. We can only guess what sorts of recent Roman experiences such reading might have gone to inspire or embellish. Certainly, as a secular person, Ameyden's freedom to indulge whatever appetites the brilliant aristocratic culture of the city might offer was limited only by his own imagination and good taste. And in the "Drama" he would have enjoyed the story of how Hysminias, the minion of Eros, daily stoked the passion of Hysmine, the herald of Zeus, by flirtatious blandishments and walks through a garden of delights decorated with suggestive paintings. And Hysmine, his attentions ever frustrated at the brink of consummation, dreamed at night, in delicious detail, of committing acts with her that he would not dare to suggest by day.

In a more serious mood, perhaps, Ameyden borrowed a copy of the works of Niccolò Machiavelli (prudently noted in our document as "N.M."), maybe in the Giunti editions of Florence, 1532–44, or even that of Aldus Manutius, Venice, 1546.[1] After all, politics was his game, and he may well have thought the game had not changed too much in a hundred years, except for the actors playing the parts. Nor was Rome exempt from it. True, Machiavelli happened to be one of the few authors whose entire production had been banned in Catholic countries since the 1564 *Index of Forbidden Books*. But ecclesiastical prohibitions had little effect at Santa Prassede. Ameyden might savor not only the irreverent lessons in pragmatic statecraft propounded in *The Prince*, but also the clear-headed historical interpretations in the *Florentine Histories* and, and with any luck, Machiavelli's libertine novel, *Belfagor*, about how the devil takes a wife.

Thanks to the diligence of the governor's court in preserving the library lending list at Santa Prassede, we know far more about the reading habits of visitors than we do about those of the monks themselves. But every reading experience outside the monastery walls that we have so far recounted, and are about to recount below, no doubt occurred a dozen times again within. Inside, as among the monastery's outside associates, interest in books extended well beyond the limits prescribed by official sanctions. And there, as outside, interest in knowledge ran the gamut from the officially tolerated to the absolutely proscribed. How was Morandi to protect this unique culture from official interference? How was he to ensure that the library might survive? By a unique stratagem based on the same policy of book lending we have been examining thus far. A few examples will show how Morandi bound readers to himself not only with ties of common interests but of co-conspiracy, of mutual involvement in one of the most extraordinarily illegal enterprises in Rome. We may then discover why the Roman authorities waited so long before closing it down.

So let us return to the discussion where we left off. While Ameyden was enjoying his Machiavelli, Padre Alessandro Gennaro, rector at the church of San Salvatore, took away with him the Giolito 1546 edition of Boccaccio's *Decameron*, our library list specifies—the one banned at the same time as Machiavelli. Indeed, Padre Gennaro's borrowing may tell a bit more about him than he might have wished to be widely known. Can we not imagine his delight upon discovering, without the mutilations introduced in the "expurgated" edition of 1573, the novel about Friar Alberto, who persuades his lady friend that the Archangel Gabriel is interested in her and later disguises himself as the Archangel for an evening tryst?[2] And if so, what is there to stop us from supposing a certain satisfaction when he came upon the scandalous novel ridiculing the Grand Inquisitor of Florence for living in luxury, later removed? With the same satisfaction, he may have considered the diatribe, in the story of Tedaldo degli Elisei, against judges who convict the innocent on the basis of confessions extracted under torture, if not the other barbs against monks who did not live by the austere rules of their founders. And so much did he and the rest of the community at San Salvatore enjoy the book, that he kept it for at least two more years, since it was still reported as "not returned" when Morandi went to trial in June 1630. To sum up:

Teod. Ameyden	1627	x	Eustazio greco latino
Teod. Ameyden	" "	x	Emblemi Franzoni in rame
Teod. Ameyden	" "	x	I romiti in rame
Teod. Ameyden	" "	x	N.M.
Teod. Ameyden	" "		Apocalissi d'Olanda, m.s.
il P. Gennaro	1627		Boccaccio del Giolito

Several months later Giambattista Castellani, a Neapolitan nobleman, borrowed the late-fifteenth-century Benedictine author Johannes Trithemius's *Steganography*,[3] an elaborate philosophical spoof claiming to show how to communicate across long distances by invoking the spirits through the aid of a certain Oriphel, supposedly the genius of Saturn. It contained, said Andrea Possevino, advising the Congregation of the Index in 1609, not a tolerable sort of natural magic like that of Giambattista Della Porta, but the most abominable sort of ceremonial magic.[4] And as such (Possevino implied) it ought to be classed with such anathematized classics as the infamous *Picatrix*, an Arabic handbook on Hellenistic magic supposedly written in the tenth century by al-Majriti, or the *Key* that circulated under the name of King Solomon, condemned already in the thirteenth century by William of Auvergne as "a cursed and execrable book."[5] And Trithemius's credit was by no means enhanced in the eyes of Possevino and fellow members of the Congregation by his reputation as the most famous alchemist of his time and possibly the teacher of the alchemical physician Paracelsus, whose works were also condemned. Much might be learned from such readings, Castellani no doubt concluded; to what purpose, only he knew.

But the library log does not yield up its secrets easily. The modern reader interested in tracing the book-lending history of Santa Prassede finds a number of perplexing puzzles. Morandi's handwriting in the slender 100-page ledger is a beautiful combination of Latin secretarial script and Italian vernacular. His abbreviations are clearly meant for himself alone and represent his own personal mental shorthand for remembering books. Thus, titles often appear without authors, as "De miraculis virorum"—referring, it turns out, to the opening treatise of Heinrich Kornmann's vastly underrated *Opera curiosa*. Authors are just as frequently represented without titles—as in "Rogeri Baconis," leaving in question exactly what work of Roger Bacon was being borrowed (the *Opus majus*? the *Opus minus*? the *Opus tertium*?). Perhaps the library possessed only one. Sometimes the riddles can be solved by referring to the list of library books in Morandi's death inventory. Other times the references are simply cryptic, as for instance "Isaco Holanda." What could that be?

Cryptic in its allusions to books, the library log seems remarkably specific in identifying persons. After all, in Morandi's mind, the library was as much a lure for influential patrons as a tool of learning, and the collection of notable names was as important for him as the collection of notable books. Whatever Pietro Accolti might borrow on a particular day was infinitely less interesting than the fact that Accolti had borrowed it. And the fact that Accolti had authored a treatise on painting was infinitely less significant than the fact that he had been secretary to Giovanni de' Medici and later joined the retinue of Cardinal Carlo de' Medici.[6] Might not the borrower contribute something in the way of favorable reports to the grand duke concerning the useful services the monks could provide for Medici interests on some future occasion? That Antonio Ricciullo, bishop of Belcastro and vice-governor of Rome, borrowed a "manuscript of diverse instructions" was far less important than the protection he might extend to the monks as the second in command to the highest criminal prosecutor in the city. From our standpoint, as no doubt from Morandi's, the influential personages so prominently noted in the lending list for easy reference furnished a precise and eloquent record of one man's—one monastery's—struggle for significance. No wonder court officials stitched the lending list into the binding of the final version of the trial record, so that it is the first document we see on opening the outsize volume.

Indeed, far more important than what the library log said, at least from the point of view of the monastery's role in the culture of its times, was what it did not say. Perhaps for reasons of prudence, only the diction "one volume in manuscript" accompanied the name of Andrea Argoli in July 1627. Anyone at the monastery would have known just how far Argoli needed to be informed about recent developments in astronomy and mathematics, beyond the limits upon learned curiosity set by his own highly placed patrons. Equally cryptic was the entry beside the name of Theodore Ameyden in February 1628: "two volumes, manuscript." By now, Ameyden's reliance upon the monastery for secret political information was common knowledge here. Where else could he find material on Roman and European political affairs to digest into the weekly reports he was sending to the Count Duke of Olivares?

We are told that Vincenzo Cavallo, of a high-ranking Calabrian family with curial ties, borrowed a *History* by Guicciardini, some time between mid-March and early April 1630. Which edition this may have been, though the list does not specify, is not hard to guess. A scion of this old family, and truly a valuable asset to the Santa Prassede circle, can be assumed to have come for the latest version, rather than for any of the earlier ones, which he or his family no doubt already possessed. A long-festering grudge against the Holy See by a clan that had never managed to field a credible *papabile* may well have sparked an interest in the rare unexpurgated version newly published by Jacopo Stoer in Geneva in 1621. There Cavallo might savor the diatribe against papal supremacy in Book Four, suppressed entirely from every other edition since the first mutilated one of 1561, published during the Council of Trent.[7]

Much of the value of the library's collections no doubt lay in the large amounts of material that could be considered dangerous by seventeenth-century standards. This is the place where Ferdinando Ughelli, whom we have already met, came to read the weekly *avvisi* or handwritten newsletters containing salacious gossip along with up-to-the-minute political information. Apparently, his interest extended well beyond the history of affairs gone by, to include also the promise of things to come. Perhaps, among these newsletters, he read the one that reported discussions between, on the one hand, partisans of the Duke of Nevers and France and, on the other, those of Spain, for a cease-fire in the War of Mantua.[8] It then went on to explain that Spain desired to maintain a foothold in Italy despite the opposition of France, the Venetians, and the pope. If Nevers, with his French background, was to be admitted as heir to the Gonzaga dominions in Mantua and Montferrat, it noted, the Spanish demanded that he be placed under the control of the Habsburg Empire—both the Austrian and Spanish branches. The Austrian Habsburgs, meanwhile, appeared ready to guarantee Habsburg control in Italy, in spite of opposition by France and the papacy. Venice, it concluded, was too weak to make open war on the Habsburg emperor but willing to send several thousand men to help the Duke of Nevers. In this case, the monastery may have provided a welcome space where Ughelli could indulge his open partisanship for France.

Here again was a place where officials close to the pope and the curia could monitor, and even savor, the malicious rumors circulating about their employer.[9] What the physician Paolo Mancini gleaned from the so-called "conclaves" he borrowed on August 23, 1627, might well have given him at least some insights concerning the political welfare of the pope whose physical welfare was his chief responsibility. After all, the anonymous authors of such writings did not always wait for a pope to die before discussing the possible party alignments among members of the special body that would assemble to elect a successor. Anything written there about the strengths and weaknesses of the possible candidates might be highly interesting to another borrower, Giambattista Doni, a protégé of Cardinal Corsini and later the secretary of the consistory itself.

If nothing else, such readings, if they pointed in the direction of an outcome favorable to France, might confirm the pro-French sentiments Doni had already expressed on behalf of his patron in an elaborate eulogy of Louis XIII.[10]

Safely barricaded behind monastery walls, readers of "conclaves" had no more to fear than readers of newsletters from the strict controls on both of these genres. Here no one worried that in February 1572, Pius V had ruled against whoever "writes, dictates, keeps, and does not destroy the infamous libels and letters called *avvisi*, containing information damaging to persons' honor, predictions of the future, or revelations regarding the government of the Papal State conducted in secret." Pope Sixtus V's extension of the same prohibitions to "any other sorts of writing" offering political information echoed ideas about political secrecy that were common in late-sixteenth-century political tracts by the likes of Giovanni Botero and Scipione Ammirato.[11] But these had no effect here.

No wonder black marketeers brought only the choicest in dangerous manuscripts on their visits to the monastery. Nothing ordinary sufficed to keep the interest of Morandi, his monks, and the library borrowers. So Giuseppe Amati discovered when he once offered some purported letters by Richelieu and a burlesque "Report from Parnassus concerning Pinerolo," a town within the Savoy state that was often the subject of contention between the Savoy dukes and the French, perhaps containing a diatribe against the Savoy's policies in the War of Mantua. To his dismay, Morandi already possessed these commonplace items; and this time, instead of coming away from the monastery with a pocket full of change, he came away with a pocket full of even more scandalous manuscripts, generously lent to him by Morandi.[12]

Dealers in dangerous manuscripts or their employees borrowed material from the library of Santa Prassede that they might later copy out by hand and sell for a profit, extending the monastery's reach far beyond the purview of any prelate or ambassador. This was surely the effect of Orazio Faliero and his brother Virgilio, after taking home a manuscript "Report by Sig. Zeno" in early 1627, probably the one Renier Zeno presented to the Venetian Senate at the end of his embassy to Rome from 1621 to 1623, no doubt originally purloined from some diplomatic pouch and now among the many such manuscripts available on demand in every major capital.[13] The acute criticisms of papal power evidently pleased more than one patron, since the two brothers borrowed the same report again on March 2 of the following year. Clearly too specialized for a scribe's own personal edification was another manuscript, whose author and argument can only be guessed from the suggestive title, "How to Deal with Princes," and again, the equally suggestive "Pretensions on Mantua," which they took home, respectively, on February 20, 1628, and

October 30, 1629. And what they might have been doing with the "Ragionamento" of Antonio Alvarez de Toledo, duke of Alva and viceroy of Naples, besides copying it, can only be imagined, although the author's appointment by Philip IV in the current mobilization against Mantua gives some idea of the contemporary importance of such a work. They may have been hired to copy it by the same customer who demanded Carlo Maria Carafa's "Instructions to Princes" borrowed on the same day, and perhaps issued by Carafa while serving as extraordinary nuncio to the Imperial Court in Vienna during the Mantua war. Hieronim Zahorowski's *Monita privata*, borrowed by Giambattista Bertolli on October 29, 1627, and again by Orazio Faliero in December of the following year, was no doubt destined to some reader who sought the ex-Jesuit author's vitriolic comments against his Order, which had led to the work's prohibition in 1621.[14]

Thus, while the library tied borrowers to Morandi by partnerships in intellectual conspiracy, in a way, it helped support a budding information industry on the edge of legality. After all, particularly fortunate single manuscripts, sold to the right purchaser by an enterprising scribe, might fetch as much as 200 scudi apiece.[15] Although a good contract for supplying some well-heeled customer with regular weekly "avvisi" was worth from twelve to forty scudi a year—good money in a city where laborers earned around twenty—back numbers of the same, bound in the volume borrowed from Santa Prassede by the scribe Giambattista Bertolli on March 27, 1628, were highly valuable items.[16] Matteo Vincenteschi, who specialized in such items, was on the payroll of several princes and prelates including the bishop of Taranto.[17] What Vincenteschi, Bertolli, and the other scribes may have learned about politics from the material they copied was less important than what they were able to spread around. The same went for Fioravanti, the official printer of the Camera Apostolica, who borrowed a volume of newsletters on February 2, 1630, perhaps for use by some of his book-buying customers.

Not surprisingly, the Venetian and Tuscan ambassadors were both regular borrowers of manuscripts from the library. Mail was slow; information could take over a week to get from Milan to Rome, at least six days more from Lyon, and nearly a month from Spain.[18] Diplomatic correspondence often got lost—indeed, robbery of diplomatic pouches was a commonplace highway crime. And for divulging what was in the mail bags that passed through their systems, postmasters were frequent subjects of bribery and extortion.[19] Manuscripts of all sorts and from all origins found their way into the clandestine market. And in Rome, Morandi was just as likely to have the latest ones as was anyone else. Accordingly, in September 1628, Angelo Contarini, the Venetian ambassador, came in to borrow a report on the Savoy's claims to the duchy of Montferrat during the current War of Mantua. Earlier that year, and probably for the same reason, the Tuscan ambassador Francesco Niccolini borrowed the same report, along with two Spanish novels and the defense argument published in 1593 by Antonio Perez, Philip II's ex-minister, then under indictment for treason.[20] If such important borrowers used the library's collections to make their missions more fruitful, could the heads of state that employed them share their interest in the library's well-being? Only time would tell.

Political manuscripts and works of literature, of course, were not the only items among the Santa Prassede collections that were lent out with an aura of danger. So were works of judicial astrology. At least until Morandi's arrest, Sixtus V's famous bull of 1586 had no effect within the monastery walls. Therein, none of the prescribed reprisals were threatened against "astrologers, mathematicians, and anyone else exercising the art of judicial astrology concerning future affairs in agriculture, navigation, and magic, or claiming to be able to use persons' nativities to predict future contingent affairs and fortuitous events or actions depending on human will." In the monastery, praise, rather than blame, was accorded to anyone "who knowingly reads or keeps these sorts of books and writings or such that contain these matters."[21] And Abbot Gherardo Gherardi, a professor of philosophy visiting Rome from Padua, was able to borrow a "manuscript of nativities of cardinals" on March 13, 1629, no doubt to satisfy the curiosity of some wealthy patron with an interest in the future of the papacy, as well as to satisfy his own.

Nor did the very name of Tommaso Campanella, as notorious for his astrological pronouncements as for his troubles with the Inquisition, strike fear into the hearts of Santa Prassede readers, though it might have done so within other circles. Instead, with Campanella's trial still going on, anyone who wished to apply to current political realities some of the most recent ideas on the interpretation of astrological signs and symbols could resort to manuscript copies of Campanella's works, perhaps deposited in the library by the author himself. With this in mind, such a manuscript was borrowed by Gherardi. If other borrowers of the same manuscript shared similar purposes, this may help us identify Francesco Usimbardi, an otherwise unknown prelate in the Apostolic Chamber, as well as one Stefano Senarego, as entrepreneurs in the same business.

The circulation of printed books on similar matters, traced in the library log, suggests a certain amount of collusion.[22] Giambattista Brogiotti returned Henrik Rantzau's astrological treatise in November 1627, just in time for Giovanni Paolo Rocchetti to borrow it on December 11. We may infer from his arrival at the monastery on another occasion with Fioravanti, the printer to the Apostolic Chamber, to borrow Rudolph

Goclenius's *Uranoscopia*, as well as from a possible connection to Andrea Brogiotti, a master at the Vatican press, that Giambattista Brogiotti, too, was a printer. Did he borrow both works to satisfy some of those who usually came to him for books printed by the press? In any case, Rocchetti in turn borrowed Antonio Magini's ephemerides on planetary positions on June 22, 1628, in time for Pietro Mulier to borrow it on September 9. Here are two other persons we can add to our list of those involved in casting horoscopes.

In this light, let us surmise that Abbot Gherardi did not borrow Kepler's *Epitome* of Copernicus in April 1630, merely for the sheer enjoyment of reading a dangerous text. Of course, that cannot be discounted entirely, since Copernicus's work had been prohibited "until corrected," as recently as 1616; and Galileo, at least according to sources close to the curia, had then been warned never to teach the heliocentric theory again. The subsequent prohibition of Kepler's *Epitome* was supposed to demonstrate just how strictly officials meant to be obeyed. Gherardi's prevailing interests may justify us in supposing that for him, Kepler's was as much a text on astrology as it was on astronomy. So indeed, according to some interpretations, was Copernicus's. In the latter, alongside a purely hard-headed demonstration of the physical centrality of the sun in the solar system was a Neoplatonic natural philosophy, dating back to Marsilio Ficino and viewing the sun as the spiritual center of the natural world.[23] Ficino himself had developed this philosophy in harmony with the notions about planetary influences common among serious astrological thinkers in his time. From Gherardi's standpoint, arguments of this sort offered valuable insights to accompany the knowledge of the stars that he gained from his readings and that he might put at the service of his own patrons and associates.

The circulation of other works adds further details to our picture of the library as a gathering place for those interested in the most dangerous aspects of the occult. Because surely Giambattista Castellani, about whom we know nothing more, borrowed Martin Antoino Del Rio's demonological manual in 1627, precisely for what the reader might learn about the anathematized arts during the course of the explanations of the permissible ones; likewise, Feliciano Silvestri, who in September of the following year borrowed Iamblichus's fourth-century disquisition on the mysteries of the Egyptians, the Chaldeans, and the Assyrians. Though the work, unlike others borrowed by Silvestri, a laureate in law and medicine and professor of philosophy at the University of Pisa, was not expressly prohibited, he might find elucidated there some of the superstitious practices to which it seemed to subscribe.[24] On the other hand, in 1627, Abbot Giovanni Angelo Beranzolo, an author of "curious manuscripts" in his own right, borrowed Oswald Croll's treatise on alchemical medicine no doubt precisely because it purported to reveal the secrets of life according to the doctrines of Paracelsus, some of whose works were on the *Index*.[25] Francesco Carducci, who much later became governor of the city of Rieti in the Papal States, showed his true interests while still a student at the Sapienza university by borrowing Ciro Spontone's manual for divining the future on the basis of physiognomy.[26]

In this company, Giambattista Gelli's scandalous *Circe* fit perfectly. Borrowed on November 25, 1628, by Marquis Domenico Bandiera, apostolic protonotary and professor of moral philosophy at the Sapienza university in Rome, this work by a Florentine shoemaker-turned-scholar had created one of the great underground sensations of the late sixteenth century. Among the scathing comments in it concerning society and morals at that time, couched in the form of purported dialogues between Ulysses and eleven characters transformed into animals by the goddess Circe, there were passages suggesting the psychological origins of religion and the hypocrisy of the Church.[27] No wonder the work had been condemned in 1590. And Bandiera's delight was no doubt matched by that of Feliciano Silvestri, who on January 30, 1629, borrowed this along with the universal history written from a decidedly Protestant point of view by Johannes Sleidanus, condemned in 1556.[28]

Booksellers as well as black marketeers knew just what Morandi's predilections were for books and manuscripts of this sort. Niccolo Inghirami, the proprietor of the "Sole" bookshop in Piazza Navona, could expect to find Morandi from time to time among other customers whose interests bordered on the dangerous, and whose discussions often turned to astrology, horoscopes, and prophesies. The same went for the proprietor of the "Luna" bookshop nearby, about whom little information has survived except the audacity of his offerings.[29] Refined tastes like the ones Morandi served required a larger inventory than even Rome could provide. And Giambattista Pusterla, bookseller in Florence, habitually sent "curious" books to him whenever they came his way. If the latter did not already have them in his library, payment would arrive by return mail. "Knowing that [the books] contained curious things," ran his typical letter to Morandi, "I wanted to let Your Lordship know about them immediately; hence I am sending them tonight by post from Florence."[30]

What mattered most to Morandi was not that the dangerous, irreverent, unorthodox, and secret material attracted borrowers of all sorts; but that the best-accredited borrowers bore the message about the library's irreplaceable value—and his own—to the most influential circles. And the number of borrowers whose accreditation included membership in the Accademia degli Umoristi in Rome seemed to suggest that he was not mistaken in this hope. Francesco Carducci, Vincenzo Cavallo, Stefano Vai, and Ambrogio Nuti, often seen in the library corridors, could thus be expected to have encountered one another also for poetry recitations at least every fortnight at the palace of Paolo Mancini, another borrower, in a large hall designated for the use of the academy since Mancini helped found it in 1608. There they could meet other literary luminaries not associated, so far as we know, with the library circle, such as Angelo Grillo, Benedictine abbot of St. Paul's in Rome and current head of the academy.[31] And there, dedicated to the promotion of new styles in literature, their activities reputedly gave a model to the French Academy.[32] Did they exchange letters with the academy's foreign correspondents, including the famous philosopher and Galileo sympathizer Pierre Gassendi, and the scholar Nicholas-Claude Fabri de Peiresc? The documents are mute; but we know both of these figures stayed briefly in Rome.

Morandi could count on other borrowers to convey their endorsements of him and his activities to fellow countrymen near and far. A definite Tuscan connection, for instance, joined Morandi to Giambattista Doni and Pietro Accolti as well as to one "Padre de' Medici," most probably Giovanni Carlo de' Medici, born in 1611 and later made cardinal. The same tie extended to another Medici, Cardinal Carlo, whose name was frequently invoked, and to the Tuscan ambassador Francesco Niccolini. And if the Bernini family's Tuscan connections meant anything, due to their origins in Sesto Fiorentino, so also did those of Giuliano Finelli, from Carrara, and Feliciano Silvestri of the University of Pisa. More evident to contemporaries than to us, no doubt, may have been the French connection, evidenced by the presence of one "Sig. Baron Francese" and others, yet unidentified but having French-sounding names like Montholon and Remion. Morandi himself, whether deservedly or not, was occasionally referred to as a French sympathizer in Roman politics, as we shall see.

Andrea Argoli most probably came on his own business rather than on that of his patron. But no one could forget that Cardinal Lelio Biscia had recently come to his rescue by appointing him as personal librarian after he lost his job at the Sapienza, allegedly for excessive attachment to astrology. His borrowing record suggests an unrepentant frame of mind. And the 1614 supplement he borrowed of Giovanni Antonio Magini's famous ephemerides of 1582, including for the first time the correspondence that passed between the author and Johannes Kepler, could just as well serve to inform Argoli's current work on critical days and astrological medicine, or even the ephemerides that he was compiling based on the astronomical hypotheses of Tycho Brahe, as it could the astrological consultations he was giving the cardinal.[33]

Still other borrowers appear to have been operating solely on behalf of the highest prelates and princes in Rome. So when a certain "Filippo" identified only as the "servant of Card. Marcello Lante" borrowed the *Eulogies* of Paolo Giovio and the *Works* of Machiavelli in September and

November 1628, it is probable that he did so for the cardinal and not for himself. Likewise, when a certain "Alberto," identified only as the "servant of Cardinal Desiderio Scaglia," borrowed Giambattista Lalli's *La Moscheide*, a burlesque poem billed as an account of "Domitian the fly-killer," on January 6, 1630, he probably took the work directly to his master without stopping to enjoy it.

Indeed, one of the most consistent groups of borrowers comprised the cardinals—in all the possible political combinations. There Cardinal Borghese might encounter his allies, Cardinals Lante, Scaglia, and Muti. The last of these came in search of Abraham van der Myl's collection of antidotes to poisons in September 1628, we do not know with what purpose in mind.[34] They all shared library space with Cardinals Spada and Sant'-Onofrio, regarded as belonging to the rival Barberini faction favorable to France. Pro-Spanish interests were represented by Cardinal Caetani as well as by his ally, the well-connected lawyer Theodore Ameyden. Interest in the library threw all these politically active figures together with cardinals whose poverty and lack of prestige prevented them from exercising any political role at all—such as Cardinal Lelio Biscia, who borrowed Schondini's complete works in folio in January 1628, and returned them in October to borrow an Italian translation of Ptolemy's *Tetrabiblos* in manuscript.

The library provided a common reference point for the most powerful congregations in Roman and ecclesiastical government.[35] Cardinals Borghese, Biscia, and Lante on the Congregation of Buon Governo, responsible for overseeing the administration of the Papal States, could expect to cross paths with Cardinals Scaglia, Medici, and Muti on the congregation concerning bishops and regulars, responsible for enforcing the decrees on Church discipline promulgated by the Council of Trent. Or else Cardinals Muti, Caetani, Capponi, and Medici on the congregation concerning Rites, responsible for judging qualifications for sainthood, might expect to run into Cardinals Biscia and Lante on the Congregation of the Building of St. Peter's, which in Sixtus V's time had taken over responsibility for architectural projects underway since Michelangelo, and which was now turning more and more frequently to Bernini.

Remarkably enough, among the best-represented cardinals' congregations in the library lending list was the Congregation on the Index, including Cardinals Caetani, Scaglia, Medici, Capponi, and Muti. Serving the congregation in an administrative post there was the Dominican friar Raffaele Visconti, mentioned in the documents. His assistant may have been the "companion of the Father of the Index," listed anonymously here. If indeed the "companion" came to the library on his own behalf, he revealed his extraordinary acquaintance with late-sixteenth-century scientific trends in medicine by borrowing, on October 9, 1627, Leonhardt

Fuchs's *Institutes*, an advanced work of medical humanism, published in Basel in 1572. Also mentioned in the documents was Niccolò Ridolfi, at this time Master of the Sacred Palace, responsible for issuing all permissions to print books.[36] And on November 12 of the same year, he borrowed Jacques en Auguste de Thou's history of his own time, prohibited in 1610 because of hostile comments about the papacy; and this he returned several months later.[37]

With Ridolfi on the lending list, not to mention the rest of the cardinals and dignitaries of Rome who appeared in the same pages and therefore could be observed walking though the same corridors of the monastery, poring over the same books in spite of their contrasting political alignments, Morandi and his monks may well have believed themselves to be safe from interference no matter what they did.

From these borrowers, Morandi and his fellow monks asked nothing in security, at least nothing in the form of collateral: only that they remain faithful members of the library's circle. Of course, lending a book was not the same as giving a gift. A gift, as Sharon Kettering has aptly suggested, is "something transferred from one person to another without compensation"—or at least without any clearly defined repayment.[38] The lender of a book, on the other hand, might expect a very precise repayment for his loan: namely, the book in return. But the obligation did not end here. In the case of a particularly dangerous book, the borrower remained obliged to the lender for the danger of keeping it. The act of restitution always required borrowers or their representatives to return to the place from which they borrowed, to renew their acquaintance with the lender, and to help keep the library populated with influential presences in case of any threat.

Not all borrowers came here looking for books. Some time between the sixteenth and the twentieth of June 1629, a painter named Giambattista Manni borrowed a "telescope of Galileo Galilei." Whether or not this was the same sort of telescope that Galileo invited Monsignor Innocenzo Malvasia, Federico Cesi, and other Roman friends to peer through in April 1611, we cannot be sure.[39] It might have been at least as powerful as the one used at that famous meeting in the Casino Malvasia atop the Gianiculum Hill for viewing the inscriptions across the river on the wall of the church of San Giovanni Laterano. Of course, by the 1620s, no such elaborate bid was necessary for the support of telescopic astronomy. In any case, all we know about this instrument's manufacture is that it was probably not one of the few models of his own design that Galileo himself commissioned in Venice for distribution to powerful patrons, nor the one with improved optics designed by a Neapolitan lens grinder named Porta that the newsletters at the time claimed to have been constructed exclusively for Galileo's demonstration in Rome. Besides astronomical instruments and books, borrowers took other objects from the convent and registered them in the library lending list. Such we must conclude, if one Padre Remigio of the convent of Santa Maria della Pace indeed walked away with a lent bundle of "diverse clothes" as noted on October 12, 1629.

Moreover, those who came out with books often went in with other purposes in mind. Surely when Cardinal Scaglia borrowed the Catholic catechism on February 15, 1629, he may well have desired to brush up on Church doctrine or to pass the manuscript around to some others of the faithful less well informed than he. But most probably, it served as a pretext for a visit chiefly aimed at renewing old acquaintances. Likewise, Father Ascanio Tambuccini, the prior of the Vallombrosans, may well have sought some particular information he had forgotten in the life of San Giovanni Gualberto, the founder of the order, which he borrowed on January 16, 1628. More likely, he sought an excuse to visit the library along with Cardinals Biscia and Usimbardi, with whom he left.

For Santa Prassede was far more than just a monastery with a library. It was a meeting place where some of the best minds in Rome, or at least the best-placed ones, collected from time to time to discuss the cultural issues of the day. There Giambattista Malaspina, bishop of Massa, invited himself one Sunday in February 1629, along with Monsignors Ghisleri and Rivaldo, as well as Vitellio Malaspina, in the hope of hearing a dramatic work performed by the monks. "They wish to come at 24 hours," Malaspina wrote, meaning at about sunset, according to the conventional method of counting time from sunset on the night before; "after the Corso, to hear a comedy and stay for dinner"—that is, after the traditional evening carriage ride up and down the main street in Rome. "Thus," he specified, "we will all have a chance to converse together."[40] There is no way of telling whether on that occasion they met Galileo Galilei, another personal friend of Morandi. Galileo in fact was invited to the monastery for the last time in May 1630, to "do penance" with the monks at table (in the genial host's facetious phrase)—more likely, to sup abundantly in the midst of the finest entertainment and the most august company a monastery could provide.[41]

More than anything else, the monastery, so Morandi hoped, was a place where persons of all sorts and all ranks could enjoy the conversation and companionship of the abbot. Even through the scraps of paper exchanged on the morrow of a fruitful meeting, Morandi managed to spread evidence of his good judgment. "I read and reread your letters," wrote bishop Giovanni Tanassi on returning to his diocese of Sebenico.[42] By sharing with them the secrets of the universe, Morandi helped his friends and acquaintances see into the secrets of their own souls. And in sharing the most dangerous secrets with all his readers, Morandi bound them to himself with ties of equal guilt. In return, the most powerful of them shielded the monastery for a while from too much scrutiny by a papal administration increasingly unable to tolerate the very cultural forces it had contributed so much to unleashing. How long could they go on?

SEVEN

HEAVENLY BODIES

May 12, 1627

Dearest friend,

The Father General came to Passignano on the way to Rome, as you know. We all agreed to ask him for permission to disperse, and in the end, he showed his saintliness by consenting. After some thought, I finally decided to go to Vallombrosa to see and enjoy my dear and beloved darling, and the caresses I received I cannot express in words.

I.F. (*Morandi Trial*, fol. 746r)

WHAT MOST PATRONS did not realize was that, since Morandi took command, the monastery's secret life throbbed in other precincts besides the library. For not all the monks at Santa Prassede found the fulfillment of their desires between the pages of a book. Some found it outside the monastery, in the fresh air, perhaps on a brief leave, granted by the abbot or the general of the order. A few found the most intense fulfillment of all in the embraces of a dear companion, a friend, a lover. So Ilario Falugi, writing back to his fellow monk Ambrogio Maggi in May 1627, recounted his latest escapade to Vallombrosa, where experimentation with the pleasures of the senses had been carried to the highest peak of excitation. He wasted no time in taking full advantage of what could only have been a furtive and breathless encounter, abbreviated by the command to return to the monastery on the following day: "Night never seemed to come, while I remained and felt those amorous embraces, sweet kisses and, in sum, all the pleasures the human body may enjoy and feel."[1]

Waiting for the next occasion to engage in the delights of the flesh, even Falugi could never forget that such practices flagrantly violated the canons of celibacy he had sworn to uphold on taking his vows. But he and the other monks who partook of similar experiences may have found at least some justification, at the monastery of Santa Prassede, from the same permissive abbot who encouraged careless infringement of norms concerning the purchase and circulation of prohibited books and free inquiry into intellectual realms strictly forbidden by the Church. The Roman authorities would soon discover what was really going on.

In the years leading up to Morandi's trial, the monks continued about their daily business with no premonitions of disaster. Their comings and goings evinced nothing of the permanent disruptions that would take place once the authorship of Morandi's last prophecy became known and the governor's court began to take interest in them. Indeed, each day that passed seemed to bring with it new opportunities for satisfaction, new avenues of enjoyment. Nor were these avenues always entirely confined within the limits of what usually passed for the conventions of monastic life. Sometimes they strayed beyond the acceptable sensations into the realm of the forbidden. Yet for the monks, this behavior was nothing less than a physical expression of the philosophical viewpoint in forming the intellectual activity they put at the service of so many satisfied patrons. Knowledge to them meant knowledge about all things; the fulfillment of all desires.

To be sure, at least as far as the search for erotic experience was concerned, what went on at the monastery of Santa Prassede was nothing new. In the early seventeenth century, priests and monks who interpreted in the widest sense the command to love thy neighbor were as common as those who misused, in order to procure amorous rewards, the influence upon the faithful conceded to them by their office. Literature has as much enshrined the figure of the randy cleric as that of the "perpetua," virtual spouse of some country pastors. The annals of episcopal visitations are rife with complaints by the faithful about the danger to their daughters' honor within the perilously close precincts of the confessional and to their own souls by the propinquity of a flagrantly immoral cleric.[2] What we now know about clerical behavior is that if the Council of Trent sought to curb worldliness and transform ecclesiastical offices into exclusively spiritual vocations, its work was very unfinished a half-century later and would remain so as long as ecclesiastical careers were regarded as survival strategies for the offspring of early modern families.

At the monastery of Santa Prassede, Ilario Falugi was not alone in his erotic exploits. Maggi was apparently his collaborator as well as correspondent, if we are to interpret Falugi's intimations literally when he says: "O how many kisses did I give, for the love of both of us. . . ? I gave them on my behalf and yours too, but you can well imagine that I was heartily sorry you were not present at these pleasures."[3] We may safely assume that the pleasure trips on which Maggi set off alone, although the general of the order was somewhat cryptic in alluding to them, were similar in nature, if not in content, to those mentioned by Falugi. Thus wrote the general to abbot Orazio Morandi: "I wish to tell you about an occasion during the last Carnival, when he left the monastery without any permission whatsoever . . . and shamelessly set out for Coltebuono. I do not wish to enter into details . . . but I was quite scandalized."[4]

Morandi, the presiding authority at Santa Prassede upon whose head any charges of laxity might fall, could have been expected to proceed severely at least against Maggi, cited specifically by the general—perhaps meting out punishments or curtailing privileges of access to the outside. As far as we know, he never did. And for good reason, if certain indications about Morandi's own behavior are more than pure coincidence. To be perfectly fair, in an ecclesiastical setting, the boundary that separated admiration from desire in relations between young people and their spiritual advisors could be narrow indeed. How frequently this boundary was crossed, then as now, was a matter between the individuals and their consciences. We may never discover the identity of the correspondent from the convent of San Giuseppe who wrote to Morandi, signing herself only "Chi Lei Sa" (Whom You Know). Nor may we ever know her real purposes in sending "a box of biscuits and twelve Seville oranges," addressed "to my love."[5] Likewise, there is no accurate way of divining Morandi's exact sentiments upon receiving these gifts and reciprocating with a very appropriate portrait of Our Lady. All we know is that in spite of "lacking nothing" in her lonely convent retreat, "Chi Lei Sa" depended on Morandi not only for affection, but also for fatherly direction in place of her parents "when they are absent." Other favors she may have desired, and that Morandi may have at least dreamed of tendering, are buried somewhere beneath the reserve that usually shrouds such stories.[6]

In general, the monks' behavior seems to suggest that certain manuscript compositions found among their possessions were more than mere imitations of standard amorous themes from Petrarch and Giovanni Della Casa. Nor did the tribunal collect them simply as evidence for the extemporaneous versifying that had been a veritable craze in academic gatherings across the peninsula, including the celebrated Silvio Antoniano in mid-sixteenth-century Rome or, still earlier in Venice, the so-called "Blind Man of Forlì."[7] If these lyrics were not intended as instruments for procuring intimate encounters or reflections upon such encounters earlier enjoyed, perhaps they contain expressions in verse of what some monks rarely dared to experience in fact. Consider the following lines, in which the reference to the heavens directed the reader to a paradise of sense, inhabited by pagan deities rather than a Christian god:

> But why between us put up palisades
> if the fiery weapon's surely bound to strike
> whoever goes out on honorable escapades.[8]

The fiery weapon in question might just as well belong to the anatomy of one of the partners as to Cupid's quiver.

In any case, the Petrarchan themes of even the chastest poems evoked an atmosphere of overripe sentimentality that added a worldly dimension to the austere monotony of monastery life.[9] There the departure of a loved one evokes pitiable lamentations:

You wished to leave,
So from my orbs might flow
streams of tears.

. . .

Woe is me, to live without hope left
And of my heart bereft.[10]

But the indifference of the beloved seals a new resolve ("Armed with fury and with pure disdain / To iron now my heart I turn"). And the fear of death recedes in the face of the challenges of daily existence without the former attentions of the companion: ("What help is death, if in the fear / Of a thousand deaths a day I live unhappy?"). The irony of youthful amorous prowess bowed down by care poisons all future expectations ("O unhappy fate, you seal my doom / Amid my verdant weapons' finest bloom"). Still, the changing seasons and the constellations' auspicious portents give reason for hope:

That was in the time when earth returns
Dress'd in lovely clothes, to contemplate
The planet, whose great pow'r makes germinate
All things, while over Taurus's horns it turns
  All the sky then seemed to undulate
Aquarius pours all beauties from its urns,
And what it is to love, he finally learns,
Who pays attention to stars' delegate.

Such sentiments, the author claimed in the title to his poem, were inspired by the memory of "the day I made friends with you, which was in springtime, with the sun in Taurus, during a downpour, as you recall."

Other snatches of poetry, this time in Latin, seem to cast all the rest in a new light, if something more than simple friendship between men and boys is suggested in the following:

Why, fawning youth, you laugh at me
You do not know that what you see
Is all the trust I have in thee.

Faithfulness toward the (male) youth in question soon appears to be somewhat more akin to love-slavery than to mere devotion:

Sick for you, in every pore;
Yet my love you know no more;
Devoted, you I do adore.

Abjection infects the mind of the lover even at a distance—as he avows, calling upon the gods:

At your service I'll be ever;
This I swear, and I'll not waver,
Even though you love me never.

Finally, absence of the beloved provokes an unbearable anxiety that cuts to the very center of the writer's being:

Far from you I can't endure;
When you're near I'm not so sure;
Woe is me, there is no cure.

These are no masterpieces of literature. The style and expression, if not the actual ideas of this last example, could remind one only of the macaronic lyrics circulated among university students since the Middle Ages.[11] Attentive listeners who recognized the rhythm from certain sacred chants of early Christian times might also have been amused to hear, in the decidedly unclassical rhyme scheme, the fateful beat of that dreadful dirge, the Dies Irae. If the writer had in mind Lubin Eilhard's recent translations into Latin of Anacreon's odes rather than the few verses in trochaic dimeter that have come down to us from the golden age of poetry in ancient Rome, none of the original poet's felicitous expression has filtered in here.[12] Nor are we strongly reminded of the powerful physical expression of sexuality suggested in poems reputedly dedicated by Catullus to the young boy Juventus.[13] These awkwardly expressed emotions may nonetheless be real.

If such verses indeed indicate an undercurrent of homoeroticism running through the monastery's culture, they were remarkably restrained. They possess nothing of the exuberant sybaritism depicted by Domenico Passignano, if we are not reading too much into his painting of Florentine men and boys fondling and embracing one another at S. Niccolò, completed some thirty years before.[14] They were far less provocative than the slightly later dialogue by Antonio Rocco, a friar at the convent of S. Giorgio Maggiore in Venice and a member of the free-thinking Incogniti academy established in 1630. In that work, Rocco celebrated the joys of pederasty, a secret passion of the authorities, he suggested, who publicly decried it in order to remove some innocent pleasure from those not belonging to the elite. Building around the story of a middle-aged professor's classroom seduction of a young student he calls Alcibiades, he humorously debunks every canon of conventional morality. Unlike in the Platonic dialogues, the relationship does not remain on a purely spiritual plane. He has the triumphant professor exclaim, on plunging lubriciously to his goal, "If this is the seat of happiness, dwelling-place of the true god of pleasure," "to this I devoutly consecrate myself." And, sounding a final blasphemous note, he has him conclude, "If there are other paradises, I will gladly exchange them for the one I'm in."[15]

Homosexual behavior of any sort implied an attitude of defiance by the very nature of ecclesiastical reactions to it. And few topics of the times excited such a mix of indignation and perplexity. In Rome, a city of men, officials were particularly sensitive about their own vulnerability to snide allusions by friend and foe alike. Sodomites were regularly executed in the public spaces, and not just the "eight or nine Portuguese of that sect" recorded by Michel de Montaigne during his visit in the 1580s.[16] The repeated papal bulls condemning the practice were summarized and glossed in these years by the famous Roman jurist Prospero Farinacci in a chapter entitled "de delictis carnis," on crimes of the flesh. At least according to some recent work, the 1620s case of the supposed lesbian nun Benedetta Carlini in a Tuscan convent not far away was regarded by ecclesiastical officials with nearly equal seriousness as cases of pretended sainthood.[17]

How much did the monks ponder the consequences of their actions? Did they worry about how to separate spiritual from physical pleasure, when the soul was confined within the worldly prison of the body? Did they wonder who, after all, could entirely distinguish the titillation of the flesh from the pain of religious austerity? Love of God convulsed the greatest mystics in the most contorted attitudes of prostration, they might have thought. St. Catherine and her chains, St. Teresa and her fasting, bore eloquent witness to the uses of the body for the purposes of the spirit. And when St. Teresa spoke of the sweet arrow that penetrated the most tender recesses of her physique, provoking waves of sensation that rocked her being and brought her to a breathless climax, how not to think of earthly love? Bernini's sculpture of the subject, completed some twenty years after his last visit to the monastery, would be condemned by the Victorians precisely on the grounds of the overwhelming sensuousness of the experience it portrayed.

Yet such behavior did not necessarily call for a theological justification. Nor did it need much in the way of a philosophical explanation. Whether the monks, while engaging in it, pondered some of the more audacious contemporary expressions regarding the position of sensual pleasure in the economy of the body is impossible to say.[18] As far as we know, Santa Prassede possessed no copy of the ex-Carmelite Giulio Cesare Vanini's exceedingly rare *Dialogues*, which inspired the admiration of seventeenth-century libertines and modern historians alike, both for their materialist overtones and for their exuberant descriptions of the varieties of copulation among all creatures, catalogued ostensibly as part of an account of the generation of living things.[19] So they were unlikely to have had any exposure to Vanini's account of human venereal stimulation as a necessary pleasure governed by a special sixth sense, in pages of the book begrimed by generations of youthful scholars in a few lucky libraries elsewhere.

Although their library possessed some of the earlier works upon which Vanini based his philosophy, such as Girolamo Cardano's *On Subtlety*, there is no way of telling whether our monks paid much attention to Cardano's inclusion of sexual practices among those sensual effects necessary for our health in Book 13. If they had, they might well have agreed not only with Cardano's purely physiological account of the sentiments, but also with his statement that "we especially love rare things, because we cannot enjoy them easily, and we always tend toward what is prohibited and prevented, and desire that which is denied to us and not permitted us to have."[20] How true, they must have thought, as they sallied forth on yet another clandestine adventure to the nearest village.

What we do know is that the monks paid close attention to the poetry of Giambattista Marino, whose account of the wonders of the human form gave the seventeenth century one of its great poetic classics. This verse romance, entitled the *Adonis*, proceeds from the education of the senses to the formation of the intellect by way of some of the most daring descriptions of organ pleasure ever offered in serious verse.[21] The monks' interest extended beyond the poem to Marino himself. They may have actually met him through the members of the Accademia degli Umoristi with whom both he and they were associated, particularly when he came to Rome in triumph after the scandalous success of his poem in France. In any case, they eagerly followed the polemic surrounding the work, sharing among themselves and among members of the library group copies of burlesque verse exchanged between Marino and his arch-rival, Gaspare Murtola, a more favorably situated but far less talented poet in Turin. Although such exchanges, even when the two poets managed to refrain from the physical violence they sometimes inflicted upon one another, were not always in the best of taste, they were at least in keeping with the mischievous environment cultivated at the monastery.

In one poem, which the monks possessed in a manuscript variant differing somewhat from the later printed edition of 1629, Marino imagined the last will and testament of the fifteenth-century Bergamo-born condottiero Bartolomeo Colleoni, whose surname aptly suggests "balls," depicted by Andrea Verrocchio in a famous statue before the church of S. Giovanni e Paolo in Venice. To the cemetery, Marino imagined, the condottiero left his bones; to his faithful squire, he left his spirit and his soul; to his enemies, terror and fright. To his sons, Colleoni left his gold and silver; to his soldiers his sword and buckler; to Venice his equestrian statue; and to Bergamo his house and home. Then, Marino imagined,

> He willed his name and honor to posterity,
> His ardor, courage and his valor bold,
> His weapon and his horse to chivalry.
>
> Last, for reform of poetry (I'm told),
> To Murtola he willed the world's supply
> Of all dick-headedness, to have and hold.[22]

All Murtola had been able to produce in response was a humorless tirade against Marino's "filth," commanding the vexatious upstart to answer for his undeserved successes by telling the world "who he was, what he thought, and who sent him."[23] An invitation Marino never bothered to accept.

Such raillery by no means diverted the monks' attention from their more serious interests in Marino's *Adonis*, an epic work in length and achievement if not in form.[24] If they cared to read the library's copy beyond the infamous Canto 8, they would know that pleasure was not everything—not even according to Marino. "The peak of pleasure, end of all desire," satisfies only part of man's nature, sang Marino. "Born to speculate," man draws upon the "fantasies [of] sense" to form the intellectual creations whereby he most resembles the divine.

> The same Divine Omnipotence whose zeal
> benign, in Man such excellence did place,
> Could well, this creature, eternally by veil
> Of incorruptibility embrace.
>
> . . .
>
> But since he's born to speculate, 'twas meet
> That in him every species did resplend;
> And that his lucid intellect should greet
> Such fantasies as lowly sense should send.
> Nor him of other stuff needs must create,
> Than what the basest elements could lend,
> So sense and mind together may reflect
> Whatever feeling, and desire, elect.[25]

Scattered references in the poem to the products of man's discoveries in cosmology, biology, optics, and every other science celebrated the products equally of man's sense and of his intelligence, ever-present in some combination in the monastery's environment.

But in the main argument of the poem the monks would have found more than enough confirmations of man's irredeemable voluptuousness to belie such philosophical pieties, and justify all manner of misconduct. The narrative traced the tragic story of the young mortal, Adonis, who wins the heart of Venus by his great beauty and gains the crown of Cyprus by her help and his own virtue. Courtship on the island eventually finds the two lovers lolling in the Garden of Pleasure, divided into five areas, one for each of the five senses. Elaborate descriptions of the sensory organs ensue, abounding in real anatomical detail from recent scientific treatises by Realdo Colombo and Fabricius ab Aquapendente. The accounts of each kind of sensation culminate in the Garden of Touch in Canto 8, where after a purifying bath together, the lovers join in the closest embrace. The next scene is metaphorically evoked by Venus, using the image of the arrow from Love's quiver:

> Be still, my heart, by now I feel arrive
> Love's pleasing tongue, sweet penetrating dart,
> And in that ruby whetstone would make sharp
> the point, thereby urging me to die.[26]

This is followed, hours later, by "Drunk with pleasure, in joyful trance they lie / Souls exhausted, borne to a heaven of love."[27] The emotions evoked here added poignancy to the later cantos, where the monks wept along with Venus on learning of the mortal Adonis's untimely death at the hunt, gored by a wild boar.

The story of Adonis must have reminded the monks about the dangers of investing too much of themselves in worldly delights. If so, this was a lesson they soon forgot. Free will gave us the choice to do good or evil, to live or die, they must have thought. Did not free will also command us to do everything in our power to live as fully as we can? The judges would disagree vehemently with the monks' interpretation of this command. Could the monastery's protectors be made to understand?

EIGHT

CLEAN TEETH, PURE SOULS

INTERROGATOR: Say whether you recognize the writings that were found today in your rooms and what name is written on them.

MORANDI: I see very well the writings being shown to me, bearing my signature and those of two witnesses, which were found in my rooms at Santa Prassede. (*Morandi Trial*, fol. 118r, July 21, 1630)

SOON AFTER THE MONKS began to explore the endless possibilities of their new-found freedom under Morandi's leadership, they conceived of new ways to shield their activities from too-close scrutiny by ecclesiastical authorities. To ensure a widespread network of influential associates, book lending was not enough—even of the prohibited kind. The monks hit upon a clever expedient, one that, by promising to draw out the thread of human mortality to the utter limit possible on earth, might also draw out the thread of their own exemption from prosecution. This brought the monastery's protectors back again and again, for nostrums, incantations, potions, and solutions to their share of the world's ills.

Notwithstanding the abundant opportunities for enjoyment and distraction, the body was, at best, an imperfect theater of delight—for the monks as well as for everyone else in their environment. There was no relying upon the senses to produce unalloyed perceptions of pleasure all the time, nor even the sort of pain that at its height might cross the threshold into pleasure. Indeed, for the most part, the body was subject to an enormous amount of unpleasantness in this period—even for those who did not blunder their way into criminal or disciplinary proceedings, as did Morandi. Nor were literati and scholars the only ones whose melancholic humors seeped up from physiques disturbed by a thousand disorders noxious to the play of fancy, the flight of whimsy, or a giddy sense of abandonment. Suffering from the same complaint, at least according to the meticulous descriptions in Robert Burton's *Anatomy of Melancholy*, were also lovers, the old, and those affected by vainglory, excessive appetite, loss of liberty, poverty, accidents, and wind.[1] Anyone perusing what is left of Morandi's correspondence, teeming with references to cataracts, watering of the eye, fistulas, headaches, constipation, and so forth, is sure to come away with the impression that we are in the presence of a century of hypochondriacs.

While they ministered to the spiritual needs of their flock in one part of the monastery, and the intellectual needs in another, in still another part of the monastery the monks ministered to physical needs. There, displayed in neat rows for ease of selection and use, stood jars in terra cotta and clear glass, arranged by size and containing whatever might be found in a well-furnished early modern apothecary's shop. Putting to use an assortment of mortars and pestles, alembics, retorts, tubes, flasks, and burners, the monks concocted secret remedies for every complaint. That such remedies should have included blasphemous incantations along with medical secrets of less than unimpeachable orthodoxy from a religious point of view was perfectly in keeping with the prevailing libertine way of life. Morandi's endorsement was the dual consequence of his experimental nature and his project for the future.

For Morandi's judges, and for the pope to whom they reported, these practices furnished just one more proof that this was a way of life gone dreadfully wrong, one that must be eradicated before its pestilential influence spread to the less privileged sectors of society. For Morandi's associates, the practices were so many more ties binding them to him, their savior and protector from all manner of earthly inconveniences. For us, they provide further evidence of the basic mentality that drove the monks ineluctably in the direction of the science of the stars.

Whatever the monks' theological errors may have been, accepted standards of public health guaranteed a steady demand for their services.[2] Monastery adherents who had managed to survive beyond infancy in fortunate enough circumstances to avoid the constant threat of war and famine were exposed to shocks to the system and contagious diseases on all sides. Even those whose occupations did not oblige them to stretch their limbs and pull their muscles to the limits of toleration were often doomed to live with chronic pain.[3] Professional physicians came to the rescue more by accident than by design; and if the Hippocratic injunction to "do no harm" was honored more in the breach than in the observance, this was less the fault of deliberate malfeasance than of mistaken care administered with good intentions. Rest cures and cleanliness were usually part of much more elaborate regimens based on one or another of the conflicting theories about the organization and function of the bodily organs. When the more sinister remedies did not get in the way of the more innocuous ones, the patient might expect some relief.

Feeling good, of course, was not enough. Advancing civility demanded not only comfort but good appearances. In a culture so highly attuned to sensual stimuli, one's own pleasure was conditioned as well by the pleasure of others. Enhancing by art the work of nature was already the goal of good breeding in the early sixteenth century, when Erasmus contrasted the bestial Germans he met with the more refined English people. The shifting sensorium, in Walter Ong's felicitous terminology, that is, the changing view of what was pleasing to which sense and when, called for close attention to whatever might help present an acceptable façade in every situation. The fashioning of the self, reduced to principles of behavior by Castiglione and Della Casa, was cultivated at least in part with this in view.[4]

Was cleanliness next to Godliness? In the mind of Juan Luis Vives it was.[5] Why not also in the minds of our monks? The body was a temple of God as well as a container for our worldly selves. Must the soul languish in a habitation that was disgusting even in human terms? Offering their remedies for the imperfections of the body, the monks may well have pondered the ramifications of their nostrums from the standpoint of the purity of the soul. Since they left no record of their thoughts on the connection between physical and spiritual perfection, we can only draw inferences from the evidence about their practices.

What we do know is that in the 1620s, to many who sought their aid, the monks at Santa Prassede offered a release from the mundane trials of life. They applied what they knew of the esoteric wisdom of the ages to every aspect of personal care—not just for solving such serious problems as seizures, syphilis, kidney stones, sterility, and difficult pregnancies, but also for whiter teeth, sweeter breath, a full head of hair, healthy lips, and luminous skin.[6] Some of what they knew they drew from books of "secrets" supposedly endorsed by the personages mentioned therein as having used the remedies included—such as Father Mattia, the Inquisitor of Brescia, named in a manuscript confiscated from the monastery by the governor's court. Naturally, the more secret the source, the more effective the remedy—at least, according to the mentality of the time. And the superiority of manuscript, as a vehicle for conveying the hidden wisdom of the ages, was attested by citations in printed works. Johann Jakob Wecker, in the collection of secrets he published in the late sixteenth century, was by no means alone in excerpting "ex libro manu scripto" with no further identification, to recommend cures for hemorrhoids and other ailments.[7]

A patron of the monastery, determined to make every sacrifice necessary for that precious ounce of comfort, might find that the remedies offered by the monks were worse than the ailment. Suppose Niccolò Ridolfi, the Master of the Sacred Palace, some time after his library visit, was afflicted by the parasitic worms that were a staple of inadequate alimentary conditions at every level of society.[8] Medical science could classify the worms, could even comment on drawings of them by the best engravers of the time; but it was as yet too ignorant of their origins and life cycles even to recommend effective conditions for prophylaxis, such as avoiding undercooked meat; much less was it able to conceive of effective cures. Most cures, consequently, were literally shots in the dark. In ancient Rome, Cornelius Celsus recommended a potion made up of crushed lupins, mulberry bark, and hyssop.[9] But times had changed. Our monks, so we gather from the book of secrets confiscated from the monastery, ordinarily recommend that the patient drink an elixir composed of the juice of the rue plant and the patient's urine[10]—hopefully adding "et sanabitur." Surely, otherwise, they might have added "et morietur."

Ridolfi would be particularly impressed by the exotic ingredients upon which some cures appeared to rely to do the trick. If he had boils, myrrh mixed with resin from the calamus draco, a plant of the palm family, was recommended. If he had a bloody nose, the skin from a hare would be carefully wadded up and stuffed into the nostril. Was his nephew a bedwetter? The solution was goat hooves. Alternatively, our visitor might find some cures to be deceptively homespun. If he suffered from a kidney stone, he might be given cassia root, the root and seed of the germander, and the seed of the bardata plant.[11] Or again, if he suffered from difficulty in micturition: two ounces of stalk cassia and one ounce of oil of sweet almonds, mixed together and "given to the patient at daybreak."[12] If he had blood from the penis he would be treated by rosemary leaves, well-mashed, mixed with white wine, then passed through a piece of white linen and given to drink.[13] Exactly what caused the difficulty, or the bleeding, the monks—like the so-called empirical physicians who devised the more coveted remedies—left up to the theorists to ponder.

Still other remedies, Ridolfi would observe, sought to place the unseen forces of the universe at the disposal of the practitioner. He might wonder how far such methods diverged from accepted structures of knowledge or the orthodox sources of religious belief. To cure his toothache he was asked to write seven powerful words (prudently obliterated in our manuscript) on a stick, then take a knife and scratch out the letters one by one, touching the tooth with the knife after each cancellation. "Thus proceeding letter by letter, touching the aching teeth, you will see the proof."[14] He could tame a horse by invoking the occult powers harbored in magic words: write on the front right foot "andrai fido"—"you shall be faithful"—then on the rear right, "idem fido," on the front left, "affido," and on the rear left, "ego idem fido." Then ride in confidence.[15] Were his gas pains unbearable? He could relieve them by saying three Our Fathers and three Hail Marys in honor of the Most Holy Trinity. Then he was to say, three times, "mago, mago, mago" ("magician, magician, magician"), and three more times, "garaliop"—a word whose entire meaninglessness only added to its magical power.[16] Suppose he wished to "find out whether he was to live or die." In this case he was to take the juice of the ortolan mint and place it on his temples and forehead. If it made him sleepy, he would live; if not, he would die.[17]

Just where many of these remedies may have originated Ridolfi would have no clue. Busy man that he was, he had no time to study the resemblance between some of the monks' procedures and those found in a book circulated in this period under the name of Albertus Magnus, the thirteenth-century Dutch theologian and philosopher who taught Thomas Aquinas, containing numerous additions from late medieval and modern sources ranging from Raymon Lull to Paracelsus. So he would not know that the basic function of the magical evocations we have just described was little different from Pseudo-Albertus's secret for attracting fish to a fishing site by detaching several mussels from their nesting spot on a rock, removing the live creature, writing on the empty shell the words "JA SABAOTH" in one's own blood, and throwing them in the designated area.[18] That both the monks and Pseudo-Albertus belonged to an esoteric tradition that, combining some elements of elite and popular wisdom, served as an undercurrent beneath official medicine was lost on him. Nor was he in any position to observe the similarity between the monks' cures for epilepsy and those of Johann Jacob Wecher, who used a paste made from oak bark,[19] attributing this cure to Antonius Mizaldus, the author of yet another sixteenth-century book of secrets.[20] Unless he himself or someone at home suffered from this disease, Ridolfi would not have noticed that the saffron and hemp seeds in the monks' version of this concoction, as well as the instruction to have the whole placed as a compress on the front part of the head, well-shaved, bore more resemblance to yet another sixteenth-century collection, that of Girolamo Ruscelli, known as Alessio Piemontese. He was more likely to have tested the monks' treatment for hemorrhoids. Like Alessio's, it recommended rubbing the affected part with a small sack made by wrapping finely mashed cooked onions and butter in an onion skin.[21] "And if [the hemorrhoids] are inside," the manuscript added, "make a suppository."

But let us suppose that Ridolfi had enough leisure to poke around the library on his own. He might have been surprised to discover that many of the remedies available in the "secrets" literature and in the monks' prescriptions had ancient roots. What else could he conclude from the close resemblance between the modern cures and the extant works from classical medicine and botany? True, the common use of cassia root, say, for curing calculi of the bladder, by the monks and by Cornelius Celsus in his *On Medicine*, was no proof of a direct link between the first century B.C. and our period.[22] Nevertheless it could indicate an indirect one either by way of now-lost medieval sources or by way of the rediscovery of the work of Celsus in the fifteenth century. Over the ages, the European pharmacopoeia, as the monks might have called it, had merely increased in volume, not fundamentally changed. If powdered stag's horn was no longer being used for cleansing wounds or curing toothache, as in Celsus's time, that was because it was now being used, our ambassador might have been pleased to find, for snakebites.[23] Similarly, if wine was the only common ingredient between the ones suggested in ancient and modern times for curing laryngitis, this may have been simply because peppercorns and saxifrage had given way to nettle seeds as the preferred infusion.[24]

Perhaps more surprising, in an environment where the latest ideas in natural philosophy were being tested and discussed, some remedies seemed to derive their power from archaic concepts rooted in popular culture. Among the people of western Europe, occult connections between tangible ojects were simply part of the way the world worked.[25] Anyone who believed that mandrake root, supposedly resembling the form of a human being, induced fertility when ingested by a woman, about which Niccolò Machiavelli built the plot of the most famous comedy of the early sixteenth century, would not be surprised to find ashes from burned linen seeds recommended as a hair-restoring tonic by our monks' manuscript of secrets.[26] After all, if the resemblance between the root and the human was the cause of the curative effect in the case of the mandrake, there was no reason not to believe that the resemblance between flax and human hair might help bring out a woolly mane where none had been. And to produce such an effect, what better way than to transmit the essence of the resemblance via the burned-down essence of the plant supplying the simile.

Such reasoning gave credit to the use, recommended by the monks, of milk from a nursing mother or even of a nursing goat as a remedy to induce parturition.[27] The parallelism between nursing and giving birth, or even the attraction of an infant to a mother's milk, somehow might call upon the mysterious forces of childbirth. Only the therapeutic ends distinguished these beliefs from persistent magical practices involving the manipulation, for the purpose of causing harm, of the little models we call voodoo dolls, formed in the approximate image of misliked persons and containing pieces of their hair and clothing. The mechanism was exactly the same: the simulacrum affected the original by the very power inherent in the similarity. There is no need to resort to James Frazer's account of the sympathetic magic of the ancient Egyptians to be convinced about the antiquity of such beliefs. Nor has the fire of love much changed across the ages, that inspires young modern Central Americans to incinerate images of their objects of unrequited affection in order to induce reciprocal feelings.[28]

But there is no reason to suggest that the monks were mere mouthpieces for popular ideas. Nor was the notion of occult connections between similar things exclusive to a popular mentality. And here the monks' intellectual background in Renaissance philosophy came into play. Of course, just how much the esoteric philosophy of "signatures," with which the monks would have been thoroughly familiar, owed to ancient folk ideas is impossible to determine. Certainly, proponents of the various versions of this philosophy took care to trace their intellectual lineage to more accredited sources, such as Hermes Trismegistus, Plato, and the Neoplatonists, especially the fragment known to the period as Proclus's *De sacrificio et magia*, with its classification of the objects in the universe according to the categories of celestial and terrestrial, good and bad.[29] In the versions offered by the monks, the correspondences between all things in the macrocosm and the microcosm formed part of more or less coherent physico-cosmological systems.

At the very foundation of the monks' whole way of thinking, in medicine as in astrology, was the notion that the human anatomy was a small replica or microcosm of the great world around. The functioning of the former could be understood best by examining the functioning of the latter, and vice versa; indeed, changes in one strongly influenced and were influenced by changes in the other. Determining which parts of the microcosm corresponded to which parts of the macrocosm called for the best efforts of the philosophers. According to some versions of this philosophy, God left occult signs or signatures on the parts of the world at the moment of creation, from which the correspondences existing between them could be discerned. On this view, the usefulness of galbanum resin for triggering a woman's menstrual cycle, suggested by the monks' practices, was no accident; it was the result of the connection between the woman's cycle and the cycle of nature, subtly revealed to us by the periodically flowing resin's musky odor and reddish color.[30]

If they wished to compare their remedies with one of the most elaborate versions of this philosophy of signatures, all the monks would have had to do was to refer to the works of Paracelsus present in their library. There they would find the therapeutic value of a substance like sulphur in the treatment of fevers attributed to its symbolization of all that was hot and fiery in the world.[31] Or else they could refer to the *Natural Magic* of Giambattista Della Porta, who, for attracting the affection of a woman, recommended presenting her with the genitals or the sperm of a dove or a pigeon—birds known for their affinity to lovemaking. An irresistible proposition indeed, the monks may have thought, pondering its application to cases familiar to them.[32]

From the contemplation and practical use of the sympathies and antipathies around them, the monks themselves as well as their more exacting patrons and admirers might hope for a measure of control over their bodies and their world as well as a higher knowledge of the universe. Such in fact had been the promise of Paracelsus, who claimed that the true adept, having become a medium for the divine light of truth revealed in nature, would acquire "firmamental power."[33] Such again, in effect, was the promise of Della Porta, who defined magic as the search for wisdom through a survey of the whole course of nature.[34] He offered a doctrine of divinely inspired instrumentality to the adept, without some of the more extravagant, not to say dangerous, claims of the fervidly iconoclastic Paracelsus. We do not know whether or not the monastery associates entirely agreed with the authors of the pseudo-Egyptian Hermetic corpus, still a fashionable source of occult information in spite of Isaac Casaubon's recent unmasking of the second-century forgery, in concluding from the proposition "like is known by like" that "if you do not make yourself equal to God you cannot apprehend God."[35] But they certainly agreed that whoever could tap into these forces ought to be able to achieve happiness on earth—or at least a less painful life. Astrology was simply another aspect of the same kind of thinking.

Supposing Ridolfi, our visiting Master of the Sacred Palace, was as demanding a patron as we are assuming him to have been, he may well have been left unsatisfied by the specific remedies so far described. In that case, the monks might offer to draw the mysterious so-called "fifth essence" out of the very marrow of nature. Known to the Pythagoreans and to Aristotle as the substance that filled the heavens, formed of neither fire nor air nor earth nor water, the fifth essence had come to be ever more coveted as theories about it had grown ever more elaborate.[36] For Marsilio Ficino it was the substance through which the world soul, drawing its energy from the sun, vivified all creation.[37] Paracelsus, on the other hand, unable to describe it directly, deferred to a series of similes. It was, he said, "the nature, power and virtue and medicine," as well as "the color of life and propriety of all things," not to mention "a spirit like the spirit of life."[38] It constituted the essence of individuality, belonging to every terrestrial thing and existing in as many different forms—in the case of iron, for instance, probably in the form of a sort of iron chloride; and in the case of emeralds, a green juice.[39] It had many uses, chiefly curative. "When the fifth essence is separate from the not-fifth-essence, as the soul from the body, and when it be taken inwardly into the body," exclaimed Paracelsus, "what infirmity is able to resist so noble, pure and potent a nature?"[40] Apart from its curative value, rivaling only that of the philosopher's stone, it was thought capable, so Cornelius Agrippa reported, of turning any metal into gold.[41] For the monks, it might be the ideal way of keeping the interest even of the most worldly of their associates.

In order to extract this essence, the monks would no doubt have reported—to Ridolfi or whoever demanded it—that the various techniques depended on highly divergent theories. Ficino suggested it might be found most easily in substances having a "warm, damp, and clear quality"—such as white sugar and wine, especially when combined with gold and the odor of cinnamon and roses. These should be ingested, he said, especially in the day and hour of the sun, the better to capture the solar power condensed in them. Paracelsus insisted that the fifth essence was obtainable in the form of a subtle liquid by "breaking the elements," earth, air, fire, and water; but he was evasive, as always, about how to do this. Any combination of sublimation, calcination, strong water, corrosive acids, and sweet and sour things might do the trick. With metals, corrosives were particularly useful; but care must always be taken that additives to the material from which the essence was to be drawn would not fatally combine with the material. Instead, opposites should be used: oil rather than vitriol for extraction from water, lest the watery vitriol become inseparable from the water.

Fortunately, the monks' secret recipe for the fifth essence did not call for anything that a monastery would not have on hand.[42] Vinegar, lye, ammonia, and silver were to be mixed with terra sigillata, a natural compound of silica, aluminum, magnesium, lye, and ferrous oxide formed by the decomposition of lava (not to be confused with the modern potters' slurry that now goes under this name). Then the whole was left to set. The maturation of the silver would bring out the earthy qualities attributed to it by the alchemists, due to its relation to the symbol of Jupiter, ruler of the propagation, growth, and nourishment of life.[43] After eight days the resulting mixture was to be distilled—the method of choice, said Paracelsus, for penetrating beyond the appearances of things and into the very viscera of nature; and the first substance to rise to the surface would be the fifth essence.[44]

Here the monks' astrological ideas and sympathetic magic combined. Taken into the body in its purest form, they promised, the fifth essence might restore the missing solar element to those in whose astrological chart the sun was occluded, even changing their material fortunes—affording wealth, for instance, "if you are too poor" (si nimis esses pauper).[45] More to the point, perhaps, at least in Ridolfi's case, it would regenerate the flagging spirits, strengthen the heart, and add precious years to abbreviated early modern lifespans. Unless, of course (it said), such was not God's will. If "Deus omnino iubeat ipsum mori," there was nothing more to do.

If ever he tried such a remedy, given to him by the monks, at least, apparently, Ridolfi survived. Indeed, he lived on for another twenty years after Morandi's arrest. If he kept his distance from miracle cures of every type, enough other persons were helped by the power of the fifth essence, of pharmaceutical secrets, of similarities and of signatures to seize the divine forces of nature and direct them into the complex routines of daily experience. Their protection could save the monastery for a time. Then what?

NINE

THE HARMONY OF THE UNIVERSE

INTERROGATOR: Do you recognize these writings?
MORANDI: Some notebooks of the cabala that were given to me so I could see what it was. Also, a discourse by a certain Domenico the Arab, now dead, concerning certain cabalistic numbers, and another sheet concerning my own life, done by the same Domenico the Arab. (*Morandi Trial*, fol. 98v, July 13, 1630)

AS THE MONKS delved ever deeper into prohibited realms of mind and matter, the monastery's ongoing strategies of self-protection became obsolete. Their riskier activities increased the danger not only to themselves but to everyone close by. Eventually, books, chemical nostrums, and incantations were no longer enough to bind the souls of prospective patrons to their precarious fortunes. Some time in the early 1620s, Morandi sought a new solution.

He did not have to go far. He well knew that the world was not just governed by the similarities that stood at the basis of homeopathic medicine. Nor was it entirely governed by the action of herbs and chemicals on the human body and its environment. It was also governed by a sovereign architecture articulated in number, weight, and measure. For understanding these articulations, the sciences of mathematics and geometry only barely scratched the surface. The same went for the still-indistinct disciplines loosely grouped under the general category of natural philosophy, including astronomy, biology, physics, and so forth. Some illumination might come from discovering the identical rules of proportion that determined such apparently different phenomena as the behavior of the heavenly bodies, the frequencies of sounds produced across the musical gamut, and the shapes of the five major solids. Such discoveries led Johannes Kepler and others to believe that the universe was the orderly product of a divine mind whose basic modus operandi was mathematical and geometrical. Even Galileo, who was far less sure than Kepler about the mystical significance of these connections, believed that the book of nature was, in his words, "written in mathematical characters."[1]

Far different from this sort of scholarship, in spirit and intention, were the efforts of other thinkers who sought in the mathematical ordering of the world a key to mastering life's challenges. And the tool Morandi eventually hit upon, one whose long history of distinguished theorists, from Pico della Mirandola to Giordano Bruno, lent it a considerable amount of intellectual cachet, was the set of beliefs and practices known as cabalistic magic. If Morandi could tap into its most secret sources, an oral tradition whose roots have since been lost, would it suffice to keep the monastery, and its contents, safe?

To be sure, neither Morandi nor the other monks had to resort to a clandestine manuscript tradition to explore the practical applications of cabalistic theory, if they did not want to. Supposing they found Pico and Bruno to be far more interested in cabala as a path to the knowledge of God and the created world than in any worldly results they were likely to achieve from such study, they might turn instead to Cornelius Agrippa's *Occult Philosophy*, present in their library. There they could learn the significance of the Hebrew alphabet and its numerical equivalents according to the standard Christian version of Jewish mysticism seen through a Neoplatonic lens.[2] Relying only upon Agrippa, they could safely ignore the original cabalistic creation story in the Sefer Yetzirah, attributed by legend to Abraham the patriarch. For their purposes they need not know how God imparted form and weight to the Hebrew letters, sending out each one respectively as an instrument or matrix for building a distinct part of the material world. Nor were they likely to seek mastery of the techniques of gematria for interpreting the Hebrew Scriptures by substituting the words in the text with other words formed from calculating the numerical equivalents of the originals.[3] Nor again were they likely to investigate the various attempts by Christian scholars to adapt and appropriate cabalistic methods for their own use.

But at least they could appreciate Agrippa's account of the significance of each number, based on a highly diverse collection of sources, ranging from authentic cabalistic to ancient Greek to Roman to modern European. They could be reminded that, for instance, the number six derives its mystic power from the number of the planets, the number of the six substantial qualities (sharpness, rarity, movement, obtuseness, density, and quiet), the six positions (up, down, left, right, forward, and backward), the six harmonic tones, the number of days the ancient Hebrews collected manna, the number of the day on which man was created, and, last but not least, the number of the wings of the cherubim. The number twelve, on the other hand, derives its power not only from the twelve apostles, the twelve tribes of Israel, and the twelve stars surrounding the head of the Virgin Mary, but also from the twelve eggs laid by the peacock, the twelve times that rabbits litter every year, and the twelve-month gestation period of a camel.

4	9	2
3	5	7
8	1	6

ד	ט	ב
ג	ה	ז
ח	א	ו

Figure 8. Cornelius Agrippa, magic square.

Agrippa's magical amulets were perhaps more directly applicable to the problems encountered by the monks. These they would have prepared by engraving arithmetical symbols for the planets upon them, derived from cabalistic sources. In Agrippa's work they would find a syncretistic distillation of pertinent information variously drawn from medieval Jewish, Arabic, and Christian sources, including the infamous magical textbook, the *Key of Solomon*, supposedly containing the concentrated wisdom of the king of Israel.[4] To each planet corresponded a group of spirits and a mystic symbol; to each symbol corresponded a table of Hebrew characters, whose numerical equivalents formed a magic square (the numbers along each column and row all adding up to the same sum).

Thus, when a member of the Santa Prassede circle complained of infertility, the monks invoked the power of Saturn. Drawing on Agrippa, they formed a square based on the number fifteen, rendered more powerful by the Hebrew equivalents (see figure 8). This they engraved on an instrument made of lead, the metal associated with the planet. Contact with the instrument would favor procreation and many other vaguely defined functions.

If someone else complained of poverty or debt, the monks sought the influence of Jupiter. Upon an instrument made of silver, they engraved a square with four numbers across and four down, based on the sum of thirty-four. Contact with this instrument was sure to bring riches, love, peace, and concord. From Mars, with its five-by-five table based on the sum of sixty-five and engraved on copper, they promised fierceness in war, wise judgment, and success in obtaining favors, as well as an excellent repellent for bees and pigeons. And so on, invoking the rest of the planets according to the case at hand, they promised everything from fame (the sun) to fertility (Venus) to a good memory (Mercury) to safety on a journey (the Moon).

Still basing themselves on Agrippa, the monks could offer a mathematical method for divining the astrological significance of personal names, should their patrons so require. For as Agrippa noted, "Letters and names . . . are not imposed haphazardly, but in accordance with a reason that we do not know."[5] God himself assigned the names of the biblical figures Abraham, Sarah, and Jacob. Christ's Incarnation, some Renaissance cabalists maintained, came about through the utterance of the letter S or ש in Hebrew, which added to the divine name JHVH became JHSVH or Jesus.[6] Just as the cabalists sought to use mathematical calculations to unlock the significance of the divine name, so also the skillful master of the occult might use mathematical calculations to unlock the significance of names given to modern persons. Since the products of such calculations referred in some way to the place of the individual in the cosmos, they could be compared to the numbers traditionally assigned to the planets—that is, 1 + 4 for the sun, 2 + 7 for the moon, 3 for Jupiter, 5 for Mercury, 6 for Venus, 8 for Saturn, 9 for Mars. The constellations were assigned the numbers 1 for Leo, 2 for Aquarius, and so forth.

Suppose a couple came to the monks to discover what planet most favored their child. The monks assigned the numbers 1 through 9 to the letters A through I; to the letters K through S they assigned the numbers 10, 20, 30, and so forth. Then they took the letters in the subject's name, plus those of the father and mother, added up the numbers, and divided by nine. They referred the remainder to a particular planet, according to the above system. To determine a child's astrological sign, they divided the above sum not by nine but by twelve, and interpreted the remainders as before.

Should any of the monastery associates come with a more specific problem in mind, the monks had a slightly more recent book ready at hand, Annibale Raimondi's *Nomantia* (The science of name-divining). Here the method of Agrippa that we have been discussing was extended for the purpose of making predictions about the course of daily affairs. For if personal names were indeed assigned by some sort of divine influence, as Agrippa had affirmed (so Raimondi reasoned in his book), "the elements of the letters possess certain letters and divine names, which, collected together, give a certain insight permitting those familiar with the technique to render a very solid judgment concerning future events."[7] Accordingly, to see if a child was to be born male or female, the names of the mother and father were assigned numbers according to the following table, and the figures added together (see figure 9).

Then, according to the same table, the name of the month of conception was calculated and added, and the result was divided by seven. If the remainder was an even number, the child would be a girl; if odd, a boy. Next, to get a quick sense of whether the baby would be born alive or dead, one might take the sum of the numerical equivalents of the name of the mother and father and the baby's day of birth, add fifteen and

A=20 B= 2 C=12 D=14	E=14 F= 6 G=10 H= 7	I=18 K=10 L=11 M=12	N= 4 O=24 P= 6 Q=16	R= 8 S=18 T=10 V= 2	X=12 Y=14 Z=14

Figure 9. Annibale Raimondi, name magic.

divide by fifteen. If the remainder was even, the baby would be stillborn. Looking further ahead to possible future hazards, to find out whether a girl child would grow up to be a whore, one might take the names of the child and her mother, add fifteen, and divide by nine. An even remainder indicated yes; an odd one indicated she would be an honest woman. Finally, to find out which of the parents would die first, one might add the numbers in their names and divide by nine. If the remainder was even, the woman would go first. And so on, with different calculations and different schemes of alpha-numerical correspondences for each set of questions.

However, for penetrating into the structures regulating everyday occurrences by manipulating the links between numbers and destiny, Morandi had a secret technique all his own. He got it from a clandestine tradition of practical magic, in this case interpreted by a certain otherwise unidentifiable "Domenico the Arab," in a manuscript he received by way of Cristoforo Bronzini, a courtier of Cardinal Pallotta best known for his prohibited feminist tract *On the Dignity of Women*. Domenico's manuscript promised to put the practitioner into ever closer contact with the real sources of number power in the universe.[8] Based loosely on a mixture of cabala and Pythagorean number symbolism, the science had been, the author claimed, "given to Israel," but subsequently lost because of "their perfidious transgressions," although "they still claim to have it."[9] From a divine science it had in recent times been "made human and terrestrial," and it could now serve "for showing everyone the road to help and to freedom from danger, for manifesting hidden thoughts, exposing traps, demonstrating offenses and, in doing so, separating happiness from unhappiness."

Morandi's method, based on Domenico's writings, called for submitting names to a still more complicated system of calculations than any we have so far encountered. The results were then to be elaborated into tables, and the tables scrutinized for answers to life's important questions. Each vowel was assigned a number, in increments of five, from A = 5 to U = 25. Thus, the name "Jacobus," with the vowels A, O, and U, yielded the series 5, 20, 25. When vowels occurred twice in a name, the second appearance was counted two times the first, and subsequent appearances were counted two times the previous one. Thus, "Antonius Villa" (the letter "V" being interpreted as "U" according to contemporary usage) gave the vowels A, O, I, U, and U, I, A, corresponding to the numbers 5, 20, 15, 25 and 50, 30, 10. "1" or "0" could be left out; and names could be utilized in either their vernacular or their Latin versions, at the discretion of the practitioner, and with the family name first or last.

Suppose a monastery associate, Cardinal Desiderio Scaglia, a frequent visitor later on in connection with astrology, came in desperation, pleading for one last consultation regarding the matters that meant the most to him. Morandi could apply his most refined technique to the name "Scaglia Desiderio." Accordingly, "Scaglia" yielded A = 5, I = 15, and A = 10 (= 5 x 2). Desiderio yielded the following results, which were tabulated in rows of four columns each. E = 10, I = 12 (15 + 15, but the digits on either side of the plus sign are added to make 6 + 6 = 12), which will be written across two columns. E = 2 (because 10 x 2 = 20, from which the 0 is dropped). I = 24 (two times the previous occurrence, which had been transformed into the figure 12, therefore, 12 x 2 = 24), which again is written across two columns. Finally, O = 20. In the table below we have designated the rows by the letters "a," "b," and "c." The series for the name Scaglia (5, 15, 10) appears as the first three entries in row "a." The series for the name Desiderio (10, 1, 2, 2, 2, 4, 2) appears as the last entry in row "a" and continues along row "b" to the second entry in row "c."

a.	5	15	10	10
b.	1	2	2	2
c.	4	2	(1)	(1)

The numbers in parentheses in the table above are entered simply to fill things out.

Even these calculations were "of little significance," Morandi might have said, repeating Domenico's comment verbatim from the manual. For the purposes of direction and divination, they had to be once more augmented and developed. But no true magical system could function without room for the practitioner to use his superior insight for understanding exactly when and how the rules applied—an insight that could not be transmitted by any conventional means. A sovereign player at dominoes, having matched the pips on his pieces to those already laid down, might, in order to form new combinations and lead the game where he would, erase a pip from his six-two piece to match a five, or add a pip to his five-three piece to match a six. Morandi, too, sought some measure of control over his results.[10] And the complexity of some of his operations, the arbitrariness of some of his choices of arithmetic to apply to a given instance, and the apparent impossibility of certain results, also seemed to point to some ineffable mystery behind this numerological technique.

To expand the table we have reconstructed so far, generating new rows that we have designated rows "d" through "i," Morandi might factor out each element in an upper row (c) by elements in a lower row (d and e), as 2 x 2 = 4, 2 x 1 = 2, 1 x 1 = 1, 1 x 1 = 1:

c.	4	2	1	1
d.	2	2	1	1
e.	1			

Existing rows could be added, or, in the following case, subtracted, to generate new rows:

a.	5	15	10	10
.....				
c.	4	2	1	1
.....				
———				
e.	1	13	9	9

Some calculations required certain entries to have two values simultaneously. Recall the factoring of the entries in an upper row to yield a lower one:

c.	4	2	1	1
d.	2	2	1	1
e.	1			

Yet row "d" in the example just shown, to be added to the next row down, yielding a still lower row, would have had to contain a "0" instead of a "1," as in:

d.	2	2	0	1
e.	1	13	9	9
———				
f.	3	15	9	10

Domenico also recommended adding digits in an upper row to produce the entries in a lower one, which in this case would yield (3 = 3, 1 + 5 = 6, 9 = 9, 1 + 0 = 1):

f.	3	15	9	10
g.	3	6	9	1

The entire series looked like this:

a.	5	15	10	10
b.	1	2	2	2
c.	4	2	1	1
d.	2	2	1	1
e.	1	13	9	9
f.	3	15	9	10
g.	3	6	9	1
h.	6	21	18	11
i.	6	3	9	2

Once he had completed the table by these techniques and by many others equally complex, Morandi could offer to pursue investigations of many sorts. If he calculated from the cardinal's own name, as we have done, he could answer questions about the future. If he calculated from the name of an associate or an enemy of the cardinal, he could reveal dangers or traps. If he calculated from a key word, he could reveal the result of a negotiation, the success or failure of a particular course of action, or even the shifts of fortune along the way. A table that began with predominantly even numbers in each cell and ended with predominantly odd ones might indicate a project that began well and later soured. A table that began with odd numbers and ended with even ones might indicate the opposite. We leave readers to guess the cardinal's fate.

For achieving the most powerful results, Domenico the Arab, Morandi's source, admitted that his manuscript alone was insufficient. He recommended the use of a "key"—like the batteries to most children's toys, not included with the device. Indeed, "the key must remain under silence, otherwise everyone would be able to gain this glorious knowledge." But without it the sublime mysteries could not "open the road to the most Intimate Sense." To whet the reader's appetite for that magical key, he dropped some hints, based, so he claimed, on the *Lesser Art* of Ramón Lull and indicating combinations of letters and numbers apparently intended as mnemonic tools for collecting and organizing various sorts of occult information. We are not told what. He ended the manuscript with a mystical talisman in the form of a scheme of the order of creation, beginning with God the Father and ending with the alchemical symbols for the substances within the earth. Magic, he seemed to imply, was the way to adjust man's place in the order of the universe and achieve the highest benefits. So the seeker after its mysteries must never rest.

Seeking, keeping, and circulating all of the occult knowledge we have described, the monks at Santa Prassede not only thought to find their own harmony within a discordant world, but to help others find theirs. They shared their results and compiled a formidable repertory of collective experience. They combined this with the transmitted doctrine of writers in every age, from classical antiquity to their own day. And they brought to bear upon the lives of those in the immediate vicinity the secrets harbored inside the monastery's precincts. What better way, so the monks must have reasoned to themselves, to fulfill the monastery's appointed task of ministering to the needs of the people around them. What better way to add this-worldly perfection to the goals of spiritual perfection assigned by the monastery's religious superiors.

For a time, the monastery's protectors seemed to agree; but their continuing indulgence depended upon the monks' ability to promise them the greatest rewards. Soon we will discover just how exacting they could be.

TEN

CHARTING THE FIRMAMENT

INTERROGATOR: Tell whether the genitures were calculated by others or by you.

GHERARDO GHERARDI: Many of the genitures concerning the present pope, the past popes and the cardinals were calculated by other persons, and also many of the genitures of other individuals were given to me by others; although there are also many done by me in order to study the falsehood of astrology and whether it might be in some small measure true, especially in regard to health or inclination. (*Morandi Trial*, fol. 105v, July 15, 1630)

AS THE SECRETS of the monastery began to build into a veritable time bomb ticking away the moments until Morandi's destruction, Morandi and the monks sought ever more radical strategies for binding their associates to themselves. And when none of the modes of inquiry so far discussed yielded infallible answers for mastering the cycles of cosmic change, the monks began to rely more and more upon astrology.

Circumstances favored such a choice. For it was precisely in this period that more causes than usual drove devout Romans to the door of the monastery for astrological advice. The need for compassion amid the ever-present tragedies of early modern life was enough to obliterate any reservations about looking outside the acceptable avenues of prayer and religious devotion. In the eyes of many, a monastery was a particularly safe place to pursue this search.

In the months before Morandi's arrest, the monks offered what they could by way of words of comfort to the bereaved and encouragement to survivors. Let us not forget that Santa Prassede was a parish as well as a monastery, a cure of souls as well as a retreat. Anything affecting the fifty-six families belonging to the parish closely affected each of the fifteen residents inside—and not just Father Ridolfo Ricciardi who happened to be the pastor of the church. To the monastery came not just potential patrons and allies, but also, especially on Sundays, parishioners, often with their children in tow. The deaths of the latter were losses for the monastery as well. In exercising their pastoral duties, the monks also demonstrated the utility of astrological knowledge in the everyday world, and, by extension, themselves. And in so doing they wove around themselves the net in which they would eventually be caught.

That misfortune fell with particular severity upon the most innocent could not escape the attention of anyone surveying the rows of miniature headstones in a seventeenth-century cemetery or perusing the parish "books of the dead," containing list upon list of young victims of the rigors of life in this period. At the monastery of Santa Prassede, the monks took as much care to record the sudden curtailment of childhood occurring in their midst by natural causes as by unnatural ones. Thus, in their astrological logbook, preserved among the documents sequestered by the governor's court, they accounted for the case of one Potentia, who died of complications at birth on October 29, 1627.[1] The physical cause of death, of course, was a cold and unrevealing fact, as far as our monks were concerned. Probing still deeper to discover what subtle forces might have determined the presence of life-threatening circumstances at a particular time and place, they drew upon their understanding of the connection between events in the microcosm of earthly phenomena and the macrocosm of the celestial spheres. They found poor Potentia's nativity, with Sagittarius in the ascendant, accompanied by the sun, to be menaced by the moon in the eighth house—a fatal combination according to the best astrological doctrine.

Whether Potentia, in departing from a hard world she had not yet entered, was actually more fortunate than some of the other tiny casualties in their logbook, the monks dared not say. Nor could they say whether, in succumbing to illness in his first two months of life, young Giambattista, son of Messer Tommaso Marmontini, was spared the misery suffered by a certain Girolamo Magino, who hung on until age eight.[2] They poured out the same compassion on these cases as they did on that of a daughter of the Aldobrandini family who managed to survive the first two years only to be struck down by a falling beam, or those of the Muscelli boy and a barber's daughter, both killed by tumbling down wells before their tenth birthdays.[3] The knowledge that human error and the latent dangers of seventeenth-century cityscapes might have been responsible for these last deaths can have offered no more consolation to the parents than it did in the case of the fifteen-year-old boy killed on March 10, 1630, perhaps accidentally, by another boy awkwardly wielding a firearm, a man's death suffered just before embarking on manhood.[4]

In every case, the monks insisted, death was inevitable, written in the very language of the stars. The Aldobrandini daughter's nativity was afflicted by a quartile of Mars with the sun in her birth sign of Cancer, an almost certainly fatal occlusion of the giver of life by a highly malcficent planet. In the Muscelli boy's chart, the planet Mercury, ruler of ages five through fourteen, was conjoined with the unequivocally destructive moon. In the barber's daughter's chart, the sun was conjoined with the moon, vitiating whatever might have been the sun's favorable effects and making Mercury a highly dangerous planet, all in the ninth house.

Dramatic and tragic though the death of a child may have been for the family, it represented only a part of the mortality experienced at Santa Prassede.[5] In fact, with the average life expectancy of adult males somewhere around thirty-five years, the death of a child may have been, for many in this period, a powerful and frequent reminder of the precariousness of life at all ages and all social levels. And in the monks' astrological logbook, we find nativities not just of children but of an elderly neighbor known only as the "Old Man of Arezzo"; and not only of a "youth who made copies" and of a servant to the Florentine ambassador, but also of bishops, archbishops, and cardinals. We find that of a student (the son of one Giambattista Carpani) as well as that of a certain "Lodovico who is in jail," and of the future Duke of Rethel and of Leopold, the Archduke of Austria.

Indeed, for the monks at Santa Prassede, astrology was not just a source of consolation; it was a matter of study. And in order to provide advice of the highest quality to those who came to them in need, they sought to widen the confines of their experience to include not only the best texts on the matter but the largest possible number of actual cases—from nearby as well as from far away, and from their own time as well as from the past.

To ensure the appeal of judicial astrology in an age better known for accomplishments in the developing fields of scientific endeavor, the monks had no need to rely on the long reverberations of fin de siècle millenarianism—although there were plenty of those. That the year 1600 had passed without a universal cataclysm put no more of a damper on such speculations than had the failure of the year 1500 to yield the same, or, for that matter, the year 1524, when the great conjunction of the three upper planets occurred in the sign of Pisces.[6] Indeed, the millennium fever toward the end of the twentieth century that spawned Centers of Study and shelves of commentary was nothing by comparison. As late as 1603, Tommaso Campanella was still as convinced as Cyprian Leowitz had been in 1564 that the year 1600 signaled the beginning of a new age. The spectacular nova that followed the great conjunction of 1603 only confirmed him in this belief.[7]

In 1628, the Sicilian virtuoso Giambattista Hodierna put a new spin on the old topos of the six ages since creation, in pages that stood close on the monks' shelves to those by Hodierna's great hero, Galileo. First came the age of gold; next came those of silver, copper, iron, and finally the age of lead in which firearms held sway. Just begun, he asserted, was the Age of Crystal, ushered in when the telescope drew us to the sphere beyond the planets, a sphere greater in nobility, prestige, and sublimity than all the others. In this age, he proclaimed, human intellect would triumph over bestiality and grossness. "Just look around at the admirable acuteness of the human mind that we observe in everyone," he pointed out, perhaps with some exaggeration, "whereas each person is able, in an unutterable way, to penetrate into the intimate recesses of the mind of someone else."[8] The monks certainly hoped they could do this and more for the members of their community.

Whatever might have been the promises of the new age, the monks well knew that the causes threatening the safety, security, and happiness of those around them were almost innumerable. Even discounting the dreaded misfortunes of death, illness, crippling accidents, and loss of limb, few persons of any rank really enjoyed the sweet placidity that modern social theorists have constructed as an ideal type of old regime society to satisfy their nostalgic yearnings for a world we have lost.[9] While social categories were relatively static and mobility was rare and slow, nonetheless, drastic changes might occur. The peasant or artisan's family was not much more exposed to confiscation of goods and sequester of persons by lawless aristocrats than the aristocrats were themselves to the rapacity of a jealous ruler.[10] Nor were the houses of the great so much less vulnerable to ransacking whenever war tore through a city or the surrounding countryside, as it did around Rome in 1614 and again in 1627. Anyone who doubted that well-being in this period hung truly by a thread had only to consult the plague chroniclers, who commented wryly on the situation of the helpless rich whose servants ran off leaving in the lurch those with no experience taking care of themselves.[11]

If this knowledge still left the monks and their community somewhat uncertain about whether the rain fell equally on the just and on the unjust, all they had to do to be completely persuaded that it fell with equal impetuosity on the highly placed as on the lowly was to pay some attention to contemporary literature. For the very doctrine of tragedy, handed down by Aristotle and developed with extraordinary virtuosity by the sixteenth-century literary theorists that were so indefatigably catalogued by Bernard Weinberg a few decades ago, stipulated that the genre could work only if it placed exalted personages in the most desperately tragic situations. Only such personages, the theorists argued, could evoke the powerful sentiments that might bring listeners to the peak of catharsis necessary for full appreciation of the tragic muse. For they alone were capable of gaining admiration by the enviable circumstances in which they found themselves before denouement set in. And they alone could gain the full sympathy of the audience for the inevitable turn of the wheel of fortune that brought them down from dizzying heights to the vilest abjection. Even the humblest among the audience might be inspired to wonder, so Bartolomeo Maranta suggested, "What is to become of us, if we see kings oppressed by travails and even death?" And the greater was the likelihood that they (i.e., the audience) might find themselves in the same predicament, "so much greater terror must they feel."[12] Such reflections, Giovanni Bonifacio added, should inspire prudence, "seeing princes, whom [people] imagined to be happy and immune to misfortunes, experience calamities because of their own foolishness."[13] But most of all, claimed Alessandro Piccolomini, such reflections might lead observers to harden themselves against the trials of life.[14] In the same way, he noted, warriors accustomed to carnage may come to "take as nothing the prospect of certain death," and, in the more immediate experience of his readers, those who observe the ravages of the plague may begin to ignore the mortality around them. To see these literary principles in action, readers could refer to recent contributions to the new genre of musical drama.[15]

Images of artificial misfortune, to be sure, might be less disturbing than images of actual misfortune. But the latter, too, were rapidly filling the library shelves at Santa Prassede. Although weekly newspapers were not to be printed in the main Italian cities until the 1640s, the number of reports on battles, victories, and sieges had doubled since the sixteenth century. Innumerable "advices," "relations," "notices," and "letters of information" bore witness to the "progress" of this or that ruler's armies in this or that neighboring state, their "success" in acquiring this or that fortified place, and the "sojourn" of this or that army in such and such a territory, followed by its triumphant "return" to the aggressor's capital. To stir up passions for the favored party, they reported on the "wickedness" of the other, only to be rebutted in even more disturbing detail by similar publications sponsored by the aggrieved.[16]

Anyone who perused the piles of such material at the library could scarcely help exclaiming with Secondo Lancellotti, the seventeenth century's equivalent of Russell Baker, that "war is a terrible thing!"[17] Nor, continued Lancellotti, contemplating the recent siege of Vercelli, along with the disaster before Gradisca and the war in the Garfagnana, did damage come only from the enemy armies. Even in the country to which an army belonged, discipline gone lax or wages unpaid could lead to excesses. So, he continued, "we hear that they robbed the chicken coop, damaged the house of that poor man, attempted to take the maidenhead of that virgin or violated that wife, or carried out similar insults." In comparing the previous three centuries, he concluded that Italy, "with war resounding on every side," had never been happy at any time. Just how much more unhappy Italy could be he demonstrated by referring to the condition of people in the neighboring Valtelline, currently caught in a vise between the warring allies of Bourbon and Habsburg.

Anyone at the monastery who crossed town to attend services at the church of Sant'Andrea della Valle on recent Sundays would have heard an urgent appeal that seemed to leave Hodierna's Crystalline Century far behind. In these times, the preacher proclaimed, "and I have never seen the like," the entire world seemed to shudder with the echo of the "thunderous irons of battle," now that a continuous call to arms under a "fierce God" made his congregation feel that an "age of iron" had returned. The earth "groans from the armed torments flooding it from every part." The sky itself, "as though afraid of its child's insults" (i.e., the earth's), determined to prove that if the child had the power to "bring forth towers of flesh to expunge the sky," the sky did not "lack lightning bolts to incinerate it." Now with the "Eumenides furiously springing forth from dark abysses upon the overturned universe and demanding audience," he admitted, perhaps a little disingenuously, "I scarcely dare to speak."[18]

Even without studying war news or listening to sermons, visitors to Santa Prassede might find plenty of other causes for anxiety. If they could persuade themselves, reading still other material at the library, that the "justifications" for Venetian ill will toward the Uskok pirates in 1617 or the "negotiations of the Savoy deputies in Milan for accommodating the affairs of Mantua" in 1622 were for the moment unlikely to lead to further hostilities, they were nonetheless assailed by descriptions of the latest contagion or fear of contagion, especially the bubonic plague that descended from Lombardy in 1629.[19] And if divine retribution seemed to work to a logical conclusion when the "lachrymose insult and parricide" committed on the person of Henry IV of France of glorious memory was followed by the "true relation of the bitter and most cruel torments and death of the wicked regicide François Ravillac,"[20] or when "many heretics" in Bamberg were killed "by the Devil, who appeared in various forms, an animal and then a giant,"[21] only the most hard-hearted could fail to be aroused to fear and wonder by the death of "a Father of the Franciscan Order who was skinned alive in Algiers, with the death of other Christians impaled, tortured and immolated"—the pamphlet specified—"alla Turchesca." A "truly piteous case,"[22] though perhaps differing only in magnitude from the likewise inexplicable "death of a coal-seller" who was "mortally burned" in 1623.[23]

For those who did not experience any interruption in their prosperity, actual economic circumstances seemed to tie the fortunate to their good fortunes more tenuously than ever before.[24] All over Europe, the 1620s began a period of relative impoverishment with respect to the previous century and a half—a depressing "B" phase, as economic historians have called it, following the triumphant "A" phase of the late Renaissance. Of course, the ever-increasing scarcity of means and the ever-wider divide between the wealthy and the poor affected the different areas with varying intensity; but the economies of the Italian peninsula appear to have been some of the hardest hit. Antonio Serra's confidential memoir to the Spanish government in 1613 would not have been known at the monastery. Nor were audiences there likely to understand that the reason "why Naples is poorer than Venice" was because of the lack of commerce and industry. Still, the same audiences could get first-hand information from Campanella concerning the outrageous unemployment rate in Naples that he had mentioned in the *City of the Sun*. From Venetian ambassador Niccolo Contarini, also in their midst, they would know that even Venice was not in such great shape. True, the unemployment rate was lower than in Naples, but in a recent report to the Senate, the ambassador looked back to the late sixteenth century as a period of prosperity from which the present economy had declined due to new trade patterns and northern European competition.[25] There, as everywhere else, the government tended to seek ever-greater fiscal slices from a shrinking economic pie.[26]

Monastery audiences who heard the news about the depression of the 1620s probably also heard about its most visible signs around the country. Few if any were likely to have observed "a thousand beggars" outside Brescia in 1619 "who say they are converts" to Christianity, while officials expressed serious doubts about whether they were telling the truth. A certain Giustinian suggested consolidating all alms collection in this and the Venetian state's other mainland territories among a small group of officials including himself, thereby relieving his fellow citizens from daily bombardment by undesirables making private solicitations.[27] New magistracies were springing up wherever they did not already exist, with wide powers to "purge the city of useless people" (and, in the case of Genoa, ship them off to Corsica).[28] Never, before the modern wave of immigration from eastern Europe, did the Italian cities seem so much like bastions besieged by those whom the denizens defined as belonging somewhere else. In Naples, the problem was so serious that one Giovanni Maria Novario drew up a kind of paupers' bill of rights—applicable, of course, only to those deserving such protection, namely: "orphans, paupers out of work, captives, prisoners, pilgrims, apprentice whores, exposed children, freed slaves, penitents, recent converts, aged virgins, scholars, farmers, merchants weighed down by taxes, those condemned to the galleys, impressed sailors, deported persons, the possessed, the blind, drunkards, madmen, idiots, lunatics," and finally "the miserable" who "fell into misery by their own fault."[29]

If such episodes elsewhere in Italy seemed very far away, monastery associates had only to look around them to find misfortune staring them in the face. Rome's economy, after all, was by no means immune to the general trend. Neither entirely agricultural nor entirely industrial, it inspired some contemporaries to wonder how it could survive at all, except by siphoning off revenue from other places. Its prosperity was only superficial, even though the Venetian ambassador insisted that "it is a sort of emporium of the universe, where from every direction, in every time and from all nations people come and congregate. . . . And everyone brings to it his best."[30] Here of all places economic hardship could be expected to be met by copious charity; and what a certain Paolo De Angelis wrote in 1611, in a tract entitled *On Almsgiving*,[31] was repeated, with elaboration, by Daniello Bartoli in 1650: namely, that helping the poor was a Christian duty teaching the more fortunate to "gain by giving," and that the "wealthy, never content" ought to learn from the "poor but content."[32] However, here, too, signs of increased suffering began to appear particularly in the 1620s, when the number of debtors in Roman prisons rose to new heights.[33] In the churches, noted a report from the parish visitors during the Jubilee Year of 1625, the "great multitude of poor around Rome" had "made prayer impossible, because as soon as the faithful kneel down, they are immediately assaulted." Indeed, "every day on the streets people die of cold or hunger, neglected."[34] In the countryside, whence a great number of peasants fled, the Venetian ambassador in transit had to admit, "We observed great poverty, and in general, indigence, not to say great hardship."[35]

Many of the wealthy families whose members frequented the monastery—the Cavallo, the Usimbardi—had managed to avoid too much damage from the economic crisis, either by shrewd financial maneuvering, by salting their money away in landed investments, by acquiring ecclesiastical benefices, or all of these things. Meanwhile they continued the previous century's trend toward ever more lavish spending. Flaunting the opulence that seemingly insulated them from the rest of humanity, the once-frugal Contarini family, to which the Venetian ambassador belonged, adopted the princely style of life that earned them and the other Venetian nobles the reproaches of observers like Fynes Morrison in 1613, "buying house and lands, furnishing themselves with coach and horses, and giving themselves the good time with more show and gallantry than was wont."[36] After all, they had to keep up with the Genoese gentry, who consumed as much resources by building stately homes for their families as by building chapels for the local churches, outfitted in the latest fashion.[37] And nowhere was consumption more conspicuous than in Rome, where papal families, the Aldobrandini, the Borghese, the Farnese, and others we have met, employing the best talents of the time, appeared to be turning a considerable portion of the city surface into a vast construction site.[38] Indeed, as spending by the Barberini nephews reached epic proportions, Roman nobles were forced to follow suit, putting themselves almost as gloriously into debt as the French nobles under Louis XIV.[39]

Ambitious families like the Morandi exercised their voyeuristic curiosity about their more prosperous neighbors by turning to writings about the so-called noble arts—by Girolamo Muzio, by Giambattista Possevino—that stacked the private shelves at Santa Prassede.[40] Old families, like the Magalotti and the Capponi, meanwhile turned to the same writings to justify their irrevocable title to positions of preeminence. What really fueled the boom in such writings, however, were the compulsions of newer families like the Scaglia, to which belonged Cardinal Desiderio, an associate of Santa Prassede whom we have already met.

Not all the new families were as fortunate as that of Desiderio Scaglia, whose father according to some sources had been an artisan. But exalted to the heights in relatively recent times, they all had to prove to themselves and to others that their good fortune was in the order of nature. Thus, if they learned grace and skill in equitation, they must also learn to fence with lethal effectiveness; and if they learned how to give the lie with a supercilious snarl and to kill a rival with the proper etiquette, they also had to learn to dance elegantly and pay compliments to others according to their station. Molière's hilarious parody of status-conscious arrivisme in *Le bourgeois gentilhomme* belonged not only to the 1640s, but also to the first three decades of the century; and there were just as many types in Italy resembling Monsieur Jourdain as there were in France. Mastery of a formidable array of leisure-time activities was everywhere used to justify the privileges of rank. A certain Roman priest named Celso Millini tried to turn an obvious social fact into a moral one, and sweeten the sour feelings that had begun to grow, by "proving that even virtuous Christians are better off born rich than poor." And the reason was that "everyone needs the wealthy."[41] At the monastery, such words were oracles.

Yet individuals seemed less and less able by their own efforts to guarantee possessions once gained. Each new regime signaled the end of the previous patronage system and the beginning of a new one. Everyone at the monastery remembered the papacy of Gregory XV, who ascended the throne at age sixty-seven and, in the brief twenty-nine months of his reign, managed to cast down nearly everyone who had been built up by his predecessor, Paul V. Among those ensconced in professional careers, opportunities seemed to be determined more than ever by the caprices of a single superior.[42] Even among those whose every wish was the command of an army of servants, circumstances that were out of control outnumbered the circumstances that were not. Indeed, fortune was a woman, the now-familiar Machiavellian commonplace proclaimed. But if ever she could have been mastered by force using Machiavelli's method, her wiles now appeared to be impossibly capricious. For noble families saddled with the most colossal debts, like the Biscia, of which Cardinal Lelio became a Santa Prassede devotee, life was no longer a race to the finish, won by the most artful driver, but a kind of lottery.[43]

Justus Lipsius, the translator of Seneca, though he wrote in the late sixteenth century, seemed to provide a perfect advertisement for the monks' wares. "Lift up your eyes and observe with me the alternate course of human affairs," he counseled in his dialogue *On Constancy*.[44] "They are not unlike the ebbings and flowings of the sea. Thou shalt rise, thou shalt fall; thou shalt command, and thou serve; be thou obscure, and thou glorious." No one, he explained, ought to think that only pleasant and profitable things were to be his lot. However fortunate he might seem, let him remember that adversity could be around the bend. Of course, few of Lipsius's readers at the monastery were likely to be satisfied by merely observing the ironies of powerlessness at the apex of power, defenselessness within the walls of the citadel. What, he asked, were the adversities most people feared? Personal discomfort rather than public misfortune? Loss of their own convenience rather than dangers to thousands of their countrymen? Fears of this kind mostly arose from mistaken attachment to worldly things. Instead, let us seek the counsels of philosophy—"the high-raised temples which the wise," in Lucretius's verse, "by learning raise up to the skies." Let us free ourselves from vainglory, pride, and self-love, and seek true constancy in lowliness, patience, and right reason. Then, "do you fall, constancy will lift you up. Do you stagger, it will support you. . . . Steer your ship into this haven, where peace and security dwell; in which there is a refuge and sanctuary from troubles and perplexities."[45] After all, "an Eternal Mind which we call God . . . rules, orders and governs the lasting orbs of heaven, the different courses of the stars, the interchangeable variations of the elements, and (in a word) all things whatsoever as well above us as below."[46]

At Santa Prassede, those not satisfied with resignation in the face of adversity and unable to quiet their souls by the consolations of philosophy turned instead to astrology. There they could find at least somewhat more concrete explanations for the fickleness of fortune. If the workings of providence seemed like a cause too vast, too distant, or too incomprehensible to serve as a guide to every day, a theory about the power of the stars might serve instead. In assigning the blame for plans and lives gone wrong, Mars and Saturn provided visible scapegoats; and the moon's evil could practically be observed through the miles of aether that separated its malignant visage from the things it affected here below. Understanding the causes of misfortune, of course, was not enough for all seekers. Some hoped to prepare better for the future by knowing what troubles or benefits might be in store. Others hoped one day to manipulate the influences of the planets, if only they could understand them. And manipulating the influences of the planets, still others hoped, might even change the course of destiny.

With this in view, Francesco Usimbardi, an official of the Camera Apostolica, came to the monastery for an astrological consultation. So did Francesco Maria Ghisleri, an auditor of the Sacra Romana Rota, and Vitellio Malaspina, son of Count Giambattista. There also came Francesco Maria Merlini, later bishop of Cervia, and Giovanni Pietro Savio, the bishop of Sebenico. No doubt they all, like the last client mentioned, awaited the results of their consultation "as the Messiah." Because "my only consolation," he added to Orazio Morandi, "is the hope of future happiness."[47]

By the time Morandi went to jail, Santa Prassede had become the astrological Mecca not only for the neighborhood but for a significant portion of the ecclesiastical aristocracy as well—and not only from all over Rome but from elsewhere. What was the key to this success? For gathering eager devotees from among the upper echelon of Roman society, Morandi came up with a unique expedient. Rather than on the half-baked speculations of street-corner charlatans, he modeled the monastery's astrology on the empirical and experience-oriented approach of the most innovative investigators of natural knowledge. This, he hoped, might bring the same form of accreditation as achieved by the best-known philosophers of his day. He thus developed a product that was as attractive as it was dangerous, and made himself as indispensable to the highest-placed individuals in his own firmament as those individuals became for him. Could his efforts keep astrology's worst enemies at bay?

ELEVEN

THE SCIENCE OF THE STARS

INTERROGATOR: Have you ever spoken to anyone else about making genitures?
MORANDI: I have often spoken to Signor Abate Gherardi about it, and especially about the great uncertainty there is in that profession, in regard to its principal foundations, especially the movements of the planets, which it seems are still very little known, as well as the identification of the true point of the geniture, since it is very difficult to obtain the proper degree of the ascendant, and also the rules given by the principal authors of astrology, which do not seem to correspond to the effects of their teachings, especially when Ptolemy discusses royal genitures, saying that the luminaries are in masculine signs or in an angle, omitting a great number of genitures of kings, who have one or both of the luminaries in a feminine sign, and outside of the angles.
(*Morandi Trial*, fol. 108r, July 15, 1630)

MUCH DEPENDED UPON whether the monks at Santa Prassede could save astrology from ecclesiastical control. And for a time, chances looked good—especially considering Galileo Galilei's success at saving science. Science, after all, rarely fails to impress. And Galileo's visual demonstrations of the laws of nature, at least mong the experts, were by now as well known as the sometimes highly polemical publications in which he discussed them. Perhaps the monks, too, could argue their way to freedom by adapting an experience-based natural knowledge to their field of endeavor.

They were not the first to make the attempt.[1] Ever since the advent of the new methods of inquiry in the latter half of the sixteenth century, the effort to bring about a reform in astrology became more and more oriented to observation and experience. Rather than simply making deductions on the basis of a given set of interpretative rules, a new generation of astrologers attempted to form conclusions on the basis of evermore voluminous sets of examples drawn from life. Consider Luca Gaurico and Girolamo Cardano, who both tried to prove the validity of their different forms of astrology by a selection of some one hundred nativities apiece, with the pertinent explanations for how they illustrated the lives in question, and compare them to Johannes Garcaeus, in the last third of the century, who included no fewer than four hundred nativities. Meanwhile, Rudolf Goclenius tried to apply to divination the same empirical methods that the astrologers were applying to astrology, by observing carefully, for instance, that a sampling of men on whose foreheads he had noted a peculiar cruciform mark included fifty-one who died violent deaths.[2]

To Morandi's way of thinking, a more experience-based astrology might not only evade ecclesiastical objections. It might also better serve his public. Those who came to the monastery had a right to know that the counsel they received came from well-tested sources. He accordingly planned an astrological encyclopedia so comprehensive that it might have impressed a pioneer science organizer like Francis Bacon. What is more, he planned to leave upon it the imprint of intellectual traditions of unimpeachable orthodoxy. Scattered notes throughout the trial record reveal the way the finished work would have looked. Had it not been interrupted almost at the outset by the police raid on the monastery, the work could perhaps have helped give astrology a second life. In the event, it only gave further evidence of Morandi's devotion to the anathematized arts.

For the monks, scientific astrology meant very much the same as scientific astronomy: a body of knowledge based on proven facts. At times, like most of their contemporaries, they found the two disciplines of astrology and astronomy very hard to tell apart. Not only did well-regarded ancients like Ptolemy write on both subjects; even the most serious modern compilers of astronomical information, such as Erasmus Reinhold, author of the Prutenic Tables of planetary motions, larded their works with astrological predictions of various types. No wonder major medical faculties were just as likely to have chairs devoted to one as to the other. And no wonder the monks situated astrological and astronomical texts side by side in their library. They, like most of their contemporaries, would have heartily agreed with Kepler's characterization of astrology as astronomy's "mother and nourisher," unable to "deny her beloved daughter" anything.[3]

Even in the monastery, astronomical developments inevitably rubbed off on astrology. The monks kept careful track of Kepler's intuitions about the usefulness of John Napier's newly invented technique of logarithms for other realms besides pure mathematics. Calculations of planetary motions that once took several days or even weeks to complete could now be carried out in a matter of minutes by consulting a few handy tables—which they carefully transcribed in documents later confiscated by the court.[4] After Galileo Galilei and Thomas Harriot, at opposite ends of Europe, first gazed at the heavenly bodies through the lenses of a new optical instrument invented for magnifying distant objects, the monks acquired an example of the instrument. They, too, like many others, entered the age of telescopic astrology, just at the dawning of the new age of telescopic astronomy. While the new observations occasioned disputes about the priority of this or that discovery of this or that celestial appearance, the same new observations demanded astrological explanations.[5]

As the new astronomy developed, one of the most persistent among the monastery's associates in attempting to apply it to astrology was Ilario Altobelli. On the basis of his new and more accurate set of tables of celestial movements, he attempted to work out a more exact division of the twelve houses than had hitherto been possible. Irregularities, due to the obliquity of the ecliptic with respect to the celestial equator, caused different houses to have different lengths. In rejecting the equal house method and eight other methods currently in use, Altobelli claimed to "confound the followers of [Johannes] Regiomontanus," the fifteenth-century German master—not to mention also those of Girolamo Cardano.[6] Had his ideas not been stolen by Andrea Argoli, another monastery associate, and incorporated into the latter's latest *Ephemerides*, so he complained to Morandi, he would surely have won credit for having restored the reputation of Ptolemy, who, in his view, came closest to the truth.[7]

The monks and their associates could not agree more with Francis Bacon, the influential theorist of the new approach to nature and putative father of modern science, who set out to clean the Augean stables of astrology once and for all. In passages of his *Advancement of Learning* that were once soft-pedaled by squeamish historians, he called for undertaking a new compilation and sorting of data: "The astrologers may, if they please, draw from real history all greater accidents, as inundations, plagues, wars, seditions, deaths of kings, etc., as also the motions of the celestial bodies . . . to . . . erect a probable rule of prediction." Such information was of course to be carefully scrutinized. "All traditions should be well-sifted, and those thrown out that manifestly clash with physical reasons, leaving such in their full force as comport well therewith." He never questioned the planetary influences themselves, upon which astrology was based—i.e., "the universal appetites and passions of matter" constituting "those physical reasons [that] are best suited to our inquiry," along with "the simple genuine motions of the heavenly bodies." This, he avowed, "we take for the surest guide to astrology."[8]

Methodological rigor implied no claim to infallibility. On the contrary, Morandi readily admitted the "great uncertainty in this profession."[9] Who could tell what was actually going on in the heavens at any particular time? After all, the celestial canopy featuring the "Medici Planets" circling around Jupiter, and other newly discovered more distant bodies like Nova Cygni and Nova Ophiuchi, was far different from any imagined by the Ancients, and likely to change still more. Another level of uncertainty

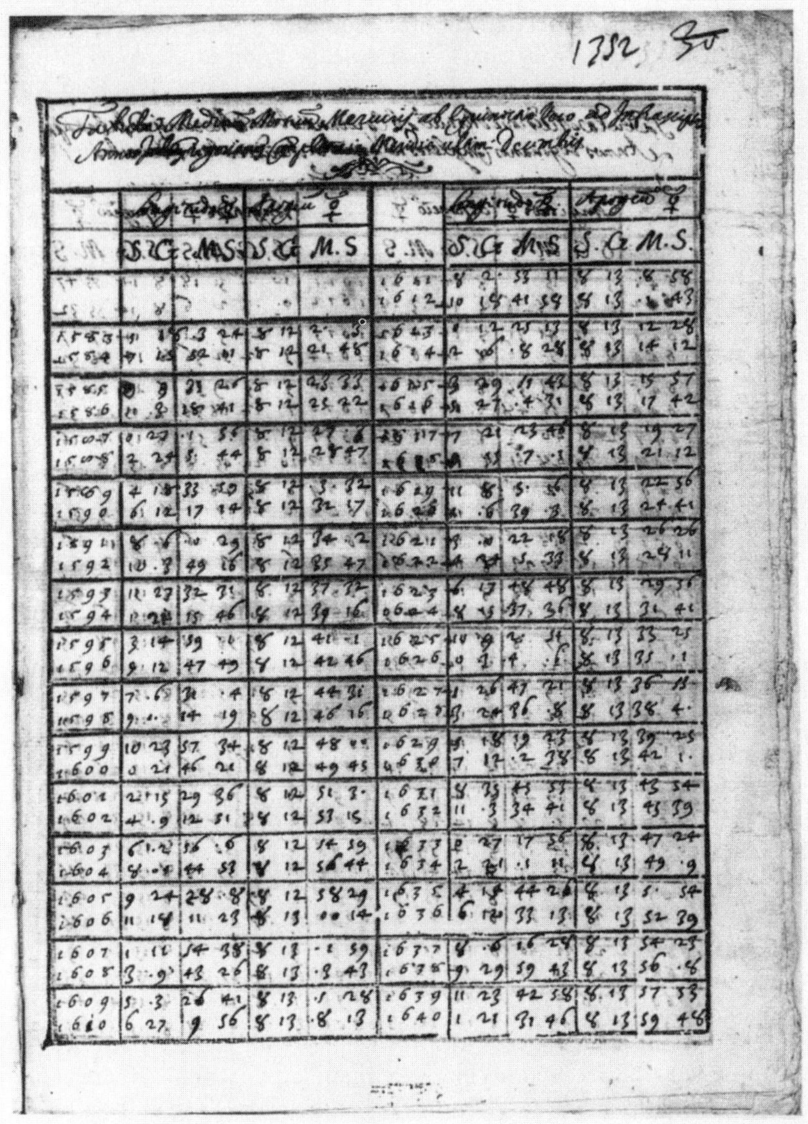

Figure 10. Table of planetary motions, from the Santa Prassede astrological treatise. (Rome, Archivio di Stato, *Governatore*, Processi, sec. XVII, b. 251.)

came from coordinating a nativity with the planetary motions. Ptolemy questioned the use of the moment of the subject's conception in the womb as the basis for a nativity chart—not an easy thing to discover, then or now. Other authors suggested various other procedures, but, said Morandi, "the effects do not correspond to their teachings." The challenge of a scientific astrology was to reduce the uncertainties by accumulating data, running tests, and finding out which theory best saved the appearances.

As chief organizer of the project, Morandi apportioned the tasks not only to members of the monastery but to experts elsewhere in Rome. Ottavio Marini, in all likelihood one of the monks from the convent of Santa Maria della Pace who frequented the monastery, would supply information about purely astrological matters, Morandi informs us in a note attached to the dossier. It would be his responsibility to explain the Part of Fortune, horizon lines and arcs, latitudes across the equator, solstice points, the aspects, the theory of the houses according to Ptolemy and according to Regiomontanus, and the theory of directions according to both.[10] Ottavio's colleague, one P. Giambattista di Giuliano, would supply more properly astronomical expertise on questions concerning meridians, the theory of the planets, the equation of natural movements, the computations of the ecliptic, the measurement of the stars, the motion of the sun at the equator, triangulation, parallax, whether right ascensions increase with their greater declination from the ecliptic, and so forth. He too was responsible for answering some hard questions concerning the recent work of Tycho Brahe, such as why the meridian at Padua, according to Tycho's computations, was a full four minutes different from that of nearby Venice.

In choosing a model on which to base the work, Morandi referred to his humanist background. His scholarly methods had not yet proceeded so far beyond the Renaissance for him to exclude a fundamentally philological and literary approach to the scientific endeavor he had in mind. Anyway, investigations and observations required some principles of organization or orientation if they were not to result in an undifferentiated morass of miscellaneous information. By consulting an authoritative and revered ancient author, he could find such principles without any more fear of compromising his freedom to innovate than had Giacomo Zabarella and others among the soi-disant Aristotelians of their time. Zabarella, after all, used the Aristotelian tradition as a template and a background for original work at the University of Padua.[11] Morandi planned to utilize Ptolemy's *Tetrabiblos* in the same way that Zabarella used the works of Aristotle.

Ptolemy's *Tetrabiblos* had several advantages as a basis for the astrological treatise Morandi had in mind. For one thing, it might confer an air of orthodoxy. Not because the most recent Latin translators, Egidio Tibaldi, Antonius Gogava, Joachim Camerarius, and Philip Melanchthon were themselves entirely orthodox writers.[12] In fact, Ptolemy was privileged by a special distinction customarily accorded to all authors of classical antiquity. Unlike the last two translators mentioned, or any number of other modern astrologers, he was not included in the Index of Forbidden Books. With Ptolemy as an armature, so to speak, whatever anyone might say about Morandi's general plan or about his other readings, at least his central structure would be unimpeachable.

Furthermore, Ptolemy's second-century text still offered the best manual of basic astrology in any language. To be sure, the continuing effectiveness of Ptolemy's astrological system as a whole had no more to do with the censure of Copernicus's heliocentric text than it did with the propagandistic efforts of thoroughgoing Ptolemaic astronomers like Christopher Clavius.[13] All Clavius was able to do was to keep the master's ideas in circulation among contemporary philosophers, urging his Jesuit colleagues at the Collegio Romano to pay a little less attention to Aristotle and a little more to Ptolemy. None of this had to do with astrology per se. Even as Ptolemy's astronomy, along with that of Aristotle, and their contrasting views of the geocentric universe, began to lose ground inexorably to the heliocentric account of Copernicus and Galileo, Ptolemy's view of the mechanisms for the influence of the planets on the terrestrial world remained unsurpassed.[14]

The monks could not have been unaware of the extraordinary adaptability of Ptolemy's view to late antique and medieval physiological conceptions that were still alive and well in the seventeenth century. He claimed that the planets exerted their influence by way of the four chief qualities of hot, cold, moist, and dry, which were essential not only to the Hellenic cosmos he had inherited but also to the version of Galenic medicine that continued to hold sway in much of early modern Europe. Here is what he said, translated from Gogava's version:[15]

> Since the foregoing is the case, and since there are four humors or first natures, two of these are fertile and vivifying, and indeed hot and humid, by which all things are brought together and increased, and two are destructive and detrimental, arid and cold, by which all things are destroyed and weakened.

The sun, he believed, and the physicians confirmed, exerted a heating and drying action, while the moon acted by cooling and moistening, and so on in different combinations for each planet. On the basis of these essential qualities, Ptolemy designated the benefic and malefic planets (as they are now called):

> The ancients likewise accepted Jupiter, Venus and the Moon as beneficent stars, because of their temperate natures and because they especially contained the hot and the humid. They held the stars Saturn and Mars to be

maleficent, for reasons of opposite natures and effects. The first they believed was exceedingly cold, and the second exceedingly hot. They relegated the sun and the star Mercury to a middling position, because they share both natures and because they accommodate their influences to the properties of the other planets with which they are associated.

The angles and modifications of these influences determined the effect the planet might have in a particular instance—and the challenge to the astrologer was to figure this out. By the sixteenth century, Ptolemy's view was combined with other late antique ideas concerning the four major personality types—melancholic, sanguine, bilious, phlegmatic—that had been further developed in the Middle Ages. No doubt the monks too viewed through Ptolemaic lenses the theory of Galen and Hippocrates on critical days and on the patterns of ebb and flow of diseases, which enjoyed a remarkable vogue long before Agostino Nifo's widely read works on the subject—if only because of Ptolemy's association with it through the spurious *Centiloqium* that circulated under his name.[16]

No one who frequented the monastery categorically denied some sort of planetary influences, and even those who mentioned them the least, we may guess, had the ones described by Ptolemy in mind. Disagreement with Ptolemy's notions about the organization of the cosmos did not prevent Galileo from suggesting that the planets "abounded in influences"—though he never specified of what sort.[17] The opponents of Ptolemy's astrological ideas across the Alps, such as Jofrancus Offusius in Germany, who tried to offer his own system, nevertheless accepted Ptolemy's account of planetary influences without too many modifications. Robert Fludd in England reinterpreted the Book of Genesis along alchemical lines and reformulated the story of creation in order to end up with planets of the sort and with the same sorts of qualities and influences as those described by Ptolemy.[18]

Present in the monastery library were some of the most flamboyant attempts to build on Ptolemy's ideas, by Johannes Kepler. At first Kepler claimed that the contrasting influences of the different planets were due to the different properties of the five nested polyhedrons that, according to his somewhat bizarre calculations, were inscribed within the spheres of the planetary orbits, determining the distance of each planet from the sun: the cube for Saturn, the pyramid for Jupiter, the dodecahedron for Mars, the icosahedron for Venus, and the octahedron for Mercury. Accordingly, the beneficent influence of Jupiter, Venus, and Mercury was due to the structurally stable faces of the sides of their polygons.

Jupiter, then, benign in the midst of the malevolent, has driven many to admiration, and also stimulated Ptolemy to enquiry into causes. We see something similar in the pyramid, which, between two solids which are partly akin and partly abhorrent to it, is so different from both of them that from our earlier reasoning its position is almost in peril. Every one of the three superior planets has hatred and hostility for the others. Also among their three solids absolutely none of their observable properties agree, though Mars conspires with Saturn in malice alone. To this I relate the variability of their angles, which is peculiar to them, and common to both. Therefore, the contrary, that is, the constancy of the angles between their edges alone, is evidence of benignity, which is evidence that Jupiter, Venus, and Mercury are benevolent.[19]

Later Kepler claimed that that the planetary aspects or angles between planets in the zodiac (i.e., opposition, trine, and so forth), were not effective in themselves as in Ptolemy's theory, but only in so far as they affected the world soul, which in turn influenced the operation of all things in the universe. Eclipses were dangerous precisely because this world soul was "strongly disturbed by the loss of light."[20] The configurations of the stars at birth reminded individual souls of their "celestial character" and endowed them with the particular features that accompanied the subject through life.[21]

Morandi hewed very closely to the Ptolemaic line even in his discussion of the categories of the objects in the heavens. Just as in Ptolemy's Book 1, chapters 1–9 (in Gogava's version), he organized his treatise so that the division of the planets into masculine and feminine, diurnal and nocturnal, would be followed by the division of the year into seasons and of the horizon into four angles:[22]

Antonius Gogava's Latin version (Louvain: Batius, 1548)	*Santa Prassede Manuscript*
Lib. I	[Bk. 1]
1. Proem	[1] Of astrology, its subject and matter
2. [Astrological knowledge is possible]	[2] Arguments about its vanity and verity
3. [Such knowledge is beneficial]	[3] The value of astrology
4. Of the powers of the planets	[4] Of the powers of the planets
5. Of the masculine and feminine planets	[5] Of the masculine and feminine planets
6. Of diurnal and nocturnal planets	[6] Of diurnal and nocturnal planets
7. Of the power of the aspects to the sun	[7] Of other planetary aspects
8. Of the power of the fixed stars	
9. Of the effect of the seasons and of the four angles	[8] Of the effect of the seasons and of the four angles of nature

Next would come the division of the signs of the zodiac into solstitial and equinoctial, solid and bicorporeal, masculine and feminine, commanding and obeying. Morandi would concur with Ptolemy's critique of the Egyptian concept of terms, or termini—places mapped out within each sign assigned to each of the five planets (excluding the sun and moon), from which the length of life could be calculated:

10. Of solstitial, equinoctial, solid, and bicorporeal signs	[9] Of solstitial, equinoctial, solid, and bicorporeal signs
11. Of masculine and feminine signs	[10] Of masculine and feminine signs
12. On the configuration of the twelve houses	[11] Of other divisions of the signs
	[12] On the aspects of the signs
13. Of commanding and obeying signs	[13] Of commanding signs
14. Of signs which behold each other, and their power	[14] Of antisigns
15. Of disjuncts	
16. Of the houses	[19] Of the meaning of the houses
17. Of the triangles	
18. Of exaltations	

Morandi would also share Ptolemy's skepticism about the Chaldean method of calculating terms, which differed from the Egyptian method only in assigning greater predominance to the maleficent planets Mars and Saturn. In the end, rather than suggesting Ptolemy's own alternative to the Egyptian and Chaldean methods, Morandi would follow Cardano in rejecting the idea entirely. But he would follow Ptolemy in taking account of the so-called applications, or planets that preceded other planets (in other words, lying to the west of them), said to "apply" to the latter—not to be confused with planetary aspects, which concerned not the real presence of the planet but its virtual presence by way of an occult connection.[23]

Morandi's discussion of the basic features of an astrological chart promised to stray a little further from the model. Following most contemporary astrological manuals, he would collect into single chapters the information that Ptolemy scattered throughout his work, adding to it whatever else he had in his files. First of all, he would distinguish the major beneficent planets, Jupiter, Venus, and the Moon, so-called because of their moderate qualities of heat and moisture, from the major maleficents, Saturn and Mars, with their excessive cold and dryness; and all these he would distinguish from Earth and Mercury, which could go either way. Then he would work through the list of heavenly bodies, one by one, beginning with the sun, the lord of action, according to Ptolemy's system—the indicator in whose presence other planets determined the particular profession or way of life of the subject. He did not follow Ptolemy in rejecting the moon's nodes as pseudo-planets and useless accretions within the classic system; instead, he embraced the view of the ninth-century Baghdad scholar Albumasar, who swore by their effects.[24] Likewise, to Ptolemy's list of five chief aspects or angular relations between the signs or planets (conjunction, opposition, trine, quartile, and sextile), he would follow Kepler in adding four new aspects—to wit, the semiquadrate, quintile, sesquiquadrate, and biquintile, referring, respectively, to angles of 45, 72, 135, and 144 degrees. On comets and eclipses, he followed the Zeitgeist in placing far more emphasis than did Ptolemy, who dismissed them in a couple of sentences. Yet he was no more certain than many contemporaries about what to do with the many new fixed stars that had appeared in the sky since Ptolemy's time, visible by the naked eye and by telescope. So he proposed only to discuss the influence of the ones mentioned by Ptolemy in the Tetrabiblos—Aldebaran in the constellation Taurus, Beta in Leo, Spica in Virgo, and so forth.

In the actual science of prediction, Morandi's adherence to Ptolemy may have been more apparent than real. After a discussion of the Part of Fortune he would add more material corresponding to the contents of Ptolemy's Book 3, chapters 1–12 and 15–18 in Gogava's translation, concerning the length of life, the form and temperament of the body, the quality and the illnesses of the soul. He would cover the standard Ptolemaic questions concerning the prediction of wealth, heredity, dignity, marriage, children, friends, and the ages of man, roughly corresponding to Book 4 of the *Tetrabiblos*, but with significant adjustments:

Book 4:	*[Bk. 4]*
	[1] Of wealth
	[2] Of heredity
1. Proem	
2. Of the fortune of the child	[3] Of the fortune and dignity of the child
3. Of the fortune of honors and dignities	[4] Of misfortune because of things not undertaken
	[5] Of misfortune because of things omitted
	[6] Of misfortune because of various troubles
	[7] Of misfortune in wealth
	[8] Of those forced to beg due to difficulties or violence

Book 4:	*[Bk. 4]*
	[10] Of misfortune due to judicial violence
	[11] Of misfortune due to violence not judicial
	[12] Of fortune due to evading dangers
	[13] Of men of various fortune
	[14] Of superiors
4. Of the actions or work of the child	
5. Of marriage	[15] Of marriage
6. Of children	[16] Of children
7. Of friends and enemies	[17] Of friends and enemies
8. Of servants	[18] Of servants and attendants
9. Of travel	
10. Of death	[9] Of death from an external cause
11. Of the division of times	[19] Of the division of times

Morandi left out entirely the branch of astrology concerned with the collective fortunes of countries and peoples. Apparently, Ptolemy's discussion in Book 2 was far too limited to provide an adequate basis for covering what the monks regarded as one of astrology's raisons d'être. Moreover, whereas Ptolemy followed this with a discussion of individual fortunes, beginning with children not reared due to death at birth or abandonment by the mother, Morandi would instead consider the death of the mother.

Morandi did his most original work when trying to discover recurrent characteristics in large numbers of natal charts. To test the various theories connecting stars to outcomes using a scientific method, he ordered the monks to begin compiling what might have become one of the most elaborate bodies of empirical evidence to date, had they not been sidetracked by the trial. Research was obviously necessary for acquiring the essential information—not only from printed compendia, but from many other kinds of sources as well. To organize the collaboration in true Baconian fashion, Morandi had the monks and their collaborators draw up questionnaires with particular regard for ascertaining exact birth times to the nearest minute, always a controversial item in the debate about astrology's effectiveness.

Even collecting birth times had its hazards, Morandi noted. Baptismal records and "books of the dead," which could be found in every city, sometimes cited only an individual's year of birth; and the most accurate ones only went so far as to add the day. If all else failed, he told the monks to ask the parents, if living—although memories could be weak. "It should be noted that many times ordinary people may recall the month and the day and the hour, but most of them do not know the exact time, saying only that 'such and such was of this and that age when he died,' often missing a year."[25] He declared only one source to be absolutely out of bounds. On no account were the collaborators to ask any astrologers—because of the latter's well-known proclivity to "accommodate things to their own purposes." No one knew this better than the monks themselves.

Afterward, the monks were to sort the nativities according to outcome. Although Morandi planned a section on individuals who obtained good fortune by evading dangers, as well as one on the varieties of fortune in general, what the monks presented for the most part amounted to a grim catalogue of possible catastrophes. In the first section they would place the cases of persons who fell from greatness or whose prosperity and happiness were interrupted by ill fortune including exile, pursuit by enemies, and wounds, as well as those who failed to gain an inheritance or other expected riches. Then they were to give cases regarding things lost due to various disturbances, persons forced into beggary, and persons placed before the tribunal. This they were to follow by a subsection on illness, including apoplexy, podagra, calculi, fluxes, spitting blood, and ruptured veins. Next would come a subsection on death by the hand of justice, including by strangulation, by iron, by contusion, and so on, and a subsection on death by another's hand including by iron, by fire, by poison, and by other means. In a final subsection on accidents, bearing witness to the triumph of fortune and the defeat of mankind, Morandi had the monks note death by fire, poison, falling from heights, ruin, and drowning.

Of course, the intentions of Morandi and the monks in all this research were more than merely scientific. Saving astrology was not enough. In an early modern world filled with unhappiness, they sought to provide themselves and their distinguished clients with what amounted, in some respects, to a naturalistic explanation of evil. Perhaps the working out of God's inscrutable will through the agency of the planetary motions might provide a more concrete theodicy than the one usually delivered from the pulpit. Not only was evil in the world, their research seemed to imply, distributed according to our just deserts; but the mechanisms for sending down this evil could be seen in operation by reading the books of human experience and of nature. Such was the consolation the monks offered to the Santa Prassede circle. In return, they hoped for at least some relief from their own portion of the world's sadness—in the form of gratitude, companionship, and eventually protection from persons in positions of power and respect.

For most of the monks, these satisfactions were enough. But Morandi himself desired greater glory and worldly rewards than local notoriety could provide. Such might accrue from a prediction about the future of an individual whose position in the firmament was of great interest not only to the usual satellites, but to others of truly planetary importance. This kind of astrology was only a very short step away from high politics. Morandi took that step in 1630—but not before it had already been taken by others around him.

TWELVE

THE BUSINESS OF ASTROLOGY

INTERROGATOR: Do you know anyone in Rome who practices astrology?
MARCANTONIO CONTI: All Rome is filled with these charlatans; and I am amazed that the pope has not given sufficient provision against these impostors. Among them is a knife-seller whose name I don't know, a certain Battelli, certain Spaniards who go around selling their opinions about nativities, as I have heard. (*Morandi Trial*, fol. 183r, August 6, 1630)

THE MONKS and their associates were obviously not the only consultants available on astrological matters in Rome. The rather uncharitable witness at Morandi's trial who listed the local "charlatans," as he termed them, was one of many who believed an astrological resurgence was under way.[1] The "various Spaniards," a "knife seller" in Monte Giordano, "a certain Battelli," as well as "Jacobelli the physician," a "son of the hatmaker at S. Pellegrino," and a "friar in S. Francesco a Ripa," whom he and another witness named as examples, would have fully agreed with the prevalence of the practice, if not the negative characterization of the practitioners.[2] Nor was another witness exaggerating when he noted, "Astrology has become a recognized profession, and almost everyone has nativities drawn up. . . . [Indeed,] there is no cardinal or prelate or prince who does not have discourses written down telling his fortune based on his nativity. . . . Of course," he was quick to add, "only for secondary causes, because everything in the final analysis depends on God."[3]

While Monsignors Francesco Nappi, bishop of Polignano, and Marco Gallio, soon to be named a cardinal, went to a certain astrologer named Lenola, mentioned in the trial documents, others, including the Roman nobleman Cesare Veralli, went to Marcantonio Conti; still others, including a patron of Santa Prassede, Cardinal Desiderio Scaglia, bishop of Melfi, went to Francesco Lamponi—with fatal consequences not only for the monastery but also for Galileo. While Morandi did everything in his power to bring the monastery into the networks of power and prestige in Rome, he could not prevent it from slipping insensibly into the sinister networks of the professional astrologers around the city.

From those who considered themselves to be the modern equivalents of Ptolemy, down to those who merely aspired to some place in the fickle

Roman patronage market, all the Roman astrologers drew upon the monastery's resources in one way or another.[4] Even before arriving in Rome, a certain Francesco Maria Samueli, a monk from the southern Tuscan town of Montepulciano, wrote to Morandi for advice. "I desire to be favored by the humanity of Your Most Reverend Lordship, to be able to come to Rome with some honorable and virtuous opportunity to serve some personage of honor and solvency."[5] Surely Morandi, with his impeccable credentials and associations within the highest reaches of Roman society, would know of any such that might arise. Samueli declared himself willing to suffer for a time even the unhealthy air around the convent of St. Sixtus, where the general of his order was sure to put him up—until a suitable offer should come forth. And, he added, he might be content to serve briefly as the confessor to one of the ecclesiastical lords, as long as, sooner or later, following the counsel of "all my affectionate friends and patrons who are knowledgeable about the things of the skies," he could "attend to the virtues of wisdom"—especially of the astrological kind—in an official capacity.

How did aspiring astrologers start out in seventeenth-century Rome? To be sure, Francesco Lamponi's undistinguished origins promised nothing of what he was later able to achieve when he brought his excellent connections along with him as a Santa Prassede associate. Born in Umbria in relatively modest circumstances and sent to Bologna for a university education, his rowdy behavior landed him in jail at least once. But he managed to finish his law degree, if not at Bologna, at least somewhere else in the papal states; and in 1620 he came to Rome to set up a private practice. His efforts to secure a position of some authority paid off in 1626, when he was appointed by Duke Giovan Antonio Orsini to be governor of the city of San Gemini within the Orsini's vast territorial estate outside Rome.

Not content merely to serve his Orsini lords, Lamponi used his new connections to ingratiate himself with the Apostolic Chamber or papal treasury. He presumed that any advice he could give, considering the dismal state in which the treasury found itself in the 1620s, would be warmly appreciated.[6] Little expertise was necessary to understand that the truly astronomical sums spent defending the papal seat of Avignon during the French religious wars, in acquiring and fortifying Ferrara in 1598, in assembling an army first against Venice in the Interdict controversy, and, again, to defend the Valtelline Catholics in the recent conflict with their Swiss Protestant overlords had all but exhausted the seemingly endless resources available to the papacy. Just in case these expenses were not enough to turn the popes into the largest deficit spenders in Christendom, there were the vast sums spent on building and decorating St. Peter's basilica and on enriching the papal nephews. To defray these costs, no regular spiritual or temporal incomes ever sufficed. Accordingly, like the other rulers of the time, the popes relied to a considerable degree on immediate infusions of cash from selling tax farmers the right to collect indirect taxes—that is, taxes and customs duties on the necessities of life. And with the tax farmers expecting to extort from hapless subjects far more than the sum laid out or the law allowed, no wonder these policies supplied some later analysts, such as Leone Pascoli, with an object lesson in fiscal irresponsibility.[7]

If Lamponi's advice, offered in the form of a private letter, tended to damage the interests of the same large proprietors who had launched his career, at least it cemented the alliance with the Chamber officials that he was to bring with him into the Santa Prassede circle. He directed attention to the large tracts of land belonging to the papacy but held by private persons throughout the papal states and even in the contiguous states. Such tracts, within the vestiges of the papacy's ancient feudal jurisdiction, were operated by families who owed little or nothing in return by way of rent or service.[8] "Many things," he pointed out, the Chamber "allows subjects to enjoy, and even to extract incomes from, without any recognition [of the Chamber] whatsoever, as instead there ought to be."[9] Indeed, "at times, the Chamber, for various reasons, even incurs some expenses." In fact, if he wished, he could have offered some examples from his own experience. His family was still fighting in the tribunals for the right to certain tributes from occupants of papal land in its possession, granted by the Chamber to a certain Ercole Lamponi as far back as 1564.[10] By proposing now that the Chamber take 25 percent of whatever tributes families drew from occupants of the papal land in their possession, perhaps he believed it might forego claiming 100 percent of the incomes from his family's holdings. In any case, some such portion to the Chamber seemed "only right, considering the profits being made." The results would be "secure and real, and could be achieved very quickly by simply collecting the money." This, he claimed, would not only "increase the income of the Chamber by many thousands of scudi." It would do so "without weighing down the people"—except those who held the land. Whether this was the gesture that terminated his Orsini connection and landed him in the palace of the Milanese Count Giovanni Serbelloni in Piazza Sciarra in Rome, where we find him in 1628, we cannot say.

Just in case his foray into political economy did not bring the expected results, Lamponi could fall back on consultations of another sort. Even before coming to Rome, he had discussed the occult arts with his cousin Agostino, a physician in the hills northwest of Ascoli Piceno. Agostino does not appear to have been particularly successful at his job, if we are to judge by the correspondence with his mother, who never failed to include a pair of socks or a handkerchief along with letters containing the usual family gossip. But he managed to accumulate a well enough stocked library to whet their curiosity for higher knowledge.[11] Not that Vesalius's work on the fabric of the human body, listed in the contents of Agostino's library, was likely to offer anything more, in the way of prohibited information, than the comedies of Plautus or the poetry of Propertius and Tibullus, also listed there. The same went for Pietro Andrea Mattioli's history of plants and Valerius Cordus's pharmacopoeia.[12] Even works providing the highest insights of natural philosophy, such as those of Marsilio Ficino, were well within the bounds of orthodoxy. Texts by Leonardo Fioravanti and Alessandro Piccolomini delivered the thrills of all-encompassing explanations and macrocosm-microcosm analogies without the dangers of confiscation. The many volumes of Galen (we do not know of which texts) were a constant reminder that the study of the heavens could no more be interdicted than could the study of how celestial movements influenced diseases—and if curious about hysteria in particular, the cousins could read Avicenna's book on the subject. Local authorities, alerted to the cousins' activities by way of the Morandi connection, and hoping to find incriminating evidence among these books, came away disappointed.

Once he began frequenting the Santa Prassede circle, Lamponi did not have to acquire his astrological expertise by learning seven languages and pondering the intricacies of works by Luca Gaurico, Johannes Garcaeus, and other modern masters of the art, which he probably would not have understood even if he borrowed them. Instead, he procured access to a tradition combining the deepest currents of popular culture with some of the shallower currents of erudite knowledge. At the monastery, this tradition was preserved in a text dictated to the monks by a certain Bernardo Fernandez, identified only as "a Spaniard." The manuscript was later sequestered by the court probably for the same reason that it is interesting to us: namely, because it might contain information of a particularly recondite or secret sort.

There, and in similar texts, Lamponi would absorb a working vocabulary to serve even the most discriminating customers. He would learn to say that the sun, lord of all the planets, might signify "potential honors" and "friendship with the great and the less great." Enterprises begun under its aegis were likely to be "fortunate"—especially on the cusp of its own sign, Leo, but also when in one of the other signs, Aries and Sagittarius, in the Triplicity of Fire.[13] When the ascendant was in the sign of Leo and the sun was on the cusp of this sign—just on the borderline with Cancer—to what might our seeker not aspire? Let him beware of the sun in Libra and Aquarius, our manuscript continues, or in the second, sixth, eighth, or twelfth houses with these signs. With a violent star or unfortunate planet like Mars in an angle (i.e., the cusp of the first, fourth, seventh, or tenth houses), it could signify a tragic finish to any undertaking. Nonetheless, "in stellar affairs, as in all other affairs," the position of the sun was not enough. "One must consider the entire figure."

Should he ever need to comment on the effects of the moon, Lamponi would be reminded that this was the most important of all the remaining planets. Baleful in some nativities, the manuscript proclaimed, it was an excellent influence in others—especially of persons born in the evening. Its general role was to supplant rationality with sensibility. "Lunacy," after all, was originally an astrological concept. In any conjunction with other planets, either in eclipse or just in the same vicinity, it was especially powerful. So also was it strengthened when found in the ninth or eleventh houses along with Scorpio or Taurus. In the tenth house, in the presence of Cancer, its natural sign, it was practically indomitable. The "Spaniard," in writing this manuscript, sided with the medieval Arab scholar Avicenna rather than with Girolamo Cardano in asserting the beneficence of the moon in the tenth house.[14]

From the standpoint of the privileged clientele Lamponi hoped to serve, the Spaniard's text was was particularly helpful in the case of Jupiter.[15] Generally fortunate, this planet was at its best in its own domain of Pisces, although in Scorpio or Sagittarius it could have good effects as well. Occasionally it might diminish the beneficence of Gemini, Virgo, or Capricorn. But it could always be counted on to favor preferment to the highest ecclesiastical offices when in the vicinity of the moon and Venus. Good news, this was, for many aspiring prelates in the Santa Prassede circle.

Not all the planets, of course, were as good as these; and Lamponi would next learn about the maleficent effects of Saturn before proceeding on to the others. Even at its best, when on the cusp of Capricorn, its own sign, it signified less good fortune than in other signs. But combined with any other planet, in any aspect, from conjunction (the closest) to opposition (the farthest) and everything in between, it signifies bad things—especially when these aspects are in relation to the sun or moon. In the second house it caused loss of earnings and of present possessions—on this the Spaniard's manuscript, Cardano, and Avicenna were all agreed.[16] In any other house, Saturn vitiated whatever might be the favorable effects. It accentuated the unfavorable effects of the moon's descending nodes or dragon's tail, the place where the moon crossed the ecliptic from north to south. Vile professions were ruled by it, the manuscript asserted, including farmers, bricklayers, morgue and hospital workers, vagabonds, and "all low people," especially in "the smelly offices" (li offitii puzzolenti). Henrik Rantzau's suggestion that Saturn's child was likely to have "great memory, experience and knowledge of many things, and practice and ability in the building of kingdoms," an important point in the case of Urban VIII, the manuscript passed over in silence.

As soon as he was able to offer astrological consultations on his own, Lamponi looked for business among the great. As the Spaniard's text seemed to recommend, he accommodated his predictions to clients' known ambitions. And again, like the Spaniard, he was never too specific about the outcome. A few of his consultations have come down to us—not, unfortunately, with the names of all the persons they concerned. But enough information is there to give a good idea of an astrological "style." In one case, under the rubric "On Honors and Dignities" Lamponi noted, "If the seeker fits his pretensions to his inclination, he may arrive at a higher stage of greatness than in the past."[17] Such was the promise of the natal chart under discussion, with the moon at Midheaven and the sun in its own exaltation. And the same was confirmed by the progressed chart of this person (i.e., advanced to a later date according to expected planetary changes), showing a conjunction of the sun with Jupiter and Mercury in the Midheaven, accompanied by "very good fixed stars."

So successful, indeed, was Lamponi at divining his clients' aspirations that he helped turn Cardinal Desiderio Scaglia, the bishop of Melfi who was among his most satisfied customers, into a Santa Prassede devotee. "There are no complimentary words or written thanks," Scaglia effused. "Only acts of the most affectionate servitude that one soul may give to another to which it is bound in perpetual obligation, as mine is."[18] And the reason was because Lamponi had "managed my stars and seen the essence of my condition." Not only did he draw ultimately flattering conclusions for the future on the basis of information Scaglia had provided. Concerning Scaglia's youthful theft of his mother's jewels at age eleven to finance a plan to run away to the Orient, Lamponi demonstrated almost uncanny insight. "You noted two things that I know I never said," Scaglia pointed out. The first was that a danger of violent death occurred in the same moment as the theft (Scaglia had only mentioned the year). The second ("and this makes me shudder") was that this danger came from his father's anger. Apparently Scaglia senior had pursued his wayward son around the house flailing "an unsheathed scimitar" from which the latter saved himself only by leaping out a window. Again, of the youthful Scaglia's adversary at age thirty-one, Lamponi not only guessed the ecclesiastical status but also the appearance: aging, with dark skin and beard—precisely the characteristics of one Fra Camillo of Vicenza, the prior of Scaglia's order at that time. "Since you discovered the facts so accurately in these and other things," Scaglia concluded, "I can only conclude that all the future events will be verified as well."

Obviously, there was nothing particularly rigorous about this kind of astrology. Practitioners at the level of Lamponi and Bernardo Fernandez, the "Spaniard" who wrote our manuscript, were running no tests, verifying no data. Their purpose was not to discover anything new about the world nor even to implement discoveries made by others. Nor did they attempt to change in any way the secret knowledge they had appropriated, lock, stock, and barrel, from whatever were its secret sources. Their only interest was in transmitting the same knowledge intact in the form of counsels and advice to whoever paid the right price. To every question they had a ready response; and as far as they were concerned, fixing a life was little different from fixing a piece of machinery. All the answers might be found in the proper manual.

The monks did their best to distance themselves from the trade in astrology as practiced by the likes of these. But as the political climate in the late 1620s began to heat up, this became impossible. What was worse, by raising Scaglia's ambitions to the heights, Lamponi managed to turn a friend of the monastery into a potential enemy later on. Appointed to the commission assigned to the Galileo case in the aftermath of Morandi's trial, Scaglia would be given a further opportunity to express his disappointment, as we shall see.

THIRTEEN

DE RE PUBLICA

INTERROGATOR: Have you seen any writings concerning the cardinals, and a discourse concerning the French monarchy in Parnassus?

CESARE TUBIOLO: Before the investigation of the copy shops, there were many scandalous writings in circulation. (*Morandi Trial*, fol. 133r, July 25, 1630)

TIES BETWEEN the monastery of Santa Prassede and Roman high society reached the last stage of complexity just as the Thirty Years War came to a crisis. In the late 1620s, the outcome of events that could be crucial to the future of Italy seemed extraordinarily difficult to predict. What was to be made of the new alliance between Catholic France and Protestant Holland, just on the basis of their shared opposition to Spain? What was to be made of Holland's recent attempts to extend its war with Spain to the intercontinental stage? Would Charles I of England continue his predecessor's efforts across the Channel on behalf of the Palatinate? Finally, what was to be made of Gustavus Adolphus of Sweden, set to replace Christian IV of Denmark as the head of the Protestant states' rebellion from the empire?[1] Surely pure military might and strategy had decided the outcome of key episodes like the siege of Pilsen and the battle of White Mountain. But all standard methods for assessing the probabilities of success on either side appeared useless. The blood of Catholic subjects cried out for vengeance from the divine defender of the Roman faith, just as the blood of Protestant subjects cried out to the defender of the Reformation. No wonder that even the Duke of Wallenstein, the Catholic champion, resorted to astrology. As surely as Providence guided the hand of humanity through the power of the planets, so the dispositions of the heavenly bodies seemed likely to hold the key to coming events.[2]

In such circumstances, considerable rewards awaited anyone who could judge the progress of states from the standpoint of the most up-to-date information. And the gratitude of princes was due to whoever could accurately predict the future. Morandi accordingly turned the monastery of Santa Prassede into a veritable political seminar. Not only did he provide access to all the available genres of political commentary, jocose and serious, verse and prose, manuscript and print. He provided his own brand of advice, based as much on secret diplomatic sources as on occult supernatural ones. Pushing to the limits the immunity from prosecution he enjoyed through his influential contacts, he dared to make pronouncements about the future failures and successes of the most powerful personages of his age. In so doing, he hoped to consolidate the substantial reputation he had already gained as a man of political wisdom beyond his station, and to merit the confidence of those who listened to his views. In fact, he began on the path that would lead to his own destruction.

For finding the political heart of baroque Europe, a monastery might seem an unlikely place to look. Subtracted from the world and isolated as much from the temptations as from the responsibilities of civil life, the monks could be expected to be better informed about the state of grace than about the state of this or that potentate, and about the new dispositions regarding the regular clergy than the new dispositions regarding particular military units. But, as we have seen, the monks at Santa Prassede were not ordinary monks. Their commitments were as much to worldly affairs as to spiritual ones, and their ministry was as much in this world as in the next. Morandi was not just their spiritual ruler, their guide in the rigors of ecclesiastical discipline and down the avenues of curial advancement, but their leader in all manner of exploits, holy and profane.

At the beginning of the year 1629, a poetry reading at the monastery might have included any number of items belonging to the distinguished tradition of political satire in Italy. This one, sequestered by the governor's court, expressed the realities of seventeenth-century state relations in terms of a popular game of cards:

> Hark! who plays there? King, emperor
> And pope, no less. But what's the game, say you?
> The game is called Primiera. And what for?
> For Italy, no less, and honor too.

The audience knew the object of the game of Primiera: to draw and pick a hand of four cards, including one card of each of the four suits of clubs, spades, coins, and cups, or else a flush of all one suit. In either case, qualifying hands were assigned points according to the value of the cards to determine the winner. So the poem goes on:

> The king, he keeps his cards; his total's high.
> The pope has forty-eight, and so he stays.
> The emperor's up short; he's going to try
> To draw one card of coins, or so he prays.
> The pope, he says to them, let's have a round.
> The king's opposed. He says, I'll see you now;

With cards like this, to win the pot I'm bound.
  It's equal. Cards are dealt all in a rush
To pope and king; and now the king, so bold,
Turns over his, to show all spades, a flush.
  And there's a hush.
The emperor puts everything at risk;
A club! No coins alas there come in his direction.
  O such discretion!
For a caprice, and a parlor game,
All Italy, and honor, lost. A shame!

According to these verses, written by Cesare Conti of Milan and circulated by Morandi, a false move from any of the three major players could be disastrous for Italy.[3] The king of France appeared to be the master of an extremely volatile situation, with some help from the pope, but the Habsburg emperor could disrupt things at any time.

Of course, Italy's predicament was no matter for sport. It was the product of a deadly mix of highly explosive forces.[4] For the first time since winning the Italian wars of the early sixteenth century, Spain was challenged in its exclusive role as arbiter of Italian affairs. The challenge came not only from France, newly freed from the Religious Wars and undergoing a remarkable political resurgence under Richelieu and Louis XIII. The challenge came also from the other half, the Austrian half, of the Habsburg empire, where declining power inspired desperate measures, to reinforce Roman Catholicism where possible, even in those Protestant regions of the empire where avenues of influence still existed, as well as to resist hegemony by Spain, whose policies were increasingly independent under the leadership of Olivares.

Echoes of European events reached the monastery through a variety of channels. Printed reports of battles, coronations, progresses, processions, and marriages, acquired from booksellers in Rome, Venice, and Florence but produced all over Europe, furnished what could be expressed openly about what was going on. Maps of countries, cities, battle scenes, and engravings of cartoon figures or portraits of major participants confirmed visually what was said in words. Clandestine publications, printed with false place name and/or date or circulated in manuscript, such as the strictly prohibited newsletters, supplied commentary far too secret, reserved, or slanderous for the open forum of print.[5]

From the monastery, Morandi directed a sort of scriptorium for the reproduction of clandestine material.[6] What he did not receive gratis from relatives like Giovan Maria Morandi in Bergamo or in exchange for cash from the newsletter writer Orazio Faliero, he occasionally received in exchange for favors in the curia on behalf of the copyist Matteo Vincenteschi or others. More often, he exchanged manuscripts for other manuscripts, which he ordered to be copied out in turn, using the services of fellow monk Calvano Vespignano when he could not use those of fellow monk Ambrogio Maggi, or those of Diego de' Franchi when he could not use Amerigo Gualterotti. To make sure the most conspicuous traces of this activity disappeared from view, he periodically recycled his correspondence, as he later recounted to the judges, "to light my fire."[7]

Thus, within the precincts of the monastery, the political situation would have been impossible to ignore, even supposing that patrons did not talk incessantly about it. If the monks were not assailed by letters from their correspondents informing them that "here we anticipate the arrival of Cardinal R., who is now at Susa with 24,000 infantry and 4,000 cavalry," and explaining that "our Venetian lords have the same number at the border at Sercino, and have conceded a general return of all exiled persons, condemning them to the field of battle at Mantua, where we fear war,"[8] they were bombarded with manuscript commentaries such as "An Advice from Parnassus Discussing the Miseries of Italy," recalled by Ambrogio Maggi to officials of the court. To dull the sharp bite of political tension by a touch of whimsy, they snickered over pieces such as the one recollected by Maggi that claimed the late-sixteenth-century poet Battista Guarino once referred to the Duke of Savoy as "caretaker of the walls of Italy." Since, the manuscript continued, "care" meant "cure" and "cure" suggested "enema," the Duke of Savoy was responsible for the evacuation of the country.[9]

Playful polemics, like the one about the game of Primiera with which we began, were no less serious, from the standpoint of the monks who recited them, than was the following, concerning the Count Duke of Olivares:

What can you say to me, O Signor Count-Duke,
You who wrote just now to Don Gonzale,
That he could always go back to Casale.
But it was all in vain, for Heaven's sake!
  And who will now withstand that army royal;
We have all France's forces under foot,
That kicked you in your rear with kingly boot,
And sent you on your way off Milan's soil.[10]

No doubt the monks thought of Charles VIII's momentous incursion in 1494 when they contemplated Louis XIII's descent in 1629 to liberate Mantua, which had been threatened by a vast campaign all over northern Italy involving the forces of Gonzalez de Cordoba and the Duke of Savoy.[11] They could scarcely fail to agree with the poet that a vast change in the balance of power on the peninsula was sure to ensue.

Figure 11. Francesco Villamena, engraving of the battle between the French and Spanish factions in Rome. (Uffizi no. 1597.)

Political contention that went on in the Roman streets and squares of course did not go on in the monastery, or at least not in the same way. The monks obviously did not affect the customary dress of one or another of the main contending factions, even though their drab ecclesiastical habits would have harmonized more perfectly with the black broadcloth customarily worn by the French faction, reflecting, according to contemporary reports, the mainly "shopkeepers and low people" who belonged to it, than with the more elaborate silk and lace of the "Spanish."[12] The monastery courtyard most probably never provided the setting for fistfights between the factions, of the sort represented in a famous engraving by Francesco Villamena, where neither side seems to be getting the better of the other, and the universal melee prevents the viewer from precisely identifying the Roman square in question.[13]

Nonetheless, the monks engaged in the political contention in their own quiet way. None of the ordinary scruples that reserved discussion only to nobles and officials—"public persons," in common parlance—held any validity here. Morandi was prone to discussing politics openly with everyone including his scribe, who later recalled, "I have often talked with the said Father Abbot about the new things of the world, and about the French and the Spanish."[14] Just what Morandi's exact sympathies may have been, at least at first, no one could really say for sure. For the sake of a good argument, he was willing on occasion to concede that the French under Richelieu and Louis XIII might deserve to play a larger role in Italy now than in the past. On the eve of Louis's descent into Italy in 1629, another scribe walked in upon Morandi and "a gentleman" who supported Spain. They talked about future prospects for a while, with Morandi and the scribe holding out for France. "Then," the scribe recalled, "we looked at a map of Piedmont and observed that the king could only come down via Carmagnola."[15] Morandi was saving his most dire pronouncements for a fitter occasion.

No one could deny that the relative success of French or Spanish power might have a powerful impact on ordinary people's lives—not just from the relatively limited standpoint of the monastery. There, to the extent that political maneuvering between the various parties in the curia, backed by one or another of the main foreign powers, might determine the choice of a pope, the monks' environment could of course be profoundly affected. A pope who happened to be partial to the order could make the road so much easier from within the monastery to the higher reaches of Roman ecclesiastical society—hence the expectations raised, for a time, by Cardinal Carlo de' Medici, who bore the title of Santa Prassede and later became pope. But every aspect of Roman life was affected by the choice of a pontiff—from the distribution of bread and presents to the distribution of the tax burden; from the beautification of Rome's streets and squares to the beatification of its spiritual heroes. No one wished for another Pius V, whom the critics accused of trying to turn the city into one great monastery.[16]

In the rest of Europe, the outcome of the struggle between Bourbon and Habsburg was watched with deep concern, and not just because the choice of a pope from among the factions dedicated to these dynasties could determine a new wave of cardinalships and abbacies for the local aristocrats.[17] The beginnings of great power politics meant that the boundaries provisionally drawn as a result of centuries of dynastic warfare and territorial aggrandizement might well be in for another revision. As yet no concept of nationhood prevented, say, French Savoy from being more or less permanently connected with Piedmont, or Norway from being connected to Denmark, any more than confessional differences prevented dozens of German principalities from pledging nominal allegiance to an Austrian emperor. But a realization more and more began to take hold that the largest dynastic agglomerations stood the best chance of survival in a changing world, that smaller states were more and more difficult to protect and defend, that taxable surface was necessary for lining a war chest capable of financing a formidable modern army, and that the future belonged to the gunpowder empires.[18]

Morandi himself became something of an expert, not only on the European situation at large, but on its significance for Rome. He was the one, after all, who compiled the list of cardinals' qualifications requested by the Venetian ambassador Angelo Contarini in early 1629, so one of Morandi's fellow monks later informed the governor's court.[19] And although Morandi's original manuscript has been lost, traces of his ideas may surely be found between the lines of the writing Contarini presented to the Venetian Senate later that year. There, for instance, we rediscover the division of the curia into four factions, based on the current and previous papacies, that was the aspect of Morandi's writing recalled by Theodore Ameyden, who consulted it.[20] A clause in the report, no doubt representing the ambassador's own point of view, somewhat hopefully suggested that Cardinal Ippolito Aldobrandini, the head of the Aldobrandini faction, was highly favorable to Venetian interests; but the document had to admit that at the next consistory the papacy would go to a favorite of the Ludovisi, Borghese, or Barberini factions, most likely the last two. Whether Morandi or the ambassador was the theorist of yet another division of the cardinals found in the report, cutting across the lines created by family alliances, namely, the division into pro-Habsburg and pro-French, is impossible to say.

Nor can we be sure whether Morandi, trying to establish a reputation for political astuteness, was the original author of some of the best passages in the report, rather than the ambassador, trying to live up to the standards he himself had previously set as Venetian emissary to Charles I of England. Fine judgments of character, especially of individuals who happened to be close to the Santa Prassede circle, were just as likely to have come from Morandi's pen as from the ambassador's. Morandi would have well known, for instance, that Cardinal Desiderio Scaglia, "a man of great affairs," was so "sweet-mannered" that some suspected him of hiding sinister intentions. All that stood between Scaglia and the papacy, the report went on, was his outspoken disapproval of Urban VIII, which had earned him the latter's particular hatred. The Venetian ambassador, on the other hand, just by reading the previous report presented by Renier Zeno in 1623, might certainly have known enough to describe Scaglia's attempts to camouflage his real origins within the Venetian territory of Brescia by a spurious show of Cremonese citizenship.[21] Even more difficult to assign to either Morandi or the ambassador was the assessment of another Santa Prassede associate, Cardinal Tiberio Muti, as "an observer of the sacred rituals without any demonstration of excessive rigor," although Morandi, a philo-Florentine through and through, might have had more reason than the ambassador to dwell on the personal friendship with the Cardinal of Savoy that made Muti the irredeemable enemy of Florence. Morandi again might have had more reason than the ambassador to elaborate on the petty pretensions of the powerless Cardinal Lelio Biscia—yet another Santa Prassede associate, "totally abandoned" only because of his lack of funds and not because of his deafness, as rumor had it, whose earnest efforts at self-promotion merely alienated the major power brokers.

We are left simply to admire the brilliant thumbnail sketches of other cardinals in this report: Cardinal Domenico Ginnasio, for instance, seeking to dissemble his personal connections to the Colonna family by allowing himself to be seen in the act of turning away a Colonna servant. If the Colonna connection did not disqualify him for the highest honors, the report stated, surely his avarice would, "since the papacy needs a benevolent person who can distribute graces and favors with a liberal hand."[22] We find Cardinal Agostino Galamino's chances even more remote, "since he allows himself to be governed in everything by his chamberlain."[23] Cardinal Laudivio Zacchia we find to have been held in such esteem that everyone already called him "pope," even though a former marriage and the existence of a daughter might get in his way. By contrast, only Urban VIII himself seemed to appreciate the exceedingly youthful Cardinal Martius Ginetti, the document went on, who received his appointment for no other reason than because he had followed Urban's every wish for the previous twenty years.[24]

What might have been his opinion at this moment regarding the future of Urban VIII, Morandi wisely kept to himself. The ambassador's report suggests that the outcome of a conclave some time in the distant future was nearly impossible to predict. With all the present factions presumably on the wane, the choice might well fall upon a prelate who had not yet even been promoted to the cardinalship.[25] On the other hand, the report noted, should circumstances arise bringing about the necessity for a conclave in the very near future, there was no reason not to believe that the main factions could be deadlocked. In this case, and here we might discern a trace of Morandi the philo-Florentine, Lorenzo Magalotti was likely to "put himself ahead and cleverly connive" with a "certain conventicle" already operating in his favor. Thus, with one of the major Florentine patricians established in the papacy, the fortunes of the city and of the Medici family might once more be guaranteed—a prospect that only Morandi could anticipate with especial satisfaction.

In fact, we know more about the enthusiasm that greeted Morandi's work on the cardinals in the curia than we do about what it actually contained. As soon as Morandi drew it up in a fine copy for the benefit of the ambassador and shared it with a few intimates, he had it reproduced by several hands and distributed to members of the Santa Prassede circle. But the boundaries between the circle and curious readers in the rest of Rome were by no means impermeable. The most interesting manuscripts soon multiplied, as the scribes hired to copy them on behalf of a library patron made up extras to sell on their own or to exchange for still other manuscripts of equal import. Morandi's anonymous manuscript was eagerly sought in at least three copy shops, where it was distributed by the scribes Giuseppe Amati, Cesare Tubiolo, and a Genoese known only as "Dragut." When Amati came around to the monastery one afternoon on a routine sales call to show what he had on hand and exchange fresh manuscripts for fresher ones, among the items he offered to an astounded Morandi was nothing other than Morandi's own work.[26]

Of course, analyzing the present political situation was one thing, and here Morandi scored high. Predicting the future was quite another. Tommaso Campanella was by no means the only competition in this far more difficult endeavor. He was simply the most vociferous. Nor were Campanella's predictions about the diffusion of Christianity through the universal monarchy of Spain the most far-fetched. Soon independent rulerships, he suggested, would be broken up and the enmities between them would be healed. A new elective theocratic federation would be created in Italy under the aegis of the pope. Thus, the Turk could finally be stopped, the natural movement of the universal monarchies from East to West could be fulfilled, and peace would reign again on earth.[27] Campanella's recommendations about how to prepare for such a future resounded from one end of Italy to the other—if not to the rest of Europe.

Within the monastery, the temptation to proceed, by whatever means, from the study of individual fortunes to the study of the political fortunes of kings, armies, and nations was almost irresistible. As it turned out, the methods for both could be substantially the same. After all, states too, like people, were subject to the eternal cycles of change in the heavens and received from the depths of the universe the forces that would determine their destruction or survival. States, too, were inscribed within an order of nature that expressed the relations and correspondences between the parts through a complex set of ultimately decipherable signs and symbols.[28]

Reading the signs and symbols that represented the relations and correspondences in the world required the expertise of the magician as well as the natural philosopher. No wonder that Morandi, looking for whatever magical shortcuts might help him unlock the secrets of the future of states in the convenience of his own study, turned to the same "Domenico the Arab" who supplied the cabalistic writings we analyzed at the end of chapter 9. From Domenico he received a series of cabalistic enigmas, deceptively simple and containing enough nuggets of profound political wisdom to turn monks into statesmen. These he made part of his repertory of political advice.

Domenico the Arab's text presented four 4 × 4 magic squares—the sums of the integers in all rows and columns of which were equal.[29] To each magic square there corresponded certain letters of the Hebrew alphabet: מ (*mem*), ב (*beth*), ו (*vau*), ט (*teth*), צ (*sadhe*), ח (*cheth*), and ל (*lamedh*). Taken together, the seven Hebrew letters represented the seven planets as well as the seven regions of the world, some of them overlapping or repeated. Thus, to the first magic square, each of the rows and columns of which added up to the number 16, corresponded the letter מ (*mem*), representing Saturn and the regions of Germany and Spain, as well as ב (*beth*), representing Mars and the regions of Milan, Montferrat, Bergamo, and Brescia. To the second magic square, the sums of which came to the number 20, corresponded the letter ו (*vau*), representing Venus and the regions of Germany and Spain (ubiquitous in this system, as in the world at large), and the letter ט (*teth*), representing Mercury and the regions of Turkey, Tuscany, and Crete. The third square, the sums of which came to 17, had as its correspondent the letter צ (*sadhe*), representing Jupiter and the regions of France, Spain, and "Amor"—"Roma" read backward, referring not to the papacy but to the Holy Roman Empire. Also corresponding to this square was the letter ח (*cheth*), representing the sun, along with the regions of Venice and the Orient. Finally, to the fourth square, the sums of which came to 12, there corresponded the letter ל (*lamedh*), representing the moon and the regions of Naples and Lombardy.

According to Domenico's analysis, these figures could be further refined by deriving their zodiacal equivalents. To derive the zodiacal equivalent of the first square, he simply spun around the signs of the zodiac until he had passed as many as equaled the square's value, 16. Thus he began at the first sign, which was of course Aries, passed this again twelve signs later, and stopped at the fourth sign after this, yielding Cancer. Performing the same operation with the second square, equaling the number 20, he got Scorpio; with the third, equaling 17, he got Leo. To the fourth, of which the sum was 12, corresponded all the signs in the zodiac put together.

From these figures Domenico was able to deduce the general cause of evil in the world—represented, according to his austere opinion, by the third letter, that is, Venus, symbol of the venereal act, adultery, and fornication.[30] Then there were the particular dangers. The fifth letter showed how trouble proceeded from and was shared between "Amor" and Spain, "since they are of one house," the Habsburg. However, the first and fifth letters showed how Germany, "Amor," and Spain were all at odds. Letters four and six showed the decline of Spain, because four represented the Turks and six represented Venice, both at this time arrayed against Spain. No doubt Domenico was also aware that a conspiracy of Spanish sympathizers against the Venetian government had recently come to light.[31] In the near future, the Turks would first attack "Amor," he suggested, but

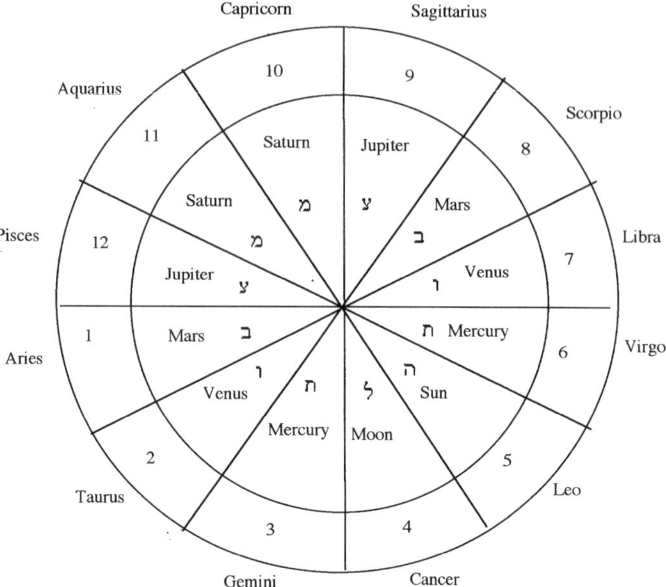

Figure 12. Domenico the Arab's Cabalistic wheel.

only that part belonging to their own state—presumably, the disputed areas of Hungary and Transylvania in which they had already made inroads. Then they would turn against Spain, as letters four and six revealed.

Some of Domenico's predictions were too far-fetched even for the 1620s. No new crusade would ever resolve the situation of Europe, contrary to his suggestion. And the "reformation of the empire" would not really take place until Napoleon's time. Other predictions, however, seem remarkably clear-sighted from our standpoint. "Much would be resolved," he noted, "by a great pestilence"—that in fact came to southern Europe in 1629. Furthermore, Spain, he predicted, would divide into separate areas—just as the rebellions of Catalonia, Portugal, and Naples in the 1640s were to prove. Meanwhile, Venice would lose "a large maritime region," which could easily refer to Crete, then known as Candia, taken by the Turks in 1669 after twenty years of warfare.

To Morandi, all this was immensely useful. But for his most demanding audiences, he needed more specific information. So instead of simply appropriating Domenico's conclusions, he struck out on his own. On the basis of the same figures, he traced the path of the plague that had just begun to make itself felt in certain parts of northern and north-central Italy.[32] The sign of Cancer in the first square regarding Germany and Spain "denotes illness," Morandi reminded readers, especially in connection with Saturn and Mars. Scorpio in the second square, corresponding to Milan, Montferrat, Bergamo, and Brescia, denoted "very great illness," while Leo in the third square, corresponding to Genoa and Spain, "denotes taking away." Thus, "the evil begins in Germany and proceeds to Milan," he explained, "then it will spread to the Veneto and to Genoa, from which it will then go to the Turk, who is on the move. From there it will begin to affect Amor and Spain; then part of France and finally Venice, Naples, and Spain. It will flourish particularly in Naples." In fact, Morandi was not too far off, if the Neapolitan and Genoese plagues of 1656 could be considered remote extensions of the present one. Regarding the prospects for the political situation, he simplified Domenico's result to produce a scheme that could just as well be a set of instructions for some modern war game:

> Spain is offended by Germany, the Turk, and by Venice.
> Venice is offended by Spain, the Turk, and Naples.
> Germany is offended by Spain and the Turk.
> Amor [the Habsburg Empire] is offended by the Turk, Venice, and Spain.
> Genoa is offended by Germany, the Turk, and France.

From this scheme, only one conclusion was possible: "Amor" and Germany would have a common affliction; Germany, afflicted, would harm Venice; and the Turk would harm both.

Characteristically, in this writing, Morandi gave no clue regarding his opinion of Urban VIII's government or any other issue of ecclesiastical politics. He would do that later on, in a piece containing his most original work. From his point of view, reinterpreting a second-hand commentary on a series of someone else's enigmas was nothing compared to offering first-hand predictions. And by now, Morandi had a reputation to protect. His admirers expected to be enlightened about future expectations for Europe, just as Morandi had enlightened them about future expectations for themselves. How far would he dare to go? What new techniques would he need?

FOURTEEN

OCCULT POLITICS

CESARE TUBIOLO: I also had a writing from a certain youth called Giuseppe Amati of Ascoli, more than a month and a half ago, which was a writing in various chapters beginning "Sigismund VIII," containing prophecies about the popes; and I remember that in chapter 30 it spoke about bees, and I considered that it must be a prophecy about Our Lord Pope Urban VIII, whose coat of arms contains the bees. (*Morandi Trial*, fol. 113r, July 25, 1630)

BETWEEN 1629 AND 1630, the fate of Italy seemed to hang in the balance; and a new demand for clairvoyance directed the search for unusual insights to the most unlikely places. Indeed, we may well wonder whether Morandi's opinion on the rain of sulfur that occurred in Naples on the evening of May 14, 1629, was solicited by a certain Giambattista Castellani with political purposes in mind.[1] Could such an event refer to the rebellious spirit of the Neapolitan people, fomented by the Spanish government's fiscal chicanery? Likewise, we may wonder whether political curiosity inspired another correspondent, one Baldassare Pignatelli, to seek Morandi's interpretation of the hieroglyphs on the obelisks in Piazza San Pietro and at San Giovanni Laterano around the same time.[2] Certainly, before Jean-François Champollion's discoveries in the early nineteenth century on the basis of the Rosetta Stone, the significance of the pictograms thickly inscribed upon the slender marble monuments was anybody's guess. What is more, political minds were no more likely to be satisfied with Pietro Vettori's fanciful analysis, present in the Santa Prassede library and based on the late antique text of Horapollo that was thought to originate from the time of the pharaohs, than with Michele Mercati's text, also present in the library, and based on Clement of Alexandria.[3] What could be less convincing, or indeed, less inspiring, than Vettori's suggestion that a drawing of a blind scarab merely referred to death from sunstroke? The same went for the suggestion that drawings of crawling cicadas referred to religious ceremonies or that two crows copulating signified human reproduction. Behind the abundance of crocodiles, pigs, and dead horses, such obvious signs of evil, surely there must lie material for far deeper reflections, as Athanasius

Kircher was to find out later on in the century. Of what sort, even Kircher could hardly explain.

If the political situation in Europe seemed far too enigmatic for the standard techniques of political analysis to elucidate, or even for the cabala, what new method might suffice? In the months before his arrest, Morandi wondered. Concentrating all his forces to delve into the very marrow of things, he sought to trace contemporary politics back to their secret source in the cycles of the universe. And the method he finally hit upon summoned up the world of symbols and similitudes that the monks had explored in administering to the health needs of monastery associates.

Indeed, in the precarious circumstances of the early seventeenth century, any particularly apt statements about a previous age were thought to contain possible keys to recurring regularities in human fortunes. And a rough-drawn woodcut entitled "I was Italy" (*Italia fui*) was just as likely to illuminate events during and after the year 1618 when it was reprinted in Rome, as events during and after the year 1554, when it first circulated.[4] Now, as then, Italy seemed to be on the brink of disaster. The depiction of Italy as a woman seated upon an empty chest with a crown at her feet, holding her face in her hands and weeping, could refer just as easily to the recent first War of Mantua as to the Habsburg conquest of the Republic of Siena and its transfer to the authority of the Medici family over sixty years before. Winds that seemed to blow at her from opposite directions were still blowing, and the terrible dragon above her head could still be imagined to be roaring, as the label indicated, "I'll devour you while the princes quarrel." Indeed, the hordes of roosters or "galli"—Frenchmen—swarming down the hills on her right, could just as well be the armies of Louis XIII as of Henry II. Venice, depicted in a corner, had not changed its aspect, and it still remained the "sola filia intacta," untouched by foreign invasion. Likewise, "quo Etruria" could still apply to Florence, torn between the gallic cock and the Habsburg eagle. Who could ever forget the Habsburg hegemony over Milan, Naples, and Sicily, represented by three nude men lying prostate while an eagle above them holds their crowns and scepters? The troubles of Italy were as well known as they were long-standing.

For answering specific questions, classic works like the spurious twelfth-century prophecies attributed to Joachim of Fiore concerning future papacies came back in vogue—and not only in the "Sole" bookstore belonging to Niccolò Inghirami and frequented by Orazio Morandi, where conversations about them were reported.[5] Whoever read the new edition of pseudo-Joachim's work, dated Padua, 1625, and adorned with the same suggestive woodcuts as the previous editions, supposedly based on the author's own drawings, would surely have found food for thought in such statements as, "The East will drink of the cup of God's anger."[6] Morandi's fellow monk, Giovanni Ambrogio Maggi, was probably not the only reader who took this to be a prophecy that the Catholic Church would disappear by the year 1632.[7] What, indeed, must viewers and readers have concluded from the statement, elsewhere in the book, that "This ugly image of clerisy will struggle against the dove"?[8] The depiction of a tiara-wearing monster rising next to an armed pope holding an olive branch in one hand and, in the other, the papal keys with a dove perched on them, could presumably refer to as many past papacies as papacies to come. The same again went for the statement, "He will give light to six planets, and one of them in the end will surpass him in splendor," accompanied only by the elucidation that "from the mountainous regions of the earth, from a bright land, there will rise a man performing singular acts, who will make some stars brighter and others darker."[9] Referring to yet another image, surely no one could resist trying to guess who was meant by the statement that "with the keys he will close and will not open."[10] Was this an invitation or a threat?

In fact, according to the cultural environment shared by Morandi and his patrons, symbols were more than just symbols. They were not just figures on a page or visual designs. Nor were they merely the product of human imagination. In fact, from this point of view, the most fertile producer of similes in the world was not the poet—not even a poet like Giambattista Marino, from whose pen they seemed to roll as easily as speech itself. No, the true mother of similes, as of metaphors, allegories, metonyms, and all other figures of speech, was nature herself. All one had to do to appreciate her handiwork was to look around at the amazing similarities: between the mandrake root and the human form. Between goats' milk and human milk, between flax and hair. What is more, as we have seen in a previous chapter, such similarities were by no means casual. They were not the result of the observer's cogitation. Nor were they placed there merely for our delight. They were signatures left by the creator during the fabrication of the world; signs of the functioning relationships that made the world work. No wonder the poets who discovered them were considered to be divine; and the creation of images was regarded as the closest Man could come to a godly act.

Writing down, building, or drawing such figures, in fact, meant tapping into the very viscera of things. And the connections thus discovered were not merely aesthetic, but operative. The symbol and the symbolized were one; what concerned the first concerned the second. The eagle did not just represent the king; it was the king—hence the reverence accorded to the objects on which the symbol was inscribed. Hence also the care with which the symbols were organized in those grand tableaux vivants of early modern society, in parades, processions, festivals, celebrations. Hence the dramatic consequences when a celebration went wrong.

Already in the late sixteenth century, analyzing the meanings of the devices that important personages commonly used as identifying symbols or, if one wishes, as trade marks, had become nearly as serious an enterprise as the formulation of the symbols themselves. Since the proper combination of an enigmatic graphic image with an equally enigmatic motto, often in Latin, could only be the work of an elevated intellect, so also was the work of deciphering the meaning. And as the materials used in the representations became more complex and esoteric, drawing upon cabala, hieroglyphics, ancient Greek and Roman culture, and all the liberal arts, not to mention whatever new flora and fauna new geographical discoveries lent to the modern imagination, the explications of the devices too became more complex and esoteric. Nor, considering the supposed natural or divine origins of symbolic representations, was there any reason why the meanings eventually drawn out might not go far beyond anything the original author could have thought he or she was putting in. If Lodovico Dolce, interpreting the chariot of Apollo depicted on Philip II's device, was able to read in the Spanish king's future greatness, this was because somewhere in the formulation of the device greatness had somehow been incorporated. The same went for his interpretation of the half-circle in the device of Henry II, symbolizing the king's future weakness. "The circle was not full," Dolce commented, "because he did not possess his whole kingdom."[11]

Morandi was not the first to consider that noble coats of arms, like the symbolic devices of important personages, bore a particular significance beyond their usefulness for designating the persons and property belonging to the families they represented. Fictive stories about the ancient origins of the practices of heraldry were still half-believed, as was the ancient origin of many family symbols still in use. That the symbols used were often commonplace objects—a thistle, a pine cone, an oak tree—made no difference. If such symbols were products of the highest ingenuity of their times, attempting to express truths too deep or too secret to be divulged, they too deserved detailed study and analysis. And they, too, like the devices, might contain knowledge that their original creators transmitted unawares.[12]

From the standpoint of ecclesiastical politics, Morandi wondered: what could be more symbolically significant than the coats of arms whereby the popes over the centuries had represented themselves and allowed themselves to be represented? Papal families, like all other notable families, were communities joining the members to a common destiny across time and space. What was true of previous generations, at least to some degree, continued to be true today. Somewhere in the various combinations of flora, fauna, celestial orbs, and geometrical designs depicted on a papal escutcheon must lie the truth about its bearer—not just about his ancestor. Something in that truth helped explain the current predicament of Europe.

Morandi accordingly set out to analyze current papal politics as a succession of past papal arms.[13] And he framed his work in the same indirect and allusive symbolic language used by others for the engraving of "Italia fui" and the prophecies attributed to Joachim of Fiore that we just analyzed. To add to the interest of this work as well as to avoid the possible dangers of making any too-explicit comments, he conceived of a clever expedient. He presented it according to the typical Baroque device of an imaginary manuscript. Supposedly written by "a certain Arab or Persian" at the beginning of the Council of Constance in 1414, it began with an invocation to King Sigismund of Germany to help resolve the Great Schism and reform the Church. The king, it explained, had warned "that the Church will either be destroyed by the tyranny of some of its sons and princes or else will return to its pristine poverty with excellent faith." And by the succeeding series of forty predictions, loaded with enough clear references for the modern reader to be impressed by how well the actual events measured up, the manuscript purported to demonstrate that the king was exactly right.

Beginning with a prediction about the fall of the antipope, John XXIII, Morandi proceeded through each of the papacies to come, dropping hints enough to fascinate well-informed readers along the way. From the epithet "de Sebete," signifying "from Naples," such readers would recognize John the antipope, as also from the comment that "he will wear a stolen stocking," referring to the leg hose on his coat of arms. That "he will enrich himself with the goods of others and will dissipate the Church" completed the description of a pope who would "be robbed of what he robbed"—meaning, of the papal title that he supposedly usurped in the Great Schism, only to lose it at the Council of Constance. Readers who managed to guess the identity of John the antipope would surely have no trouble recognizing Martin V. "The once-darkened light will now shine on a solid column" clearly referred to Oddone Colonna's coat of arms as well as to his role as the restorer of the papacy after years of schism. "And it will bear," the manuscript continued, referring to the column, "the crowns that had been deprived of their adornments." And if that was not sufficient confirmation for their conjectures, readers would find the next pope indicated clearly enough by Eugenius IV's origins in "the lagoon," that is, Venice, and by the suggestion that "he will smite his son," that is, Francesco Sforza, whom Eugenius created marquis of Ancona and later destituted. "By his clemency," they would read, "he will bring about magnanimity in people," no doubt mainly in Rome, where Eugenius stemmed the tide of civil war.

Morandi reserved particularly harsh criticism for the popes best known for simony, nepotism, and susceptibility to foreign influence. No reader with a passing knowledge of Church history could fail to recognize Alexander VI in "a viper full of venom, a great serpent, and not a cow nor a calf," as in the Borgia arms. "And with the divine Empire situated between cadavers and wicked evils, he will die at a banquet"—indeed, where poison was served, readers acquainted with the legend would have known to add. Names had their hidden meanings too, and soon afterward, a "clement physician" or *medicus*—Clement VII of the house of Medici—would "make war in the Clementia"—that is, as part of the league against Charles V. "Fleeing in the face of war, he would see the city destroyed and vanquished by new barbarians," obviously, during the sack of Rome. He would then "conspire with the princes," and by applying "their medicine" to Italy's infirm body, he would allow the country to be "made the shame of a new Empire," clearly, as Charles took over Lombardy and Naples. Readers could then join Morandi in admiring the "lilies" in the Farnese coat of arms, that "will bloom in the city," engraved (he might have added) in the very stonework of many a wall and fountain, and yet disparage Pope Paul III, who would acquire "more for his relatives than for Peter" and would "fight against princes." A "dishonest soldier," presumably referring to Paul III's natural son Pier Luigi, "would luxuriate in the name of Jesus," the manuscript commented, without specifically mentioning the principality Pier Luigi set up for the family in Parma. Those who had followed the story up to now were sure to join Morandi in exclaiming, "Woe to you, O Church, when the monarchy of the oppressors will surround its wealth and its poverty."

Viewed from either side of the international political spectrum bounded by Bourbon and Habsburg, such commentary was calculated to win nods of assent for its disenchanted assessment of papal power. Readers familiar with works by the Venetian friar Paolo Sarpi concerning state sovereignty against ecclesiastical interference could delight in the depiction of Pope Paul V. Identified only by the Borghese coat of arms, which in his case, the manuscript specified, bore not a dragon and an eagle but "an evil dragon and a vulture," he would introduce "new laws" into Italy. What could this be but a reference to his definitive redaction of the bull *In coena domini* proclaiming Church rights and his various attempts to assert the independence of ecclesiastics in their own states? When he finally put the recalcitrant republic of Venice under an Interdict, the international community, informed by Sarpi's tracts, joined in forcing him to back down.[14] And for those readers who recognized "new wars" as the first War of Mantua, the portrait of Paul V was completed by the overall characterization of a reign in which "charity will be destroyed, faith will diminish, injustice will become justice, and tyrannies will strengthen against the poor and innocent."

Readers could almost guess what was coming next; but the radical departure of Morandi from his customary reserve regarding Urban VIII's government must have shocked even those who knew him best. In this section Morandi and his manuscript moved into the area more properly defined as prediction. And to those readers who, with Paolo Sarpi, objected to the increasing worldly dimension of the papacy, Urban's whole Barberini clan was as easily recognizable by the buzzing bees on its coat of arms as they were by the damage widely attributed to their actions:

> They will be changed into bees, and they will make honey only in the corpse of Christendom. War will increase under their aegis, powerful kings will fight, arms will thunder, trumpets will blare; even asses will cry out. Italy will languish, Rome will be changed, and people will say, "where is our shepherd?" and the father of peace will be sorely beset by violence and by death. Finally, roaring through his teeth, he will be destroyed.

Attentive readers would easily recognize the pope who took advantage of the confusion caused on the peninsula by the beginnings of the Thirty Years War to incorporate the duchy of Urbino into his state and add to it the counties of Gubbio and Montefeltro. His fiscal oppressions earned him the nickname "papa gabella"—the tax pope. And that he would eventually "be destroyed" while "roaring through his teeth" practically no one doubted. The question was, when and how?

With readers' attention galvanized by these daring pronouncements, Morandi next embarked on a series of prognostications about papacies to come, based on the arms of the probable candidates. In the paragraph following the discussion of Urban VIII, Morandi foretold that "between black and white" and "from a combination of the eagle and the dragon" there would emerge a "fleet-footed canine, borne away by his own speed." Who could that be but Desiderio Scaglia, one of the most eminent *papabili* in the Borghese faction, for whom Lamponi had given such favorable notices about the future? The allusion to the running greyhound in the Scaglia coat of arms was clear; and the probability of an alliance between the imperial faction, represented in the prediction by the Ghibelline dragon, and the opposing faction, represented by the Guelf eagle, seemed good enough. What remained to be seen was whether Scaglia as pope would indeed "incite Mars against the Orient," probably referring to the Ottoman Turks, only to have his "good will" thwarted by "the depraved desires of the faithless belligerents"; and, worse yet, whether, on his watch, "the palaces of Rome" would indeed "burn by the fault of the barbarian armies"—no doubt, the Germans—and "drip in blood."

In any case, the sense of impotence in the face of danger would, the manuscript continued, motivate the consistory to "choose inappropriate candidates" until peace could be restored once again by foreign arms. Scaglia, the first "canine," would thus be followed by "other canines"; and these would run toward the light of the stars—the stars, one might conjecture, adorning the upper part of the escutcheon of Fabrizio Verospi, under which were depicted two silver controrampant and affronted dogs, collarinated with red. Among the cardinals *papabili* in 1630 belonging to the Barberini faction, Verospi might have seemed a longshot. But he was only fifty-nine—young enough to survive at least one other papacy after Urban's death. Would he indeed "foment" the Barberini bees and increase the scope of the present wars, as Morandi foretold? If so, one could only hope, as Morandi suggested, that he would "die like a dog" without so much as uttering "an imprudent bark."

Nor would the series of evils end there, at least according to Morandi's predictions. Next would come what could only be a brief pontificate, considering the age of the candidate—that of Pietro Paolo Crescenzi, unmistakable for the castle and two towers in his coat of arms, to which the manuscript's thirty-fourth paragraph alluded. But these "towers," providing "a bulwark against projectiles," would be "leveled" and would "fall miserably before the flood of the enemy army." In the end, "the waters of the Tiber" would "run with blood."

Morandi's predictions became ever more Delphic as the popes in question were more and more expected to have been made cardinals by the popes to come. Which pope would be "caught in the tracery of the walls," presumably, of Rome, where he would allow the Church to "run among the thorns"? Under his rule, perhaps in an ironic allusion to the present time, "people will incite pseudo-prophets against other people," and "the name of Jesus will be afflicted in society by the worst tyrants." But the "eagle" that symbolized him was common enough among noble families' coats of arms to provide a fertile field for speculation as to which one it metaphorically evoked. The subsequent pope designated as "a veiled horse" was as enigmatic as his destiny was bleak. "Tinged with blood," he would "run among the lions over the cadavers, amid the tears of the people." Affairs in Christendom would fall into total disorder, and in his time "whoever rises will come crashing down." The multitude of the people will "luxuriate faithlessly in the goods of the Church." And the search for peace would be in vain.

Only once the "ancient lines were extinguished," presumably referring to the most powerful families in and around the papacy, would things begin to improve. Then there would come "a lamb," no better identified than by the indication that he would be "sitting between two lions." He would "strike at the dragons and the eagles," perhaps at what remained of the Guelf and Ghibelline factions, and peace with the Turk would return. The "spouse," namely, the Church, "having been rejected by the adultery," indeed, by the faithlessness of the papacy, "would be reconciled to its true husband," the pope, and its youth would be restored.

Finally, there would arise a "man of justice and strength," and although neither Morandi nor his readers could know it, his prediction here came closest to the truth. For the new pope would indeed be "a dove," bearing the name and arms of the Pamphili family, originating from within "the dead and salty swamps" of the Umbrian springs. By the standards of the time, he would indeed reign for "many years." Whether this "dove" was in fact entirely "innocent" while at the same time "powerful as a lion" and "wise as a serpent" would be for the flatterers of Innocent X to decide. Likewise, wide open to interpretation would be Innocent's role in reducing the laws "to the image of his own candor" and receiving into his own breast the dove of peace that had been "blackened by the impious" and "sending it out to fly over the wheels of the heavens." The power of the papacy to play any role in preserving "smaller states" and preventing their destruction, foretold by Morandi, was surely on the wane by the 1640s, even if Innocent managed to "renew the city and the world." In any case, with "Peter returned by Peter to his rock," the days of iniquity would end.

The sensation these prophecies must have made among the "group of men" in Morandi's chambers to whom it was first read, according to the testimony of Francesco Ripa, is not difficult to imagine.[15] Morandi himself was so pleased with the reaction that he had the work drawn up in several copies for distribution to the Santa Prassede circle. When the scribe Giuseppe Amati came around to the monastery to barter fresh manuscripts for fresher ones, Morandi supplied him with this. Before long it began circulating as widely as his report on the cardinals. Amati thereupon took it to another scribe, Cesare Tubiolo,[16] who kept it for three weeks; and when the latter returned it, Amati gave it to Aurelio Adami of Fermo, yet another scribe, for another copy. Adami returned the two copies, reminding Amati that he had "paid for that writing," that is, the copy, so Amati was obliged to requite him with "the next writing that comes out," should he manage to find anything nearly so interesting.[17]

Of course, anyone seeking specific answers to the political issues raised by the current circumstances might have been disappointed even by Morandi's Latin prophecies. In the sections devoted to the next papacies, the author gave no hints about how long the popes in question might last, nor about how many decades might go by before "Peter was returned by Peter to his rock" so the new era of reform might begin. More important, Morandi gave no hints about exactly when Urban VIII's destructive effects would lead Rome over the brink of disaster. He even left in doubt the precise date of the pontiff's death.

However, in yet another writing Morandi made good the promises left unfulfilled—the writing by which he hoped to launch his new career as a curial Cassandra. Daring in its conception and frightful in its implications, it could either make or break the individual to whose authorship it might be attributed. Following his usual habit of self-concealment, he wrote his prediction in the form of an anonymous letter from Lyons dated February 1630, although its author and place of origin soon became as widely known in Rome as the prophecies it contained.

FIFTEEN

THE LAST PROPHECY

INTERROGATOR: Where did you get the geniture of Our Lord Pope Urban, and how long have you had it?
MORANDI: I have had Our Lord's geniture for a very long time, and I do not remember where I got it. But in Florence it is very easy to get, and it is noted at the Merchant's Guild, where books are brought belonging to the Oratory of S. Giovanni, where the Baptistry is.
INTERROGATOR: Would you say when and on what occasion you rectified the said geniture?
MORANDI: I do not remember precisely when I rectified that geniture of Our Lord, although it was after His Holiness Pope Urban VIII became pope, but I only did it for pure curiosity.
(*Morandi Trial*, fol. 109v, July 15, 1630)

PREDICTING THE DEATH of a personage as eminent as Urban VIII was bound to be risky. And not just for the obvious reason that the prediction might fail. Only three years before, the pope's health seemed to be so sound that a previous Venetian ambassador saw no reason not to expect a "long pontificate."[1] However improbable a prediction of death might be, it was almost certain to encounter strong disapproval from the personage in question. Julius Firmicus Maternus was by no means the first astrologer in history to deny nativities to eminent persons on the grounds of possible retaliation. Nor was Luca Gaurico the last to suffer for having done them. Half a century after Gaurico went to the torture chamber in Bologna for having predicted Guido Bentivoglio's problems with Pope Julius II, Thomas Harriot was thrown in jail in England for having cast nativities for the king and crown prince on the eve of the Gunpowder Plot that narrowly missed destroying them both.[2]

No matter. Morandi pressed ahead. Emboldened by his own reputation, he rushed into an area of political prophecy where even the greatest experts feared to tread. Perhaps convinced by his own growing myth, he dared to match wits with the cleverest intellects of his time. Borne away by the flattery of his admirers and the expressed appreciation of his patrons, he apparently assumed that his high connections made his judgment as infallible as his person was unassailable. Could he win this desperate gamble? And if not, was it worthwhile?

Of all possible subjects for astrological prophecies, Urban VIII was perhaps the most sensitive. Even those who knew him well admitted that the rumors about his singular dedication to this science were partly true. Two years before, when some of the Roman astrologers, including Francesco Lamponi, a member of the Santa Prassede circle, had foreseen an imminent threat due to a solar eclipse followed by a lunar eclipse, the Tuscan ambassador reported that "the pope has begun to calculate his nativity more than ever."[3] To counter the fatal astral influences, he called in none other than astrology expert Tommaso Campanella, who happened to be enjoying a rare period of relative freedom from the prisons of the Inquisition. Only Campanella's own later testimonies stand as proof that their collaboration involved nothing to arouse suspicions of witchcraft or necromancy.[4]

Exactly what Urban may have done with Campanella in a special room in Castel Gandolfo, fitted out as a veritable magic chamber, the pope kept carefully concealed from public scrutiny. Campanella provided the only information we are likely to get, while describing a similar room in his manual *On Avoiding Destinies Inscribed in the Stars*. First, to cancel the "pestiferous influences" sent down from the heavens, the air was to be sprayed with rosaceous vinegar and filled with pungent odors produced by burning laurel, myrtle, rosemary, cypress, and other aromatic woods as incense. "Nothing has more effect against the power of the stars," he noted, "even if the poison has been administered diabolically." Next, the place was to be adorned with white silk cloths and budding branches. Two lamps and five candles were to be lit, representing the planets in the heavens. Around them were to be drawn the twelve signs of the zodiac, although Campanella gave no hint about what he meant when he advised going about this "philosophically" and not "superstitiously, as the vulgar do." Friends were to be summoned, whose nativities did not threaten evil effects, in this case presumably Campanella himself. Music characterized by Jupiter or Venus was to be played so that the evil in the air would be dissipated (a duet between the multitalented friar and his pope?). Stones, plants, and other objects of various colors were to be scattered about, whose symbols were most apt to attract the forces of the benefic planets and repulse the malefics. Provided all these things were done three hours before an eclipse and three hours afterward, and until the benefics had arrived at the angles and achieved their strength, the seeker was safe. Considering Urban VIII's indignant reaction to Campanella's treatise, and the author's hasty self-defense, we may assume it contained a reasonably

Figure 13. Bernini, bust of Urban VIII. (Palazzo Barberini, Kunsthistorisches Institut von Florenz.)

accurate account of what may have been a rather embarrassing moment for the pope.

In spite of the pope's volatile state of mind, death was one matter about which the astrological teachings studied at Santa Prassede left little room for doubt—provided that the proper data could be found.

Of course, interpretation of the data was no easy matter; and Ptolemy, upon whom Morandi and his fellow monks often relied, had added endless complications to the earlier Greek idea that the birth planet determines life span.[5] Instead, he calculated the life span on the basis of the geometrical distance between two highly variable and movable points in the zodiac, beginning with the aphetic, also called the prorogating or life-giving point, where the planetary giver of life was situated. This could be in a number of different places, most properly in the Midheaven, but also in the ninth house. The planetary giver of life itself was usually either the sun or the moon, but not necessarily. The natural life span according to this theory was calculated from where the planetary giver of life was situated in the life-giving point, as far as the descendant (i.e., the opposite side of the nativity from the ascendant), unless interrupted by an anaretic planet, a planet with death-giving properties. Such planets might include the quintessentially unfortunate planets Saturn or Mars; they might include the moon if the sun happened to be the life-giving planet. A sign could also be anaretic—especially when in a quadrate (i.e., three signs away from the sign where the giver of life was located). Determining which sign or planets were relevant, and how dangerous, demanded all the skill of the experienced astrologer. The number of years of expected longevity was equal to the number of degrees of longitude between this place and the aphetic point.

Morandi was presented with a nativity for Urban VIII drawn up for April 5, 1568, at 1:29 P.M., with the sun in Aries in the ninth house and Leo in the ascendant.[6] According to the writing that he pretended to have been addressed from "Lyons," the sun was the life-giving planet in this configuration, but its favorable effects were entirely vitiated by the presence of Mars and the Moon. Venus, though favorably situated, was no match for these evil planets, especially because it in turn was blocked by the opposition of Saturn in the eighth house. Urban was very fortunate, said Morandi, to have lived beyond the age of seven.[7] Things started looking better if these directions were progressed to the year 1630. The ascendant would be unaccompanied by any unfavorable planets, and Venus would be in its own house and in a good position to counteract Saturn. But none of these benefits were of much use if Urban was doomed to die in any case. That year, a solar eclipse would occur in June in the sign of Gemini, in the vicinity of Mars, the planetary ruler of late middle age, Urban's current stage of life. Concerning the influence of solar eclipses, Morandi overlooked Ptolemy in

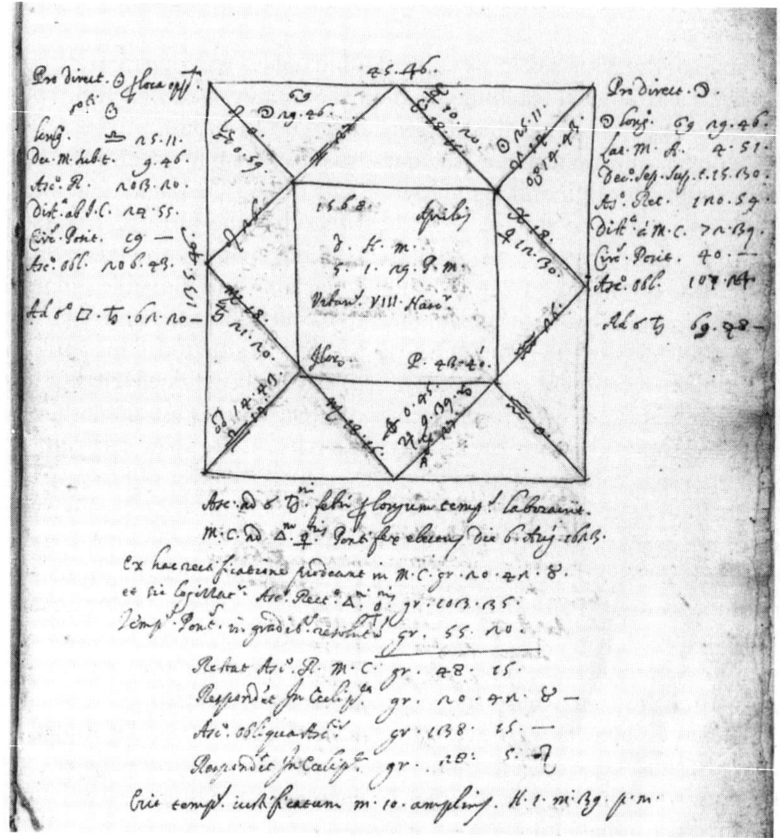

Figure 14a. Horoscope of Urban VIII.

favor of the medieval *Centiloquium Hermetis* (in fact a Latin translation by Stephanus of Messina of a work by Albumasar, which uses ancient Hermetic and other astrological traditions).[8] On the basis of this reading, his conclusion was inescapable: Urban VIII was doomed. The fact that Rome was under Taurus, a whole sign away from Gemini, where the eclipse would be occurring (although Italy itself was sometimes said to be under Libra), was not enough to save his life.

This prophecy did not go unchallenged, even at the monastery. One frequent visitor who objected was Raffaele Visconti, an advisor to the Holy Office. He explained the reasons for his dissent in an anonymous letter that he too pretended to have been sent from Lyons, dated February 21, 1630, in reply to the previous one of Morandi.[9] According to him, Mars in a right quartile with the sun—that is, four signs away, a disharmo-

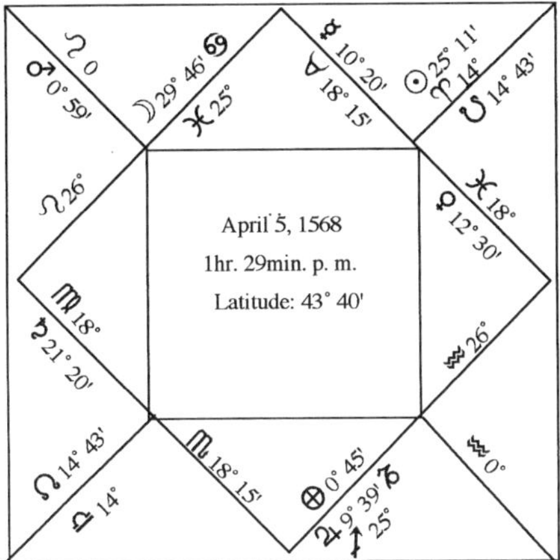

Figure 14b. Horoscope of Urban VIII.

nious position tending to accentuate the bad in whatever revolutions were occurring—when combined with the moon, the sun's natural antagonist, in almost the same place in the sky, was far more significant than Morandi realized. Rather than simply offending the sun, this double check removed the sun entirely from its position as the giver of life in the chart. Moreover, Visconti found the negative effects of Saturn to be counteracted by the vicinity of the dragon's head and the edge of the house of Virgo, not to mention the antiscia or corresponding point opposite Venus. The progression to the year 1630, he contended, was far more favorable than Morandi made out. Not only would the ascendant be unshadowed, and in a good position with respect to Saturn. Mars too would be in an aspect with Saturn, whose excessive frigidity it would temper still further by its own excessively dry effects.

The crucial question, according to Visconti, was whether the solar eclipse of 1630 would do any harm. In fact, two eclipses had previously occurred in the year 1624—one in Urban's ascendant and another in quadrates with the sun and moon in his nativity; and he was never better. Most likely, Visconti suggested, the new eclipse would be harmless unless the pope happened to find himself in a city badly situated with respect to the area of the sky where the eclipse occurred. Thus, if Urban went to where Gemini ruled, he could die; but in Rome he was safe for now. The first signs of real trouble Visconti was able to find only in the years 1643 or 1644, when the combination of negative planets could well be fatal. The future would prove just how accurate this prognostication actually was—if not in its attribution of the cause of Urban's death, at least concerning the time.

But Visconti's view was drowned out in the universal chorus of assent that greeted Morandi's analysis within the monastery. No one, it turned out, could convince Monsignor Francesco Usimbardi, recently made an official of the Camera Apostolica, and two academicians, namely, Vitellio Malaspina and Bartolomeo Filicaia, that the prediction conveyed *viva voce* to them by Morandi might not be true.[10] And whereas the poet Francesco Bracciolini believed the prophecy because of the authority of its bearer, the astrologer Francesco Lamponi believed it because he had reached the same conclusions on his own—to the delight of his patron, Cardinal Desiderio Scaglia, whose papal aspirations suddenly seemed less fanciful than ever.[11] As if news about the prophecy did not spread far enough spontaneously, Morandi himself communicated it by mail to Simon Carlo Rondinelli, librarian to Cardinal Carlo de' Medici in Florence, and perhaps to many other correspondents whose identities he was reluctant to reveal to the court.[12]

Such a remarkable piece of news inevitably found its way into the clandestine manuscript newsletter network; and just as inevitably, it went through a few transformations along the way. With mediocre comprehension, an anonymous writer on the payroll of the duke of Modena attributed the prophecy to Tommaso Campanella, much to the chagrin of the latter, who immediately rushed to defend his already precarious position at the papal court.[13] Antonio Badelli, on the payroll of several Roman aristocrats, attributed the prophecy to "the astrologer" Galileo Galilei, exemplifying once again the typical confusion between celestial observations and celestial predictions. For the first time, the fate of Galileo and Morandi would be truly linked. It was only the beginning.

Galileo, according to the version of Badelli the newsletter writer, happened to be in town "trying to publish a work against the Jesuits"—presumably, the *Dialogue Concerning the Two Chief World Systems.* Not satisfied with the prediction about the pope's death, Badelli went on, "the astrologer" had apparently added another prediction about the death of Taddeo Barberini, the pope's nephew, not to mention yet another one about the birth of a male heir to Donna Anna Colonna, Taddeo's wife, and about the future peace of Italy.[14] In many forms and in many cities, the prediction made the news, and Naples was by no means the only place besides Rome where it was widely reported as a proven fact.[15]

As the prediction about Urban VIII rapidly slid out of its author's control, it became a part of the bitter factional struggle in Rome. And among those of the pro-Spanish faction who could hardly contain their joy at the prospect of an imminent conclusion to Urban's notorious French favoritism was Ludovico Ridolfi, brother of the outgoing Master of the Sacred Palace. He forthwith recruited Raffaele Visconti to help communicate his sentiments "by day to the princes" (so Tommaso Campanella later recalled) and "by night, to the Spanish." With Urban's fate apparently decided, the question arose of who might be the next pope;[16] and a flood of clandestine publications concerning the possible outcomes of the next conclave encouraged further speculation.[17]

When the Spanish cardinals forthwith set sail for the coast of Italy and the German ones began the difficult journey across the Alps in order to be in Rome in case a new conclave was called, Campanella's reaction was severe.[18] He may have had his own reasons for drawing attention to Morandi, as we shall see. But truly, "no one ignores how many disorders were caused," as he complained, "by the vain mutterings of the astrologers, and the superstitious predictions they made concerning the life of the pope and the state of the Church." How "souls rose and fell," he exclaimed, as the vanity of those who expected the greatest rewards was alternately enflamed or cooled. New things were meditated and connived behind the pope's back, mostly encouraged and influenced by the great powers in Europe. It was not the first time, he concluded, that "false prophets" had been turned into instruments for "agitating the souls of the vulgar and inciting seditions, wars and schisms."[19] Nor would Morandi be the last.

No doubt, had Urban VIII died in 1630, Morandi could have built a career around this single prophecy, just as William Lilly was to do around the prophecy of the death of King Charles I of England. Since this did not happen, he could at least take some satisfaction in having played a dangerous game and lost without dishonor. Indeed, defying the ban on judicial astrology and meddling with the stars of a powerful ruler was not only the biggest risk of his life. It was a risk worth comparing to the wildest spendthrift escapades of the debt-ridden aristocrats of the age. Making a prophecy whose failure promised disaster was surely tantamount to building a costly palace for which one could never pay. It demonstrated a courageous soul and a heart far greater than any mere worldly comfort could console.[20] It placed Morandi exactly where he always wanted to be, in the company of the men of his generation who aroused in others the most powerful sentiments of wonder, esteem, respect, and, sometimes, of envy—if only for a moment.

SIXTEEN

THE VENDETTA

Minutes of the high council of the Vallombrosa order, at Vallombrosa, December 17, 1630:

"At twenty-four hours, the official went to Our Lord, Pope Urban VIII, who told him to place the abbot in custody at the Tor di Nona. The official thereupon sent a coach and four horses to the monastery, where the abbot was apprehended, along with his associates. After interrogation at the palace of the Governor of Rome, they were sent to prison. Innumerable letters, indeed, an infinite number of them, circulated concerning [Morandi's] imprisonment and the reason for it, especially since many members of the curia had been sent to prison with him. Correspondence sent by secular persons divulged that a Dominican friar had performed this charitable act, telling the authorities that many persons interested in politics frequented the monastery, and often spoke ill of the pope." (Vallombrosa Archives, cod. 6 II 5, fol. 73r)

THAT THE MONASTERY'S astrological activities should have gone on indefinitely was too much to expect, even though the monks continued to carry on business as usual well into the month of July—at least, if we are to judge by the entries in the library log. There we find Stefano Senarega on hand on July 7 to borrow Campanella's manuscript *Astrology*, where the week before, the poet Francesco Carducci, rising star in Urban's court and later bishop of Rieti, had stopped by to borrow Cherubino Ferrari's eulogy of St. Cecilia.[1] Morandi's relations with his patrons had never been better, if the invitation sent to Cardinal Desiderio Scaglia's nephew for a dinner party to take place in March is any indication.[2]

Who was the "Dominican friar" that the Roman rumor mill blamed for the tipoff leading to Morandi's arrest? At first, many suspected Raffaele Visconti, secretary to the Master of the Sacred Palace and a chief censor for the Congregation on the Index. An accomplished astrologer in his own right, he was among the few dissenting voices we heard when Morandi announced his prediction of Urban VIII's imminent death. After the spirited discussion among the members of the Santa Prassede circle in the last chapter, Morandi and Visconti had each written up their theories about the pope's future in the form of letters supposedly dated at Lyons. As news of Morandi's prediction began to spread, frightened by the consequences of his association with the monastery, Visconti, according to one version, would have gone to the authorities to clear himself by indicting Morandi. Jealousy against a rival astrologer would have sweetened the blow and helped justify the betrayal. In carrying out a deed that would bring down nearly as many fellow Dominicans as Vallombrosan monks, he would have been able to vent some frustration at having been passed over in favor of Niccolò Riccardi for the job of Master of the Sacred Palace. Yet the initial suspicions concerning Visconti proved to be unfounded. After all, the vast net of curial responsibility for the crimes at Santa Prassede involved parties that he could scarcely have dared to accuse, even if his position as the sole dissident in the discussions about Urban VIII did not guarantee his own immunity no matter what happened.

How Tommaso Campanella came to be recognized as Morandi's true nemesis is difficult to say. The legend, preserved for over three centuries at the Vallombrosa headquarters in the hills of Tuscany, no doubt drew at least some inspiration from traditional inter-order rivalry. However, it was also based on solid intuitions concerning a vast machine, devised by the genial yet half-mad philosopher, in which Morandi, an acquaintance from days in Florence, played only a small part. What finally put Morandi in Urban's sights was a vendetta of truly Roman proportions. What destroyed him was Roman society's peculiar way of caring for its own.

By the time the events we are narrating took place, nearly three decades had passed since Tommaso Campanella led a ragtag horde of sympathizers in the desperate enterprise of overthrowing the Spanish government in Calabria. The dust had long settled on the tiny town of Stilo where the conspiracy began. All that was left behind was the memory of what he had attempted to achieve there, during his exile from Naples for errors in matters of dogma aggravated by attempted escape. Whatever remained of the hopes he had raised for the foundation of a communitarian theocracy were rekindled from time to time—perhaps in the rebellions of Naples in 1620 and all over the kingdom in 1648. The astrological configuration of a new century had passed, and so also the moment for realizing the fantastic ideas he expounded in the *City of the Sun*. At the time, only a famous simulation of madness, made more convincing by forty hours of resistance to the famous torture called "the waking" (suspension of the body with muscles taut over a pointed stake), saved him from the decapitation and dismemberment inflicted on others who were caught. But his troubles were far from over.

Campanella had no complaint against Morandi. He was, however, the inveterate enemy of the Congregation of the Index. Nothing less could be expected of a spirited thinker whose every written word had been so carefully scrutinized over the past thirty years and mostly faulted on philosophical, theological, or moral grounds. Nor was he much of a friend to the Roman Inquisition, which had ordered him hauled to Rome for an abjuration in 1594, while his trial before the Inquisition's Neapolitan branch was still going on. The prison term following the Calabrian uprising gave him plenty of time to reflect on all this. Then came Cardinal Desiderio Scaglia's damning report, in 1627, on one of the productions that was closest to Campanella's heart, entitled *Atheism Defeated.* Campanella's fellow Dominicans, sitting as the chief officials of the tribunal, instead of defending the presumptuous friar, had merely nodded their assent and added still more charges to the swelling dossier.

The last straw came in August 1629. Four years before, Campanella had authorized the Prost brothers in Lyons to publish the six books of his controversial *Astrology* at a safe distance from Rome; but so far nothing had been done. Niccolò Ridolfi, then the general of the Dominican order, and Niccolò Riccardi, the Master of the Sacred Palace, eventually received news of the manuscript's troubled history, as well as a copy of the manuscript itself. They also managed to gain possession of a copy of Campanella's *On Avoiding Destinies Inscribed in the Stars.* To ensure the downfall of their wayward fellow friar, they connived with the Roman printer Antonio Brogiotti to rush through a pirate edition of both texts in Rome, with false imprint of Lyons.[3] There for all to see was new material describing an incantation scene that Urban VIII was sure to find uncomfortably familiar: a pope so deeply concerned about his public image was unlikely to take kindly to the local newsletters' rude but inevitable suggestion, in early May 1630, that he had just now gone off to Castel Gandolfo "to perfume himself and do everything prescribed" in the book.[4]

What was Campanella to think? Clearly a campaign of defamation, inspired by an egregious sin of envy, was under way. And where could these trammelers of evil all be found? Where was Antonio Brogiotti's favorite haunt, when he was not busy as the official printer to the Apostolic Chamber? From whom else might Riccardi and Ridolfi have obtained copies of the dangerous manuscripts for the pirate edition? Indeed, where did the manuscripts circulate most freely, if not at the monastery of Santa Prassede?

Moreover, what single place was frequented by the Dominican Master of the Sacred Palace, the secretary to the Congregation of the Index, and the members of the Congregation itself, including Cardinal Scaglia? Yet where was justice, if all these figures were allowed to dabble in forbidden knowledge that they only half understood, while he, Campanella, a true

Figure 15. Francesco Cozza, Portrait of Tommaso Campanella. (Rome, Collezione Caetani di Sermoneta.)

Jeremiah, was made their scapegoat? The time had come to turn the tables, to reveal the convent of Santa Prassede for what it was: a hornet's nest of adulators who dealt with Urban's adversaries behind the pope's back.

The opportunity soon presented itself. Campanella knew he could not count on the pope's favor for much longer. In early June, he took advantage of one of his last moments as a free man to let fall a few chosen words about the monastery.[5] The seeds of suspicion fell on fertile ground.

No one could deny that the climate in Rome, at least as far as astrology was concerned, was about to change anyway. Although Urban had not yet decided what to do about Campanella's insinuations, a previous trial in April 1629 certainly did not bode well for Morandi. There, a young boy had dropped the abbot's name as a source for dangerous writings and as the author of a prophecy foretelling the same boy's incarceration. "O how many dangers there are," a correspondent wrote to Morandi on that occasion, "and how vigilant one is constantly forced to be—and even sometimes this is not enough."[6] Soon Morandi would stand in as the symbolic victim representing astrologers and freethinkers of every kind.

With whatever hidden end in mind, Urban went to Castel Gandolfo in early May 1630, on a very important mission; and already in June word got around that, while there, he had written a long bull against the astrologers—the same bull later published under the title *Inscrutabilis*.[7] Alberto Del Vivaio, a Florentine musician who dabbled in astrology, wrote to Morandi beseeching him to help deter Urban from a perilous resolution. Not only the welfare of themselves and their friends was at stake, Del Vivaio pointed out, but that of all Christendom.

What would happen, Del Vivaio asked, anticipating some of the protests that would be made against the bull *Inscrutabilis*, if astrology was no longer there to encourage persons to study the stars? "I think few people really care about Mars or Jupiter unless they can incorporate this knowledge into a prediction."[8] Without this motive, he suggested, there would be no stargazing, no planetary calculation, and eventually no means even of determining the proper time for the Easter cycle (based on the vernal equinox and the phases of the moon)—with grave consequences for religion, for faith, and for the Holy Catholic Church.

Urban's mind, however, was made up. Activities of the sort observed at Santa Prassede could no longer be tolerated.

The chief danger of astrology, and anything connected with it, from Urban's point of view, did not come from its spiritual, theological, or philosophical consequences. That debate had reached an impasse already in the Renaissance. Since Pico Della Mirandola's famous treatise in the late fifteenth century, few new arguments were likely to be alleged on either side.[9] Once the standard criticism of the astrologers' inaccurate prophecies had been parried by the standard Ptolemaic response that everything depended on the accuracy of the very complicated observations involved, there still remained the nagging question of free will versus planetary determinism. Once the argument about the astrologers' frequent disagreements among themselves had been effectively refuted by noting that some astrologers were better than others, there was always the question of whether stellar destiny was compatible with Christianity. The persistent complaint about the many different fortunes of persons born under the same celestial configuration had just as persistently been sidestepped by the response that the stars create dispositions and not concrete realities, but this gave no relief to those who wondered whether human beings could ever divine the mysteries of celestial causation. There had been the apparent contradiction between the traditional organization of the houses and the changing positions of the signs in the heavens due to the precession of the equinoxes, but this had been deflected by pointing out that such changes merely created new challenges without destroying astrology. Once resolved, there still remained the problem of whether humanity was a part of the grand machine of nature or outside it. And once Ptolemy and the other ancient astrologers had been defended for the arbitrariness of their conclusions on the grounds of their having offered them as hypotheses and not as certainties, there was always the question of whether astrology put limits on Almighty God.

Even the pope, if he followed the remaining spiritual, theological, and philosophical questions down to the last detail, would have been impressed by the thoroughness of the Venetian mathematician Domenico Scevolini, writing in the closing years of the Council of Trent.[10] Far from limiting the power of God, Scevolini argued, the astrological hypothesis actually illustrated it. For to attribute to the planets the ability to do this or that could hardly be any more blasphemous than to attribute to fire the ability to cause heat. Such expressions were simply other ways of explaining how God acted in the universe. Indeed, if all the cosmos was part of a great chain of being, from God down to the tiniest thing on Earth, what could be more natural than to suppose that the planets were put here in order to regulate human life? Surely, Scevolini remarked, they could not exist merely for the sake of decoration. If their movements were far too intricate to suggest their having been left bobbing around in the aether like so much celestial flotsam and jetsam, they clearly deserved the attention of humankind. Anyone who doubted that stargazing was in harmony with the Scriptures had only to look at Jeremiah chapter 10, Isaiah chapter 44, and Paul's Letter to the Galatians, chapter 4—not to mention a host of passages in the Church Fathers, from Albert the Great to Duns Scotus to Thomas Aquinas.[11]

How could Urban gainsay Giambattista Della Porta, writing at the turn of the seventeenth century, who thought he could solve the problem of free will and planetary determinism to the complete satisfaction of astrologers and inquisitors alike? The different choices made by individuals in their lives, Della Porta said, clearly depended in one way or another on their personalities. Their personalities were in the last analysis the effects of the soul, not of the stars. No one could deny that the soul, before original sin, was a perfect reflection of God's goodness sent from on high to exert sovereignty over the body. During the course of humanity's sojourn on earth, the body and the passions had come to usurp more and more authority for themselves. Once master, the soul was now the body's slave. Let no one be surprised, therefore, Della Porta insisted, that variations in physical types might have a far more powerful effect on character than any changes in the heavens. Nor should anyone wonder that the saturnine personality, noted for quietude, patience, sincerity, and reasonableness, as well as a certain irascibility and rebelliousness, was usually accompanied by a large, slow, and ungainly physique.[12] Such were the obvious effects not of Saturn but of a cold and dry temperament, brought about when a surfeit of black bile fills the seat of the mind with darkness and melancholy. Likewise, no one should wonder that the jovial personality, noted for virtue, generosity, happiness, and grand gestures, was usually accompanied by a majestic and beautiful body. Such were the effects not of the planet Jupiter but of a moderately warm and humid temperament, with abundant aeration and sexual energy.

Fortified by the knowledge of these and other natural laws, Urban might well have followed Della Porta in advancing to the prediction of how individuals with the traits so analyzed might behave. Since the soul was the mirror of the body, the shape of the body and especially of the facial features was a guide to the shape of the personality. Since similar shapes reflect similar customs even between humans and animals, one could easily guess from ass-faced persons what their stolidity and vileness of spirit might compel them to do.[13] Yet Della Porta left open the question of whether the many variations in physical types and temperaments might themselves have an underlying astrological cause. In the last two chapters of his book, without reference to any of his previous physical explanations, he simply crammed in as much material as he could from Ptolemy, Firmicus Maternus, Haly (i.e., the eleventh-century Egyptian scholar Ali ibn Ridwan), and anyone else who had discussed the effects of the signs of the zodiac on human lives. Nor did he ever exclude the possibility that variations in the celestial spheres, at one point or another in a person's early growth, might be decisive for the future.

Yet all this philosophizing left Urban still uneasy. What to do in the case of a prediction of death? If the astrologer had, by some amazing accident, managed to gain the slightest insight into the obscure workings of the divine Mind, was not the subject bound to respond? Must he not use his free will in any way he could, to counter those fatal astral influences? Did this not mean contacting the easiest available expert on deflection techniques, even if that expert—Campanella—happened to be suspected of heresy by the Inquisition? Who was to ensure that those very deflection techniques, including lighted tapers, aromatic essences, and strange symbols on the floor, were not themselves a form of diabolical magic? Surely a pope could not engage in them without serious danger to his own immortal soul. And the effect, should news about them be divulged, could be highly dangerous. Better not to put himself into that situation in the first place.

The political and social issues at stake were enough to turn Urban decisively against astrologers, if not against astrology. Anyone with the temerity to make pronouncements about a personage as important as himself was a dangerous threat, whatever might be the intellectual dress of those pronouncements. That such a one should dare to consider whether he might live or die was even worse. As he said in his letter to the judge, the "grave penalties imposed by the sacred canons and civil laws and apostolic constitutions against those who presume to study and practice judicial astrology" were specifically intended to discourage "the prediction of future occasions of war, revolutions of states and princes and the deaths of the latter."[14] Allowing such unacceptable opinions to escape from someone's brain, into the streets and squares, was unpardonable. Not only might such opinions, coming to the notice of foreign powers, provide a potent source of embarrassment on the international scene, as happened in this case. Moreover, coming to the notice of the Roman plebs, whose fickleness and hypersensitivity were well known, they might provide material for discussions about politics. And discussions about politics could easily degenerate into actions tending to provoke violence and revolt.

To his great indignation, Urban discovered that Morandi had not only made the predictions attributed to him by Campanella, but had allowed them to spread far and wide. He was all the more incensed at having made the discovery not on his own, nor even by way of the many informants he had scattered around the city, but by way of a message from Cardinal Richelieu, in the course of negotiations between France and Spain concerning the War of Mantua—as Urban himself later related to Theodore Ameyden, who once frequented the Santa Prassede circle.[15] If Richelieu already knew what Urban had learned from Campanella about monastery activities, and knew others who knew, the French were better informed than the pope himself. And if the international community was as saturated with the rumors as Richelieu claimed, there was no wonder the Spanish cardinals were already en route to Rome to take part in conclave

Figure 16. Urban VIII, order for Morandi's arrest. (Rome, Archivio di Stato, *Governatore*, Processi, sec. XVII, b. 251.)

preparations that were secretly under way. Richelieu's very presence before him on that occasion, Urban must have suspected, was probably intended to gain favor for the French cause by portraying the Spanish as shameless intriguers. The conclusion, in any case, was inescapable: Morandi must be stopped and his punishment made an example to the others.

Rather than waiting for the clumsy Roman bureaucracy to run its course, Urban demanded immediate action. To Antonio Fido, lieutenant governor of Rome, "We order you," he wrote on July 13, "to make the necessary incarcerations and investigations of the said abbot and any other person you may consider appropriate."[16] No holy place was to be spared, regardless of the degree of ecclesiastical immunity it was supposed to enjoy—not even "the monastery and the church of Santa Prassede" itself. To ensure "the unity and perfect order of all the above mentioned proceedings already under way and still to begin," Urban ordered the trial to take place in the governor's court and not be split between that court and the Inquisition. And the same evening just after sunset, under the terrified gaze of his fellow monks, Morandi was led off by two policemen, driven to the prisons at the Tor di Nona, near the eastern end of the Ponte St. Angelo, and charged with "exercising judicial astrology, composing political and malicious writings and keeping prohibited books."

No sooner was Morandi apprehended than his highly placed associates began to abandon him one by one. Morandi as a demi-god was a tolerable companion; as a mere mortal, fallible and human like the rest, he was worse than a bore. All the signs of esteem and promises of support vouchsafed in better days suddenly disappeared. From darling of the Roman intellectual community, Morandi at once became a pariah. Even Galileo kept his distance. Bernini, Cassiano Dal Pozzo, and Ughelli, on the topic of the monastery, were never heard again. Morandi's many correspondents were stunned into silence. The cardinals in the curia who had once flocked to the monastery for information and counsel continued about their daily business as though he had never existed. Except for the company of his intimates within the monastery, his fellow monks, he was left alone to meet his doom.

Doomed and alone, but not forgotten—at least, not immediately. To many who were close to him, Morandi's arrest cast a pall over an increasingly troubled city. He had fallen victim to the same nervous environment that had made his astrology business possible. Now, if the greatest astrologer in Rome could be so wrong, who could know when the next disaster might strike? As Urban VIII's behavior became more and more erratic, who indeed, among those who flourish today, might still be flourishing tomorrow? A bleaker future than ever seemed to beckon.

SEVENTEEN

THE BODY OF THE ACCUSED

DRAWN UP TO a height of fifteen feet by his wrists tied behind his back in the torture known as the "strappado" or "rope," the suspect usually began experiencing excruciating pain in the shoulders and wrists. The first searing stabs came from the tearing of the ligaments from the deltoid muscles. Depending on body weight and musculature, dislocation of the humerus was sometimes immediate, other times more gradual. After the first few minutes, the pain spread to the chest, as the pressure traveled to the collar bone, while the pectoral muscles' pulling against the sternum and ribs constricted the lungs so breathing came in gasps. All this Matteo Maiani might have avoided, had he confessed the truth from the outset of the interrogation. Instead, to the question of whether he had been present when the police seal was pried off the door of an armoire in the library of the monastery of Santa Prassede from which incriminating books and papers were removed to a hiding place, he had replied with an indistinct mumble.[1]

Prosecutors on this gloomy afternoon of August 26, 1630, had enough information to suppose that the principal suspect, abbot Orazio Morandi, was guilty of predicting the death of Pope Urban VIII. Indeed, what particularly hardened the hearts of the judges against Morandi, and, in their minds, turned his case into more than a typical instance of astrological misbehavior, or even of political chicanery on a grand scale, was the abundant evidence concerning the entire way of life at Santa Prassede. Once the general tendency had been revealed, they could scarcely have been too surprised to find love letters and erotic poetry among the possessions confiscated from the monks' cells.

Yet there was still not enough to secure a conviction. Nor could they torture the abbot himself, since his high ecclesiastical status necessitated proofs far beyond what was required for tormenting someone of inferior social prestige. So to bring the missing evidence to light they fell upon young Matteo, servant to the current prior of the monastery, Francesco Ripa. Once again, showing him the broken police seal and a hammer obviously used to break it, they asked: Who left these tools at the scene of the crime? Once again, Matteo answered by spitting a few unintelligible syllables between clenched teeth.

The interrogators knew exactly what to do next, even without consulting the well-known manual by Prospero Farinacci. "When the suspect is interrogated by the judge about the crime for which he has been indicted and incarcerated and he either refuses to respond or responds imprecisely," noted Farinacci, "in order to obtain a precise response, either affirmative or negative, apart from other evidence, the judge may certainly use torture."[2] And so they did.

In this case, the crime was concealing evidence, since the rules prevented the judges from torturing Matteo to discover his complicity in the more serious crimes imputed to Morandi, or anything else for which they had no more than a suspicion of guilt. In order for the evidence to justify torture even in the case of a humble servant, Farinacci commented, "it must be realistic, probable, not trivial or perfunctory, but much more weighty and urgent, certain and clear, indeed, clearer than the noonday sun." The broken police seals and the insinuations of his accomplices were Matteo's undoing.

So Matteo was led to the torture chamber next to the interrogation room—*ad locum tormentis*—to confess to the crime of concealing evidence. And once he was stripped to the waist, great care was taken to ensure that the knots on his wrists might be capable of resisting several hours of tension from the weight of his swaying body, as well as from occasional violent pulls of the rope, should such be necessary for extracting the requested information. The same went for the binding that joined the wrists to a rope hanging from a pulley fixed to a transverse beam in the chamber and attached to a winch at one end. After all, the slightest mistake could lead to the most dreadful accidents—even though, as Farinacci noted, "if the torture rope breaks and the tortured person falls to the ground and dies, the judge will not be held responsible."[3]

Warned of the consequences of his refusal to cooperate and drawn up by the rope, for a while Matteo writhed in silence. Then, the trial record specifies, he exclaimed, "O Jesus, I'm dead!"

They told him to tell the truth. He repeated, "I don't know anything" and was silent.

Asked again to tell what he knew, he repeated, "I don't know anything," and, after a few moments of silence, he shouted through the sweat that by now must have been dripping from his bloated face, "O Jesus, you make me suffer for nothing." This he repeated three times and then was silent.

When the question was put to him once more, he said, "O Jesus, I know nothing. O Annabeatabenedetta!" This last ejaculation he repeated several times. Shortly afterward, he cried, "O madre benedetta, the pain! And you men, put me down and I'll tell the truth."

But when told to tell the truth, he prevaricated, saying, "I said what I know. I don't know anything else." Again he said, "O please put me down! I want to tell the truth."

At this point the judges could see that Matteo was only playing for time, hoping to gain a few seconds of repose for his aching limbs, which may already have been distended beyond repair. It was one of many similar ruses they and the others of the profession knew only too well. "In the case of a suspect who does not wish to respond to the questions put to him and asks for time to deliberate," Farinacci commented, "such a delay should certainly not be granted."[4] Otherwise, the torture might drag on until even the torturer was entirely worn out.

So the judges told Matteo to tell the truth now. But all he would reply was "I already told the truth." They had him held up for about another half hour, but they could get nothing more out of him—*et aliud ab ipso haberi non potuit*. So they had him brought down and his arms reset into their sockets as well as possible, and sent him back to his cell "to repose his soul"—probably, in a dead faint.

But if Matteo seemed conspicuously ill-informed about episodes in which he himself was known to have taken part, other members of the Santa Prassede community soon began to talk. With the monks' resistance worn down to the breaking point, and plenty of circumstantial evidence to suggest that they were merely bit players in the drama directed by Morandi, the judges finally played their best card: immunity from prosecution to whoever told the truth. Benigno Bracciolini immediately stepped forth; and his testimony told the whole dramatic story of the cover-up.

After the material was removed to the sacristy, as we explained in the opening chapter, it was Bracciolini who found a semipermanent home for it the next morning in the usually vacant rooms reserved for Cardinal Ubaldini, the protector of the order. Halfway through the transfer operation, he learned that Ubaldini was en route to the monastery for the feast of the monastery's patron saint, having sent an auditor ahead to prepare his rooms. Bracciolini then hid what he could in another room belonging to the gardener of the monastery's main tenant, and what he could not hide there he carried to the holy oil closet in the sacristy. The next day he took the larger trunk into the Colonna chapel and dragged part of the contents up a ladder and behind the painting in back of the statue of Blessed Margherita Colonna. The rest he put in a large chest in a corner of the oil closet. Other books he carried up to the organ loft, where he wedged them into the sides of a window and walled them up with bricks and mortar. "And I have to tell you," he continued, "that I myself threw certain printed books taken from the said armoire up on top of another armoire in the sacristy." What remained of the books and correspondence, he brought into the gardener's room and burned in the grate.

This is not to say that the search for better material evidence had not been going on right from the outset. The court's attempts to secure a copy of the infamous letter from Lyons, containing Morandi's original prophecy, to which Visconti had replied, proved entirely futile. The first hint that Morandi might have communicated his ideas about Urban's death in yet another, perhaps still existing writing, besides the Lyons letter, also supplied the first hint about the existence of Morandi's pseudo-Joachimite Latin prophecies concerning the popes. According to the deposition of the scribe Cesare Tubiolo, the most striking feature of those Latin prophecies was the part regarding Urban VIII. "In the thirtieth chapter," he specified, "it spoke of bees, and I believed it was a prophecy about Our Lord Urban VIII, whose coat of arms depicts bees; and then there are other chapters, but I do not know how many."[5] Could this document contain the incriminating prediction of Urban's death? For the time being, all efforts to locate it turned up nothing.

Another scribe, Aurelio Amati, reported having copied an enigmatic writing he got from Morandi for distribution to his correspondents. His recollection of it as "concerning certain stones with Arab writing representing prophecies" seemed to point to something entirely unrelated. Since it, too, like Morandi's Latin prophecies, was written in such a fashion as to persuade the reader that it had been "found in the time of the Great Schism," an amazing coincidence, the court officials decided to go after it anyway.[6] But the two messengers they sent to intercept it at the post office could only find yet another enigmatic document, nothing to do with Morandi, containing various symbols including "an eagle and others of the same sort," which, the hopelessly myopic messenger was embarrassed to report, "I was unable to make out."[7]

Armed with the new information from Bracciolini, the court officials now set about recovering the missing material. What they found behind the painting in the chapel, behind the bricks in one of the windows in the organ loft, and in all the other places so carefully chosen by the monks put the case against Morandi on an entirely different footing. Even without the key piece of evidence—the putative Lyons letter predicting Urban VIII's death in 1630—here was material enough to prove there had been significant trafficking in astrological predictions. No judge would be able to ignore the disorderly sheaves of esoteric writing embodying the monastery's whole project on unnatural death. Here too was material enough to prove significant trafficking in prohibited books. No judge could fail to be persuaded by the physical evidence of the books themselves, now transferred to the courtroom—texts by Machiavelli, by Boccaccio, by Trithemius, by Copernicus and all the rest. To confirm the circulation of such books was the library lending list, a tiny but precious ledger so unique that it was immediately made a permanent part of the whole trial record.

However, the judges' enthusiasm as they surveyed the piles of new evidence now before them must soon have given way to dismay. Just on opening the library log and making out the first few borrowers' names, they had to realize there was more at stake here than even the pope had anticipated. Gian Lorenzo Bernini, artist to the Borghese and Barberini families, Pietro Accolti, the Medici courtier, Niccolò Ridolfi, former Maestro of the Sacred Palace and now general of the Dominican order, Giulio Mancini, the pope's physician, and Cardinals Capponi, Scaglia and Lante were only a few of the distinguished members of the library circle who now came to light. As the same names, with their equally distinguished addresses, began turning up in the newly discovered correspondence, the court officials could see that the Morandi case was not just against a monk or a monastery. It was a case against a good portion of Roman high society. And it was not about astrology, prohibited books, or political information per se. It was in part about how Roman high society protected its own. If Roman high society let Morandi go to the gallows, who in Rome was safe? Perhaps not even the judges themselves.

Exactly what Urban VIII's sentiments might have been, as the investigation began to spread like oil on water, is impossible to say. Surely, from the standpoint of the ecclesiastical hierarchy, the embarrassment from Morandi's crimes was bound to be slight compared to the embarrassment from the trial itself, should revelations about the libertine culture of the monastery become public knowledge. And anyone could imagine what fodder for the ruminations of skeptics and critics of the Roman Catholic Church might be provided by the spectacle of eminent cardinals collaborating with their astrologers to launch themselves into higher spheres, even in their imaginations, at the expense of the reigning pope. Should the curia's diet of prohibited literature be demonstrated as a concrete fact rather than bruited about as a fantasy of courtly wags, the effect could be disastrous. Also nefarious were likely to be the repercussions of the circulation of information about the cardinals' political machinations with foreign powers. From the standpoint of the ecclesiastical hierarchy, the Morandi case was about discipline—discipline of which the culture of the monastery and the people around it represented an amazing lapse.

Clearly, the expedient ordered by Urban VIII at the beginning of the trial, of allowing the court recorder to leave blanks for the more important names "of previous popes, of cardinals, living or deceased, and other personages," in order to protect the Roman political and ecclesiastical hierarchy in the final redaction of the trial record, was not sufficient to guard against the ill effects of this story.[8] It was thus most probably not without a considerable amount of satisfaction that Urban and his associates learned of Morandi's sudden death on November 7, 1630.

Whether news of Morandi's death in jail came as a total surprise is another matter. After Michelangelo Soderini officially recognized the corpse of his fellow monk, the prison doctor, Bernardo Messoni, reported having treated Morandi for twelve days.[9] The rumor attributing his death instead to poisoning, ordered from on high to protect the reputation of the ecclesiastical hierarchy, seems not beyond the realm of plausibility. That he managed, in his last hours, to bequeath to the monastery a precious painting by Bernini, whose subject and subsequent history will never be known, does nothing to remove this suspicion.[10] We will leave readers to speculate for themselves.

The trial proceedings thus came to an abrupt halt, and so does our account of them. Admittedly, many questions still remain. We have attempted to bind together, by way of possible assumptions, conjectures, and hypotheses, the disparate elements of an unfinished story. This does not mean we know with any more certainty whether Morandi was indeed merely the instrument of some political mastermind, a bungling zodiacal pope-killer sent by one or another of the major powers battling for superiority in Europe during the Thirty Years War. We may never know for sure whether the first Lyons letter containing a prediction of Urban's death in 1630 was indeed a figment of the judges' imaginations—or indeed, our own. No document explicitly attests to Campanella's role as an informer, in spite of the many suggestive hints. Nor may we ever know for sure whether the trial record, as we have it, represents a reasonably accurate account of what transpired in the courtroom. According to contemporary custom, it was drawn up after the fact on the basis of minutes taken during the proceedings—the accuracy of which could vary considerably depending on the court recorder. Questions are put in Latin, we cannot be sure how faithfully translated from the Italian original; and responses are truncated. Interrogations that must have taken many hours are reduced to a few pages. In spite of these reservations, the story as we have told it seems to be the best one we can get.

One thing is certain: in April of the year following Morandi's death, Urban VIII finally published the most severe bull to date against the astrologers.

"The inscrutable judgment of God the Highest," declared the pope in the bull *Inscrutabilis*, "does not suffer that the dusky human intellect, constrained in the prison of the flesh, should arrogate itself to explore, with nefarious curiosity, the arcana hidden in the divine mind."[11] For this reason, he went on, Sixtus V had wisely prohibited anyone from performing judicial astrology or dealing in or keeping any books about it—"especially those persons who presume to pass judgment on the welfare of the greatest republics or princes," thus furnishing pretexts for rebellion.

"And yet, we have heard," he thundered, "that not a few sons of iniquity, perhaps forgetting their own puniness, made more daring by talk or connivance and seeking a vain temporary esteem, do not blush at publicizing prognostications and predictions by word of mouth and even by writing, to the deplorable perdition of their souls and the grave scandal of Christendom." Particularly serious, he noted, was the practice of these arts among "clerics, priests, and other ecclesiastical persons." These, if convicted, must immediately be expelled from their orders, deprived of their benefices and excommunicated. And lay persons were to be treated as guilty of *lèse majesté*, subjected to the worst torments, deprived of all their goods, and destituted of any civil or feudal jurisdictions they may enjoy.

Tommaso Campanella was dismayed by the consequences of what may well have been largely his own handiwork. To save what could be saved, he argued as strongly as he could against any excessively broad interpretation of the bull. Considering his own precarious position and his intention to submit his philosophical treatises for approval to the highly orthodox censors at the Sorbonne in Paris, he could scarcely avoid declaiming against those "calumniators, both on this and the other side of the mountains," who suggested that the bull, along with Sixtus V's earlier one, "might in some way be open to criticism."[12] In fact, he said, no two bulls could be more holy and correct. For astrologers who pretended to predict the main events in peoples' lives were subject to the same reprehensions as the Protestant proponents of predestination. The latter encouraged people who believed they were destined for salvation to live their lives without good works, while the former encouraged believers to perform all their good works on the last day before their destined day of death. Daily Christian living, under such premises, Campanella argued, could not go on.

However, Campanella protested—repeating some arguments he had already made in his *Astrology* and prefiguring others that would be made later on by Placido Titi, whom modern astrologers cite as the founder of the commonly used "Placidean system"—that astrology itself, as a science of the stars, was still safe.[13] No one could deny that the bible and the Holy Fathers of the Church, especially St. Thomas Aquinas, expressed astrological ideas from time to time. So "anyone who removes astrology combats Christ."[14] Nor could anyone deny that all knowledge here below comes from attending to causes, effects, or signs placed in the cosmos by nature or by God. Since astrology was based on all these, Campanella exclaimed, citing an astrologers' topos dating at least to the time of Albertus Magnus, "whoever overthrows astrology removes all philosophy." Galileo had made a similar argument in favor of astronomy sixteen years previously, in his *Letter to the Grand Duchess*, on the eve of the censure of Copernicus's book. Furthermore, no one could deny that in order for doctrines to be reprehended they must be discussed—an argument that was later to be developed in regard to much different matters by John Milton in the *Areopagitica*. So a narrow reading of the bull was self-defeating. It gave believers less capacity for understanding what was wrong with astrology than they had for understanding what was wrong with the doctrines of Luther and Mohammed. Studying the way the stars and planets affect things here below is unexceptionable, as long as we limit our inquiry to physical causes, leaving the supernatural ones up to God alone. Therefore, let not those who study astrology be anathematized, Campanella concluded. Let those be punished instead who, "in order to further the designs of the [infernal] Enemy," attempt to tar the many serious astrologers and the few dangerous charlatans with the same brush.[15]

But all such protests were in vain. Urban VIII cared nothing about the future of philosophy if it happened to conflict with the future of himself. And just in case there remained any doubts about his intention in the bull, soon enough, a new case came up, one that might put an end to promiscuous stargazing once and for all: the case of Galileo. On the outcome of that, much would depend—and still does.

EPILOGUE

AS IT TURNED OUT, following Morandi's arrest, the monks at Santa Prassede did not simply burn a few books and papers. With this desperate act, perhaps a kind of unwitting expiation, whatever was left of the independent intellectual life at the monastery went up in smoke; and the long season of free exploration came to an end. No more would notorious prohibited texts stand side by side on the library shelves with the chastest and best-approved works of Catholic apologetics. No more would the pleasures of the body be joined with the pleasures of the mind in a mutual search for the most intense forms of expression available to humanity's fallen nature—at least, not openly. No more would the secret arts of the cabala and the best techniques of judicial astrology be placed at the service of the monastery's circle of friends and advisors, or of the neighborhood around.

Finally, no more would Morandi's familiar form, gliding through the half-lit halls, remind visitors that divine illumination was not to be attained by contemplation alone; nor entirely by reciting the offices and engaging in acts of devotion. Something in the world had changed. And if epochs may be made by the creative agency of a few individuals, so also they may end by the disappearance of the environment in which those individuals lived and worked.

To Galileo Galilei, the events of 1630–31 could only have proven more conclusively what he had come to suspect: that for winning the curia over to the conclusions of the modern astronomers, time was running out. Although his opinions on the Morandi case have not come down to us, we know he followed the trial "about which Your Lordship wishes to be informed" (in the words of a correspondent), as the hopeful news of early August began to give way to the more guarded prognostications of later months. By March 1631 he knew that Raffaele Visconti and Gherardo Gherardi, close members of the Santa Prassede circle and deeply compromised in the trial, had been exiled from Rome, "more because of the hatred for judicial astrology than for any particular charges against them," said another correspondent.[1] Surely Galileo could no longer look to Visconti for support, even though the latter was still the assistant to the Padre Maestro or Master of the Sacred Palace while the post passed from Niccolò Ridolfi to Niccolò Riccardi, derisively dubbed "Padre Mostro" or "Father Monster" by Campanella. And Visconti's pre-publication approval of the *Dialogue Concerning the Two Chief World Systems*, Galileo's latest attempt to win support for his doctrines, was not likely to be of much help in steering the troublesome book amid the various clashing opinions in the ecclesiastical bureaucracy that the theories in it had begun to arouse. Perhaps the contrary.[2]

Nonetheless, Galileo persevered. Armed with the approval of Visconti and the signature of the Padre Mostro, he next obtained the consent of the Florentine Inquisitor. Using the recent death of his Roman friend Federico Cesi as a convenient excuse to get away from the increasingly impossible Roman environment, he had the book published in Florence instead of in Rome. In February 1632, then, the *Dialogue* came out under the imprint of the local printer Giovanni Battista Landini. Galileo's troubles seemed to be over.

To be sure, the book Galileo published was a far cry from what the Padre Mostro had anticipated. Their conversation had led the Padre to expect a cautious account, offering conclusions hypothetically and not definitively, defending the propriety of the decree of 1616 that had condemned the writings of Copernicus on the grounds that the sun-centered universe was theologically incorrect. Galileo instead published the most powerful defense of heliocentrism ever compiled—far more persuasive even than that of Copernicus, because its arguments were couched in everyday terms, based on commonplace experiences and not exclusively geometrical or astronomical. Publishing the work in vernacular Italian rather than in Latin, he had obviously intended it for a broad audience.[3]

As the cumbersome Roman bureaucracy rolled into action, many circumstances conspired to ensure Galileo's downfall. For one thing, any time or energy Urban VIII himself might have had left over for contemplating the long-term consequences of leaving the Galileo case to a small band of disgruntled theologians was entirely occupied in contemplating the short-term consequences of the French victory in the War of Mantua and the new opportunities now open to the papacy. Worse yet, Cosimo II de' Medici in Florence was no longer alive to protect Galileo from the fury of a foreign court. And even if the next grand duke had been remotely interested in natural science, the great plague of 1629 that had already annihilated a third of the population of the Tuscan capital, while threatening still more destruction in the provinces, captured all of the young Ferdinando II's attentions.

But Galileo's real problem was not the absence of help from Florence. Nor was it the impact of the Thirty Years War. Nor again was it Urban VIII's bureaucracy. Still less did it have to do with supposed suspicions about Galileo's attachment to the doctrines of atomism in some earlier works, as a recent study has suggested. For there is no doubt that atomism was regarded as highly dangerous because of its connection with the materialist philosophies of Lucretius and Epicurus. What was more, it was viewed as incompatible with current views about the Eucharist that drew their arguments and language from the traditions of medieval Scholasticism. How, one version ran, could Transubstantiation take place if not by a change of Substance, leaving the Form intact? But an anonymous document of spurious origin, found among the Inquisition papers, and a cryptic reading of some of Galileo's letters, are not enough to prove that heliocentrism was not the real issue all along.

What is more, Galileo gave his most explicit defense, not exactly of atomism but of a corpuscular theory of matter, in the *Assayer.* This book was published not in Florence but in Rome, in 1623, under the noses of the Roman censors who approved it, and dedicated to Urban VIII when relations between the two men had never been better. Indeed, at the time, not even the book's implicit heliocentrism and explicit attacks on some Galileo adversaries, including those who sustained the Scholastic doctrines, were regarded as significant reasons to prevent the book from appearing on the world scene.

In the case of the *Dialogue*, Galileo's disobedience of a supposed directive by Cardinal Roberto Bellarmino issued on the occasion of the 1616 condemnation of Copernicus may well have played a role. Galileo always believed that Bellarmino had simply warned him, as a friend, to steer clear of dangerous topics, and that the condemnation did not regard him personally. Investigators at the trial insisted that Bellarmino instead had enjoined Galileo specifically, in light of the condemnation, to avoid speaking and teaching about heliocentrism. The more successfully he did this in the *Dialogue*, according to this view, the guiltier he was. Documents were produced at the trial to support both interpretations of the Bellarmino meeting, and no definitive answer has ever been given.

What finally tipped the scales against Galileo was Urban VIII himself. When news of the publication of the *Dialogue* first came out, as the Florentine ambassador later recorded, "His Holiness exploded into great anger, and suddenly he told me that even our Galilei had dared entering where he should not have, into the most serious and dangerous subjects that could be stirred up now." Nothing the ambassador could say would mollify the pope. It made no difference that Galileo had spent nearly two years trying to steer the book through the meandering paths of Roman officialdom before finally getting the go-ahead from the Padre Mostro. Urban VIII cared nothing that the book had been approved both in Rome and Florence. Can we hypothesize, given the new information we now have, that Urban attacked Galileo with Morandi in the back of his mind?

That Galileo proved to be a disappointing courtier, as other scholarship has suggested, may have had something to do with changing Urban's humor so decisively. Courtiers were expected to be amusing and ironic, without actually being self-deprecatory. Galileo's constant insistence on the veracity of his views rather than their vivacity, on their truth rather than their wit, on their capacity to produce edification rather than their capacity to produce pleasure, may well have changed him from a good courtier to an annoying gadfly in the eyes of the patron, Urban VIII. Never mind that Galileo was never exactly a courtier of Urban VIII; and never mind that, as far as the environment around the pope was concerned, there were many versions of what might be acceptable behavior. And we can be sure that some actual courtiers, such as the antiquary Ferdinando Ughelli, were far more pedantic on their best days than Galileo could ever have been even at his worst.

Far more pertinent may well have been Galileo's alleged portrait of Urban VIII in the character of "Simplicio" as one of the interlocutors in the *Dialogue*. Seeing himself depicted, reputedly, in the guise of the irreducible traditionalist who fails to be won over to Galileo's eminently reasonable arguments, placed in the mouth of the far more intelligent "Salviati," must have been a hard blow to a pope who prided himself on his philosophical understanding. Yet nothing Galileo could have said came even close to matching the virulence of the infamous anonymous pasquinades pasted every morning on the statue of Pasquino in the square of the same name, spreading insinuations about the pope's artistic programs, his political policies, and even his libido.

Is it possible that Urban changed his mind about Galileo when the Morandi affair was added to all the other motives we have mentioned? To view astronomy and astrology as indissolubly intertwined, he did not need to consult the esoteric works of Kepler and Campanella. Even Tommaso Garzoni's often reprinted manual on the trades found the two fields to be "like sisters, bound in close embrace."[4] He would certainly not have been alone in seeing Galileo less as a modern scientist or mechanical philosopher than as another Renaissance magician. Like the Roman newsletter writer we have met, he too may well have seen him as "the great astrologer" at least as much as the great astronomer. If so, the two trials of Morandi and Galileo can only have been closely connected in his mind.

And if Urban was as dedicated a believer in astrology as we have shown, he may have found some cause for dismay in Galileo's *Dialogue*. There, not only was the Ptolemaic basis for astrology utterly destroyed. Astrologers of all sorts were treated with undisguised disdain. Whether Urban also suspected that Galileo's new cosmos might call for yet another embarrassing afternoon in a magic chamber in the papal palace, such as the one designed for him in 1628 by Tommaso Campanella, protecting himself from who knew what fatal new astral influences, we cannot say. In any case, the bull of 1631 was supposed to put an end to astrological meddling of every kind. And who was to define Galileo's world-shaking conclusions as anything else?

To ensure Galileo's destruction, Urban did not have to go very far out of his way. All he had to do was to avoid diverting the new trial from its tragic conclusion. Then Galileo's adversaries would be given free rein. And so would a disgruntled associate of the Santa Prassede astrological circle who was now on the Inquisition committee: Cardinal Desiderio Scaglia. For when Orazio Morandi had made his famous prediction about Urban VIII's death in 1630, to whom had the other astrologers in his orbit promised the vacant see? In the most fulsome terms, Scaglia had thanked the bearer of those good tidings, Francesco Lamponi, and by extension the whole group of monastery devotees. Now was the chance to cut down the most ambitious astrologer of them all.

If all this is true, the Morandi case may have made the outcome of Galileo's trial virtually inevitable. Why has it so far been ignored? Antonio Bertolotti first discovered the documents in 1878 as part of a larger study on the curiosities of seventeenth-century Rome, including "journalists, astrologers, and necromancers."[5] Subsequently, the case shows up from time to time in research dedicated to other subjects, such as A. Bastiaanse's study of Theodore Ameyden.[6] For Luigi Fiorani, writing in 1978, Morandi's astrological activity gave evidence of the superstitious mentality typical of Baroque piety.[7] For Germana Ernst, writing in 1993 one of the most illuminating surveys, the case furnished an episode in the troubled life of Tommaso Campanella.[8] But among scholars of Galileo, apart from a footnote here and there, nothing has been done.[9]

This is hardly surprising, since over the years, the Galileo case itself has been examined largely from the point of view of the history of philosophy. To some, it is an example of a colossal shift in the hierarchy of learning on the threshold of modernity. A view of truth as one seamless and unambiguous whole, revealed in the Scriptures interpreted by the theologians, was giving way to a view of truth as many-sided, reachable by many different methods, using many different forms of expertise.[10] Or else the case is an example of the conflict between faith and reason. The world of belief, of conformity, of religious orthodoxy collided with the world of intellectual speculation, of new ways of verifying facts, of ever-progressing ideas. Although the outcome was never in any doubt, the old world would demand sacrifices from the new; and Galileo was one of them.[11] To yet other scholars the Galileo case is an example of the dangers of free inquiry in a hegemonic regime. Free-ranging curiosity, of the sort exemplified by Galileo, cannot be tolerated where the jealous concerns of a power-thirsty bureaucracy hold sway. New ideas, in such regimes, are less important than the ideologies necessary for inducing conformity and preventing sedition.[12] All these perspectives have shed revealing light on the events; all have helped us understand an important episode in the history of science.

However, in recent years the Galileo case has been examined from the point of view of the history of elites within the culture and society of Baroque Italy. And all the facts of the case begin to make sense for the first time. The personalities now appear in full relief—the paranoid pope, the obedient servants, the vengeful rivals. The human causes of a calamity that, both in fact and in the mythology that quickly enveloped it, made an indelible impression on Italian—and European—intellectual life now come into view. And we are finally beginning to discern the true contours of the complex cultural world in which new ideas were explored, a world in which the winners and the losers, the innovators and the traditionalists, the heroes and the villains, were far more difficult to distinguish than according to the textbook view.

In the heat of the conflict between the philosophers and their accusers, the various strands within Renaissance culture that had been bound together by a thread began to come undone.[13] Nor were there any signs of what might replace them. The campaign against astrology cast a shadow over the whole practice of natural philosophy that had been built on unified theories concerning the relation between the celestial and terrestrial worlds. If investigations of the future significance of occult forces in the universe could be proscribed, there was no telling what other investigations regarding the forces in the universe might be proscribed along with them.[14] At the same time, the campaign against heliocentrism and against Galileo cast a shadow over the culture of experience, of real data, of experimentation, that had in some way supplied a method and a program where grand theory had begun to wear thin. But the proposition that all questions were to be answered by reference to the Holy Scriptures, as interpreted by theologians with no expertise in the laws of natural causation, was no more acceptable now than it had been when Galileo had expressed his reservations about it in a celebrated *Letter to the Grand Duchess* of Tuscany in 1615. Clearly, free-thinking philosophers, of whatever sort, were going to be an inconvenient presence for the custodians of both sacred and secular power, even if religion might seem an easily controllable terrain for carrying on the struggle to rein them in.

Just as clearly, philosophers were not going to go away.

ACKNOWLEDGMENTS

THANKS GO TO the many friends, colleagues, and others who have commented on previous versions of these chapters or in other ways aided the research, including Peter Burke, James Hankins, Ed Muir, Paola Zambelli, Owen Gingerich, Rab Houston, Ted Rabb, Mario Infelise, Laurence Fontaine, Wolfgang Hübner, Wolfgang Haase, Barbara Marti Dooley, Brigitta Van Rheinberg, Tim Sullivan, Eric Schramm, Pierdamiano Spotorno, and Giuseppe Casetta; audiences at the Fogg Museum, the Center for Literary and Cultural Studies at Harvard, the Universities of Tübingen, Glasgow, and Manchester; Bennington College; and graduate students in the seminars of the Department of History and Civilization at the European University Institute in San Domenico di Fiesole, where the author was a Jean Monnet Fellow in 1998–99.

NOTES

Except where indicated, classical sources are cited in the Loeb editions.

INTRODUCTION

1. Rome, Archivio di Stato, *Governatore*, Processi, sec. XVII, b. 251 (hereafter, *Morandi Trial*), fol. 525r.

2. Giacinto Gigli, *Diario romano (1608–70)*, ed. G. Ricciotti (Rome: Tumminelli, 1958), p. 118.

3. We wonder whether Stanley Fish takes seriously his own suggestion that understanding the lives of historical persons is no longer necessary, and that in any case only autobiography can furnish a true account of the past, in "Just Published: Minutiae Without Meaning," *New York Times*, September 7, 1999, p. A23. The dialogue here is with Stephen Greenblatt, *Renaissance Self-Fashioning: From More to Shakespeare* (Chicago: University of Chicago Press, 1980).

4. On this last point, Anthony Grafton, *Cardano's Cosmos: The Worlds and Works of a Renaissance Astrologer* (Cambridge, Mass.: Harvard University Press, 2000); D. P. Walker, *Spiritual and Demonic Magic from Ficino to Campanella* (South Bend, Ind.: Notre Dame University Press, 1975); Eugenio Garin, *Astrology in the Renaissance: The Zodiac of Life*, trans. Carolyn Jackson and June Allen, rev. Clare Robertson (New York: Arkana, 1990); Wayne Shumaker, *The Occult Sciences in the Renaissance* (Berkeley: University of California Press, 1979); Fabio Troncarelli, ed., *La città dei segreti: magia, astrologia e cultura esoterica a Roma (secoli XV-XVIII)* (Milan: F. Angeli, 1985); and *Scienze, credenze occulte, livelli di cultura* (Florence: Olschki, 1982). Compare the English case: Bernard Capp, *English Almanacs, 1500–1800: Astrology and the Popular Press* (Ithaca: Cornell University Press, 1979); Patrick Curry, *Prophecy and Power: Astrology in Early Modern England* (Cambridge: Polity Press, 1989); and Ann Geneva, *Astrology and the Seventeenth-Century Mind: William Lilly and the Language of the Stars* (Manchester: Manchester University Press, 1995). Still fundamental are Keith Thomas, *Religion and the Decline of Magic* (1971; reprint, Oxford: Oxford University Press, 1997), chaps. 10–12, and Franz Böll et al., *Sternglaube und Sterndeutung. Die Geschichte und das Wesen der Astrologie* (Leipzig: Teubner, 1931).

5. Concerning the state and civic structures, I have in mind Laurie Nussdorfer, *Civic Politics in the Rome of Urban VIII* (Princeton: Princeton University Press, 1992); and Alberto Caracciolo and Mario Caravale, *Lo Stato pontificio da Martino V a Pio IX* (Turin: UTET, 1978).

6. In general, the articles in Stacey B. Day, ed., *The Communication of Scientific Information* (Basel: Karger, 1975); Trevor J. Pinch, "The Sun-Set: The Presentation of Certainty in Scientific Life," *Social Studies of Science* 11 (1981): 131–58, and "Toward an Analysis of Scientific Observation: The Externality and Evidential Significance of Observation Reports in Physics," in *Social Studies of Sci-*

ence 15 (1985): 3–36; and the contributors to Stevan Harnad, ed., *Peer Commentary on Peer Review: A Case Study in Scientific Quality Control* (Cambridge: Cambridge University Press, 1982).

7. Compare Peter Burke, *The Fabrication of Louis XIV* (New Haven: Yale University Press, 1992), chap. 9. In addition, Michel Foucault, *The Order of Things* (New York: Random House, 1970); as well as Steven Shapin, *The Social History of Truth: Civility and Science in Seventeenth-Century England* (Chicago: University of Chicago Press, 1994).

8. See for instance Brian P. Copenhaver, "Natural Magic, Hermetism and Occultism in Early Modern Science," in David C. Lindberg and Robert S. Westman, eds., *Reappraisals of the Scientific Revolution* (Cambridge: Cambridge University Press, 1990), 261–303; Wayne Shumaker, *Natural Magic and Modern Science: Four Treatises, 1590–1657* (Binghamton, N.Y.: Medieval and Renaissance Texts and Studies, 1989); Brian Vickers, ed., *Occult and Scientific Mentalities in the Renaissance* (Cambridge: Cambridge University Press, 1984); and Charles Webster, *From Paracelsus to Newton: Magic and the Making of Modern Science* (Cambridge: Cambridge University Press, 1983). For a particularly critical reading of the relation between science and the occult, see Paola Zambelli, *L'ambigua natura della magia* (Milan: Il Saggiatore, 1991), esp. chap. 1.

9. Another example of natural philosophy and its commercial relations is Pamela H. Smith, *The Business of Alchemy: Science and Culture under the Holy Roman Empire* (Princeton: Princeton University Press, 1994).

10. Mario Biagioli, *Galileo Courtier: The Practice of Science in the Culture of Absolutism* (Chicago: University of Chicago Press, 1993), chap. 2.

CHAPTER ONE
CRIME AND MEMORY

1. Bracciolini's deposition, dated September 2, 1630, is in *Morandi Trial*, fols. 409v and following.
2. Ibid., fol. 110v.
3. Ibid., fol. 110v.
4. Ibid., fol. 481r.
5. Ibid., fol. 90r.
6. Ibid., fol. 136r.
7. Ibid., fol. 404v.

8. Prospero Farinacci, *Praxis et theorica criminales, pars 1 et 2* (Frankfurt: Endter, 1622), p. 7. Concerning early modern criminology in general, John H. Langbein, *Prosecuting Crime in the Renaissance* (Cambridge, Mass.: Harvard University Press, 1974); concerning Italy in particular, Mario Sbriccioli, "Fonti giudiziarie e fonti giuridiche: riflessioni sulla fase attuale degli studi di storia del crimine e della giustizia criminale," *Studi storici* 29 (1988): 491–501; Edoardo Grendi, "Sulla storia del crimine: risposta a Mario Sbriccioli," *Quaderni storici* 25 (1990): 269–75; Claudio Povolo, "Aspetti e problemi dell'amministrazione della giustizia penale nella repubblica di Venezia, secoli 16–17," in Gaetano Cozzi, ed., *Stato, società e giustizia nella repubblica veneta (secoli 15–18)* (Rome: Jouvence, 1980), 1:155–258; and Thomas V. Cohen and Elizabeth S. Cohen, *Words*

and Deeds in Renaissance Rome: Trials Before the Papal Magistrates (Toronto: University of Toronto Press, 1993). Concerning inquisitorial procedures, G. Henningsen and John Tedeschi, eds., *The Inquisition in Early Modern Europe: Studies on Sources and Methods* (DeKalb: Northern Illinois University Press, 1986). Interesting reflections may be found in Carlo Ginzburg, *Il giudice e lo storico. Considerazioni in margine al processo Sofri* (Turin: Einaudi, 1991), pp. 3–14.

9. Prospero Farinacci, *Praxis et theorica criminales*, p. 645.

10. Ibid., p. 4.

11. Galileo Galilei, *Edizione nazionale delle opere* 20 vols., ed. Antonio Favaro, 3rd ed. (Florence: Guinti-Baroéra, 1967), 14:135, letter from Vincenzo Lanzieri, August 17, 1630.

12. Farinacci, *De testibus* (Venice: Giorgio Varisco, 1609), p. 47r.

13. *Morandi Trial*, fol. 384r.

14. Ibid., fol. 433r.

15. Ibid., fol. 514r.

16. *Praxis et theorica criminales*, p. 644. I refer the reader to the literature cited in the Prologue.

17. *Morandi Trial*, fol. 251r.

18. Ibid., fol. 258r, testimony of Niccolò Inghirami, August 17, 1630.

19. Ibid., fol. 265r (Maggi); 289r (Zuccagna), 289v (Falugi).

20. Ibid., fol. 306r, interrogation of Vincenzo Gandolfi on August 20, 1630, concerning venality. Concerning sidetracking techniques, ibid., fol. 386r, interrogation of Scipione Leoni.

CHAPTER TWO
THE ROAD TO VALLOMBROSA

1. *Rule of St. Benedict*, chap. 53; contained, with commentary, in *Costituzioni dell'ordine di Vallombrosa* (Florence: Vangelisti, 1704), pp. 168ff. The present-day remains of the monastery are described in Carlo A. Kovacevich, *L'Abbazia di Vallombrosa, Itinerari dei musei e monumenti d'Italia*, n. 85 (Rome: Libreria dello Stato, 1951).

2. *Morandi trial*, fols. 563ff. Cf. Peter Thornton, *The Italian Renaissance Interior, 1400–1600* (London: Weidenfeld and Nicholson, 1991).

3. The Morandi case has been discussed most recently by Germana Ernst, "Scienza, astrologia e politica nella Roma barocca," in Eugenio Canone, ed., *Bibliothecae Selectae, da Cusano a Leopardi* (Florence: Olschki, 1993), pp. 217–52; in addition, Antonio Bertolotti, "Giornalisti, astrologi e negromanti in Roma nel secolo XVII," *Rivista europea* 5 (1878): 478–79; Luigi Fiorani, "Astrologi, superstiziosi e devoti nella società romana del Seicento," *Ricerche per la storia religiosa di Roma* 2 (Rome: Edizioni di Storia e Letteratura, 1978), pp. 97ff.

4. Biographical information is scarce. Some clues are in Benigno Bracciolini, *Oratio . . . de laudibus . . . Horatii Morandi Romani* (Rome: Francesco Corbelletti, 1626); Torello Sala, *Dizionario storico-biografico di scrittori letterati ed artisti dell'ordine di Vallombrosa*, 2 vols. (Florence: Istituto Gualandi, 1929), pp. 76–77; D. F. Tarani, *L'Ordine Vallombrosano. Note storico-cronologiche* (Flor-

ence: Scuola Tipografica Calasanziana, 1920), p. 127; Antonio Favaro, *Galileo Galilei e lo Studio di Padova*, 2 vols. (Florence: Le Monnier, 1883), 1:7–8.

5. On whom, Pietro P. Ginanni, *Memorie storico-critiche degli scrittori Ravennati*, 2:1769, son of Alessandro. Concerning Alessandro, Vincenzo Forcella, *Iscrizioni delle chiese e d'altri edificii di Roma dal secolo XI fino ai giorni nostri*, 14 vols. (Rome: Tip. delle scienze matematiche e fisiche, 1869–84), 10:160.

6. Forcella, *Iscrizioni*, 9:279.

7. Florence, Archivio di Stato, Archivio Mediceo del Principato, f. 5149, fol. 653, April 16, 1616. On the origins of the urban patriciate there is the lucid chapter in Laurie Nussdorfer, *Civic Politics in the Rome of Urban VIII* (Princeton: Princeton University Press, 1992), chap. 6; and Peter Partner, *The Pope's Men: The Papal Civil Service in the Renaissance* (Oxford: Oxford University Press, 1990).

8. *Le visite "ad limina apostolorum" dei vescovi di Bergamo, 1590–1616*, ed. Ermenegildo Camozzi (Bergamo: Provincia di Bergamo, 1992), p. 203; and Bortolo Belotti, *Storia di Bergamo e dei Bergamaschi* (Bergamo: Poligrafiche Bolis, 1959), 2:401. A reference to a homonymous Morandi of nearby Castel S. Pietro is in Forlì, Biblioteca Comunale A. Saffi, "Carte Romagna," 696.25: "Copia dell'atto dotale fatto da Orazio Morandi di Castel S. Pietro, 20 viii 1616. Notaio Urbano Bertazzoli. Copia del 1647."

9. Concerning the university in this period, Nicola Spano, *L'Università di Roma*, preface by Pietro de Francisci (Rome: Casa editrice "Mediterranea," 1935); Paolo Cherubini, ed., *Roma e lo studium urbis: spazio urbano e cultura dal Quattro al Seicento, Atti del convegno Roma, 7–10 giugno 1989* (Rome: Ministero per i beni culturali e ambientali, Ufficio centrale per i beni archivistici, 1992). In addition, Italo De Feo, *Sisto V: un grande papa tra Rinascimento e Barocco* (Milan: Mursia, 1987); Paolo Prodi, *The Papal Prince: One Body and Two Souls: The Papal Monarchy in Early Modern Europe*, trans. Susan Haskins (Cambridge: Cambridge University Press, 1987); B. Dooley, "Social Control and the Italian Universities, from Renaissance to Illuminismo," *Journal of Modern History* 61 (1989): 205–39; Fiorenza Rangoni, *S. Ivo alla Sapienza e lo "Studium Urbis"* (Rome: Istituto nazionale di studi romani, Fratelli Palombi, 1989).

10. Charles Déjob, *Marc-Antoine Muret: un professeur français en Italie dans la seconde moitiè du sixième siècle* (Geneva: Slatkine Reprints, 1970).

11. On Parisetti, Emanuele Conte, *Accademie studentesche a Roma nel Cinquecento. De modis docenti et discendi in iure* (Rome: Edizioni dell'Ateneo, 1985), chap. 1.

12. Still useful is Biagio Brugi, *Per la storia della giurisprudenza e delle universita italiane: saggi* (Turin: Unione tipografico-editrice torinese, 1915).

13. In general, Donald Kelley, *Foundations of Modern Historical Scholarship: Language, Law and History in the French Renaissance* (New York: Columbia University Press, 1970), pp. 90–103. On the Renaissance philological tradition, Anthony Grafton, *Joseph Scaliger: A Study in the History of Classical Scholarship* (New York: Oxford University Press, 1983), vol. 1, chap. 1.

14. Niccolò Del Re, "Prospero Farinacci, giurisconsulto romano," *Archivio della Società Romana di Storia Patria*, ser. 3, vol. 29 (1975): 135–220.

15. The standard source on the Cenci affair is Corrado Ricci, *Beatrice Cenci*, 2 vols. (Milan, 1923).

16. Niccolò Del Re, "Prospero Farinacci," p. 175. On prelates in this period, A. V. Antinovics, "Counter Reformation Cardinals: 1534–90," *European Studies Review* 2 (1972): 301–29.

17. In general, Jean Leclerq, *Momenti e figure di storia monastica italiana* (Cesena: Badia, 1993).

18. Nicola Vasaturo, *Vallombrosa. L'abbazia e la congregazione*, ed. Giordano Monza Compagnoni (Vallombrosa: Edizioni Vallombrosa, 1994). Concerning the Medici connection, Carlo Fantappiè, *Il monachesimo moderno tra ragion di chiesa e ragion di stato: il caso toscano (XVI–XIX sec.)* (Florence: Olschki, 1993), pp. 131–41.

19. G. Sommi Picenardi, "Don Giovanni de' Medici, governatore dell'esercito veneto in Friuli," *Nuovo archivio veneto*, n.s. 7, 25 (1907): 104–42; 26 (1907): 94–136.

CHAPTER THREE
AD ASTRA PER ASPERA

1. *Prose*, ed. G. Martellotti et al. (Milan: Ricciardi, 1955), Book 2, p. 453.

2. Eric Cochrane, "The Renaissance Academies in the Italian and European Setting," in *The Fairest Flower: The Emergence of Linguistic Consciousness in Renaissance Europe, Proceedings of the Conference at UCLA, December 1983* (Florence: Accademia della Crusca, 1985), pp. 21–39; and specifically relating to Florence, Eric Cochrane, "Le accademie," in Giancarlo Garafagnini, ed., *Firenze e la Toscana dei Medici nell'Europa del Cinquecento* (Florence: Olschki, 1983), 1:3–19.

3. Severina Parodi, ed., *Catalogo degli Accademici della Crusca dalla fondazione* (Florence: Accademia della Crusca, 1983).

4. Concerning the Crusca: Severina Parodi, *Quattro secoli di Crusca, 1583–1983* (Florence: Accademia della Crusca, 1983), p. 13; P. B. Diffley, *Paolo Beni: A Biographical and Critical Study* (Oxford: Oxford University Press, 1988), chap. 8.

5. For biographical details, Silvio Adrasto Barbi, *Un accademico mecenate e poeta (Giambattista Strozzi)* (Florence: Sansoni, 1900).

6. On Allegri, Alberto Asor Rosa, entry in *Dizionario biografico degli Italiani* (1960): 2:477–78. Concerning the Spensierati, Michele Maylender, *Storia delle accademie d'Italia* (Bologna: n.p., 1929–30), vol. 5. Concerning other monks mentioned here, D. F. Tarani, *L'Ordine Vallombrosano. Note storico-cronologiche* (Florence: Scuola Tipografia Calasanziana, 1920), p. 124.

7. *La prima parte delle rime piacevoli di Alessandro Allegri, raccolte dal M. Rev. D. Orazio Morandi; e da Francesco Allegri date in luce* (Verona: Francesco dalle Donne, 1605), preface signed by Morandi.

8. Ibid., pp. 3–4.

9. Ibid., p. 54.

10. On the late-sixteenth-century occult revival in Europe, Allen Debus, *Man and Nature in the Renaissance* (Cambridge: Cambridge University Press, 1978),

chaps. 1–3; Brian P. Copenhaver, "Astrology and Magic," in Charles B. Schmitt et al., eds., *The Cambridge History of Renaissance Philosophy* (Cambridge: Cambridge University Press, 1988), pp. 264–300; Nancy G. Siraisi, *The Clock and the Mirror: Girolamo Cardano and Renaissance Medicine* (Princeton: Princeton University Press, 1997), chap. 7; as well as Frances Yates, *Giordano Bruno and the Hermetic Tradition*, 5th ed. (Chicago: University of Chicago Press, 1991).

11. Indeed, Marino's *Rime*, the first version of his fabulously successful *Lira*, had been published in Venice in 1602.

12. *La prima parte delle rime piacevoli*, p. 16.

13. Ibid., p. 6.

14. Ibid., Francesco Allegri's preface, unnumbered pages.

15. *Summa contra Gentiles* 3:82–86, 104–6.

16. Lynn Thorndike, *History of Magic and Experimental Science* (New York: Columbia University Press, 1941), 5:480.

17. On what follows, Paolo Galluzzi, "Motivi paracelsiani in Toscana," *Scienza, credenze occulte, livelli di cultura* (Florence: Olschki, 1982), pp. 31–62.

18. Pier Filippo Covoni, *Don Antonio de' Medici al Casino di San Marco* (Florence: Tipografia Cooperativa, 1892); Francesco Inghirami, *Storia della Toscana*, vol. 13 (Fiesole: Poligrafia Fiesolana, 1844), p. 154.

19. This version appeared in a manuscript entitled *De sensitiva rerum facultate*, composed in 1590 and later lost. In 1604 he reconstructed the lost work, composing it in Italian; this has been published as *Del senso delle cose e della magia, testo inedito italiano con le varianti dei codici e delle due edizioni latine*, ed. Antonio Bruers (Bari: Laterza, 1925). Biographical material is from the entry by Luigi Firpo in *Dizionario biografico degli Italiani* 17 (1974): 372–401. Concerning Campanella's philosophy, the authoritative work is now John M. Headley, *Tommaso Campanella and the Transformation of the World* (Princeton: Princeton University Press, 1997).

20. Although only per accidens—free will being exempt. D. P. Walker, *Spiritual and Demonic Magic from Ficino to Campanella* (London: Warburg Institute, University of London, 1958), p. 216.

21. Tommaso Campanella, *The City of the Sun: A Poetical Dialogue*, trans. with introduction and notes by Daniel J. Donno (Berkeley: University of California Press, 1981), p. 123. On Telesio, Raffaele Sirri and Maurizio Torrini, eds., *Bernardino Telesio e la cultura napoletana* (Naples: Guida, 1992).

22. Gérard Simon, *Kepler: Astronome, Astrologue* (Paris: Gallimard, 1979), pp. 55–64. In addition, Edward Rosen, "Kepler's Attitude toward Astrology and Mysticism," and Judith V. Field, "Kepler's Rejection of Numerology," both in Vickers, ed., *Occult and Scientific Mentalities*, respectively at pp. 253–72 and 273ff. Galileo's position is explained in Germana Ernst, *Religione, ragione e natura: ricerche su Tommaso Campanella e il tardo Rinascimento* (Milan: Angeli, 1991), chap. 10. Compare Stillman Drake, *Galileo at Work: His Scientific Biography* (Chicago: University of Chicago Press, 1978), chap. 6.

23. Galluzzi, "Motivi paracelsiani," p. 55; and F. Jacoli in *Bollettino di bibliografia e di storia delle scienze matematiche e fisiche di B. Buoncompagni* 7 (1874): 377–415; Giovanni Casati, *Dizionario degli scrittori d'Italia* (Milan: Ghirlanda, 1934), 3:55.

24. Raffaele Gualterotti, *Discorso sopra l'apparizione della nova stella e sopra l'oscurazione del sole e della luna nell'anno 1605 con alquanto di lume dell'arte del oro* (Florence: Giunti, 1605), A3v.

25. Gualterotti, *Discorso*, chap. 6. James Lattis discusses this model in *Between Copernicus and Galileo* (Chicago: University of Chicago Press, 1994).

26. *Scherzi degli spiriti animali dettati con l'occasione dell'oscurazione dell'anno 1605* (Florence: Giunti, 1605), chap. 22.

27. Galileo's early career is analyzed in Mario Biagioli, *Galileo, Courtier: The Practice of Science in the Culture of Absolutism* (Chicago: University of Chicago Press, 1993), chaps. 1–2, and Giovanni Santinello, ed., *Galileo e la cultura padovana: convegno di studio* (Padova: EDAM, 1992).

28. *Edizione nazionale delle opere di Galileo Galilei* (Florence: Giunti-Barbera, 1967), 11:530, letter dated July 6, 1613.

29. Concerning the seventeenth-century fortunes of Castiglione's work, Peter Burke, *The Fortunes of the "Courtier"* (University Park: Penn State Press, 1995), chap. 6. Concerning courtiership in general, Cesare Vasoli, *La cultura delle corti* (Florence: Il Portolano, 1980); and, a critical review of the literature, Pierpaolo Merlin, "Il tema della corte nella storiografia italiana ed europea," *Società e storia* 27 (1986): 203–35.

30. *Seconda parte delle rime piacevoli d'Alessandro Allegri* (Verona: Francesco dalle Donne, 1607), f. D1.

31. Concerning Giovanni de' Medici's cultural interests, Domenica Landolfi, "Don Giovanni de' Medici, 'principe intendente in varie scienze,'" *Studi seicenteschi* 29 (1988): 125–62.

32. Florence, Archivio di Stato, Archivio Mediceo del Principato, f. 5149, fol. 716, dated May 1, 1620; here Morandi refers to books existing in Giovanni's collection. Prohibited texts by these writers are discussed by Franz Heinrich Reusch, *Der Index der verbotener Bücher* (Bonn: Max Cohen, 1893), 1:497 (Paracelsus's *Libri tres chirurgiae*, 1573, and *Chirurgia magna*, 1570, both forbidden in 1583–4); 1:536 (Telesio's *De rerum natura* and other works, forbidden in 1596); 1:62 (Reuchlin's *Augenspiegel*, *Speculum oculare*, *De verbo mirifico*, and *Ars cabalistica*, prohibited in 1557). In addtion, Florence, Archivio di Stato, Archivio Mediceo del Principato, filza 5158, c. 534r, and filza 5170, pt. 1, c. 169r, both included in the Documentary Sources database of the Medici Archive Project.

33. Florence, Archivio di Stato, Archivio Mediceo del Principato, f. 5149, fol. 632, dated December 29, 1615. In addition, fol. 669, dated October 12, 1618.

34. Florence, Archivio di Stato, Archivio Mediceo del Principato, f. 5149, fol. 625, dated June 20, 1615.

CHAPTER FOUR
THE ASTROLOGER'S BOOKS

1. *Morandi Trial*, fol. 605r, letter dated August 3, 1629.

2. Ibid., fol. 595r, dated June 30, 1629.

3. The inquiry of 1600 is recorded in Biblioteca Apostolica Vaticana, mss. Vaticani latini 11288, fols. 211r-215v. On these episodes, especially in Venice, Antonella Barzazi, "Ordini religiosi e biblioteche a Venezia tra Cinque- e Seicento,"

Annali dell'Istituto Storico Italo-Germanico in Trento 21 (1995): 141–228. Still useful concerning Italian libraries in this time, Romeo De Maio, "I modelli culturali della Controriforma: le biblioteche dei conventi italiani alla fine del Cinquecento," in his *Riforme e miti nella Chiesa del Cinquecento* (Naples: Guida, 1973). In addition, Danilo Zardin, *"Donna religiosa di rara eccellenza." Prospera Colonna Bascapé: i libri e la cultura nei monasteri milanesi del Cinque e del Seicento* (Florence: Olschki, 1992).

4. The list appears in duplicate in *Morandi Trial*, 556r-62v.

5. In *Il cane di Diogene* (1689), excerpted by Ezio Raimondi in *Trattatisti e narratori del Seicento* (Milan-Naples: Ricciardi, 1960), p. 957. Concerning this metaphor, Ann Blair, *The Theater of Nature: Jean Bodin and Renaissance Science* (Princeton: Princeton University Press, 1997), chap. 5.

6. Vitruvius, *On Architecture* 6:5, cited in the excerpts from Giambattista Piazza's *Eusevologio romano, ovvero delle opere pie di Roma* (Rome: 1698), edited by Valentino Romani, *Biblioteche romane del Sei e Settecento* (Rome: Vecchiarelli, 1996), p. cxliv.

7. On which, see Roger Chartier, *The Order of Books*, trans. Lydia Cochrane (Stanford: Stanford University Press, 1994), chap. 3.

8. On ecclesiastical courtiership, Gigliola Fragnito, "Cardinals' Courts in Sixteenth-Century Rome," *Journal of Modern History* 65 (1993): 26–56; Renata Ago, *Carriere e clientele nella Roma barocca* (Rome: Laterza, 1990), and Maria Antonietta Visceglia, "Burocrazia, mobilità sociale e 'patronage' alla corte di Roma tra Cinque e Seicento: alcuni aspetti del recente dibattito storiografico e prospettive di ricerca," *Roma moderna e contemporanea* 3 (1995): 11–55.

9. Concerning Italian libraries in general, Mario Rosa, "I depositi del sapere. Biblioteche, accademie, archivi," in P. Rossi, ed., *La memoria del sapere* (Bari: Laterza, 1988), pp. 165–210.

10. M. Morci, "Del bibliofilo Angelo Rocca," *La bibliofilia* 2 (1908): 357–62. In general, Enzo Bottasso, *Storia della biblioteca in Italia* (Milan: Editrice bibliografica, 1984).

11. Marino Zorzi, *La libreria di San Marco: libri, lettori, società nella Venezia dei dogi* (Milan: A. Mondadori, 1987); Christine Grafinger, *Die Ausleihe Vatikanischer Handschriften und Druckwerke (1563–1700)* (Vatican City: Biblioteca Apostolica Vaticana, 1993), Ian Philip, *The Bodleian Library in the Seventeenth and Eighteenth Centuries* (Oxford: Clarendon Press, 1983), and E. Apollonj et al., *Annuario delle biblioteche italiane*, 5 vols. (Rome: Palombi, 1969–1981). In general, Paul Raabe, ed., *Öffentliche und private Bibliotheken im 17 und 18 Jahrhundert: Raritätenkammern, Forschungsinstrumente, oder Bildungsstätten?* (Bremen and Wolfenbüttel: Jacobi Verlag, 1977), especially the articles by Ian Willison and Maurice Piquard.

CHAPTER FIVE
THE SUN POPE

1. Concerning Ameyden: Alexandro Bastiaanse, *Teodoro Ameyden (1586–1656). Un Neerlandese alla corte di Roma* ('s Gravenhage: Staatsdrukkerij, 1968).

Concerning Bracciolini: Michele Barbi, *Notizia della vita e delle opere di Francesco Bracciolini* (Florence: G. C. Sansoni, 1897). Cincerning Finelli, see below.

2. Here and below, *Morandi trial*, fols. Ir–IXv.

3. Vallombrosa, Archivio dell'Abbazia, D. V. 3, c. 373r–376r and 377v.

4. *Edizione Nazionale delle Opere di Galileo Galilei*, 12:206, dated December 5, 1615, Piero Guicciardini to Curzio Picchena. For what follows, Ludwig von Pastor, *The History of the Popes* (St. Louis: Herder, 1923–69), vol. 25; William Bouwsma, *Venice and the Defense of Republican Liberty: Renaissance Values in the Age of the Counter Reformation* (Berkeley: University of California Press, 1968); Wolfgang Reinhard, *Papstfinanz und Nepotismus unter Paul V (1605–1621): Studien und Quellen zur Struktur und zu quantitativen Aspekten des papstlichen Herrschaftssystems*, 2 vols. (Stuttgart: A. Hiersemann, 1974); Volker Reinhardt, *Kardinal Scipione Borghese (1605–1633): Vermögen, Finanzen und sozialer Aufstieg eines Papstnepoten* (Tübingen: M. Niemeyer, 1984).

5. Apart from sources mentioned more specifically below: Pastor, *History of the Popes*, 28:408ff.; Torgil Magnusson, *Rome in the Age of Bernini*, 2 vols. (Atlantic Highlands, N.J.: Humanities Press, 1986); Francis Haskell, *Patrons and Painters: A Study in the Relations between Italian Art and Society in the Age of the Baroque* (New Haven: Yale University Press, 1980), chaps. 1–5; Marilyn Aronberg Lavin, *Seventeenth-Century Barberini Documents and Inventories of Art* (New York: NYU Press, 1975); Pietro Redondi, *Galileo Heretic*, trans. Raymond Rosenthal (Princeton: Princeton University Press, 1987), pp. 68ff.; Frederick Hammond, *Music and Spectacle in Baroque Rome: Barberini Patronage under Urban VIII* (New Haven: Yale University Press, 1994); Louise Rice, *The Altars and Altarpieces of New St. Peter's: Outfitting the Basilica, 1621–1666* (New York: Cambridge University Press, in association with the American Academy in Rome, 1997); on the contradictions of Counter Reformation religious careers, A. J. Antonovics, "Counter Reformation Cardinals, 1534–90," *European Studies Review* 2 (1972): 301–28.

6. Leone Allacci, *Apes urbanae: siue De viris illustribus, qui ab anno MDCXXX. per totum MDCXXXII. Romae adsuerunt, ac typis aliquid evulgarunt* (Rome: Ludovico Grignani, 1633). Concerning Allacci, the authoritative work is Thomas Cerbu, "Leone Allacci, 1587–1669: The Fortunes of an Early Byzantinist," Ph.D. diss., Harvard University, 1986.

7. Benedetto Castelli, *Carteggio*, ed. Massimo Bucciantini (Florence: L. S. Olschki, 1988), pp. 1–27; in addition, Antonio Favaro, "Amici e corrispondenti di Galileo. Giovanni Ciampoli," *Atti del R. Istituto Veneto di Scienze, Lettere ed Arti*, vol. 62, pt. 2 (1902): 91–145.

8. On the Barberini library, Jeanne Bignami Odier, *La bibliothèque Vaticane de Sixte IV à Pie XI. Recherches sur l'histoire des collections manuscrits* (Vatican City: Biblioteca Apostolica Vaticana, 1973). Concerning Holstein: Alfonso Mirto, ed., *Lucas Holstenius e la corte medicea: carteggio (1629–1660)* (Florence: Olschki, 1999).

9. *Poemata* (Rome: Typographia Reverendae Camerae Apostolicae, 1637), p. 158.

10. "Io raggiro per la mente cose di qualche momento per la repubblica letteraria, le quali se non si effettuano in questa mirabile congiuntura, non occorre,

almeno per quel che si aspetta per parte mia, sperare d'incontrarne mai una simile." Letter to Federico Cesi, dated October 9, 1623, in Giuseppe Gabrieli, ed., "Il carteggio linceo della vecchia Accademia di Federico Cesi," *Memorie della R. Accademia Nazionale dei Lincei, Cl. Sci. Mor. Stor e Fil.*, ser. 6, vol. 7 (1938–42): 683.

11. For what follows, Giorgio Spini, *Galileo, Campanella e il 'divinus poeta'* (Bologna: Mulino, 1996), pp. 41–58; and in general, Germana Ernst, *Religione, ragione e natura. Ricerche su Tommaso Campanella e il tardo Rinascimento* (Milan: Angeli, 1991), chap. 4.

12. Concerning the academy, Giuseppe Olmi, " 'In essercitio universale di contemplatione e prattica': Federico Cesi e i Lincei," in Laetitia Boehm and Ezio Raimondi, eds., *Università, accademie e società scientifiche in Italia e in Germania dal Cinquecento al Settecento* (Bologna: Mulino, 1981), pp. 169–236; and Jean-Michel Gardair, "I Lincei: i soggetti, i luoghi, le attività," *Quaderni storici* 16 (1981): 763–87. On Cesi's life, *Dizionario biografico degli Italiani* entry by A. De Ferrari, 24 (1980): 256–58.

13. Relevant portions of *Del naturale desiderio di sapere* (1616) are in Ezio Raimondi, ed., *Narratori e trattatisti del Seicento* (Milan-Naples: Ricciardi, 1960), pp. 39–64, 66–70.

14. On these topics, see Donata Chiomenti Vassalli, *Donna Olimpia: o, del nepotismo nel Seicento* (Milan: Mursia, 1979); Susanna Akerman, *Queen Christina of Sweden and Her Circle: The Transformation of a Seventeenth Century Philosophical Libertine* (Leiden: E. J. Brill, 1991). On the demographic composition of the city, see articles by Eugenio Sonnino, Manuel Vaquero Piñero, and Giampiero Brunelli in E. Sonnino, ed., *Popolazione e società a Roma dal medioevo all'età contemporanea* (Rome: Calamo, 1998).

15. Roman social divisions are the subject of Laurie Nussdorfer, "Writing and the Power of Speech: Notaries and Artisans in Baroque Rome," in Barbara Diefendorf and C. Hesse, eds., *Culture and Identity in Early Modern Europe* (Ann Arbor: University of Michigan Press, 1993), pp. 103–18; Gabriella Bonacchi, *Legge e peccato: anime, corpi, giustizia alla corte dei papi* (Rome: Laterza, 1995).

16. Still useful concerning Bernini, apart from sources specified below, are Domenico Bernini, *Vita del cavalier Gio. Lorenzo Bernino* (Rome: R. Bernabo, 1713), and Filippo Baldinucci, *Vita di Gian Lorenzo Bernini: con l'inedita vita del Baldinucci, scritta dal figlio Francesco Saverio*, Sergio Samek Ludovici, ed. (Milan: Edizioni del Milione, 1948). For his early career, Irving Lavin and Marilyn A. Lavin, "Five New Youthful Sculptures by Gianlorenzo Bernini and a Revised Chronology of His Early Work," *Art Bulletin* 1 (1968): 233–48; as well as Rudolf Wittkower, *Gian Lorenzo Bernini: The Sculptor of the Roman Baroque*, 3rd ed. rev. by Howard Hibbard, Thomas Martin, and Margot Wittkower (Ithaca: Cornell University Press, 1981). Also useful: Maurizio Fagiolo dell'Arco, *L'immagine al potere. Vita di Giovan Lorenzo Bernini* (Bari: Laterza, 2001).

17. The following discussion accepts the arguments for the attribution of the work to Gian Lorenzo Bernini, as suggested in Howard Hibbard and Irma Jaffe, "Bernini's Barcaccia," *Burlington Magazine* 106 (1964): 159–70.

18. *Ab urbe condita*, 26:51; they were repeated again at Syracuse, 29:22:2.

19. On Pietro's career, *Pietro Bernini, un preludio al Barocco: 16 settembre-30 novembre 1989, Sesto Fiorentino, Teatro la Limonaia, Villa Corsi-Salviati*, ed. Scramasax (Florence: G. Capponi, 1989); and Giovanni Baglione, *Le vite de' pittori, scultori et architetti dal pontificato di Gregorio XIII del 1572 in fino a' tempi di Papa Urbano ottavo nel 1642*, 3 vols., ed. Jacob Hess and Herwarth Rottgen, (Vatican City: Biblioteca Apostolica Vaticana, 1995). For Pietro's role in the Barcaccia project, see Cesare D'Onofrio, *Le fontane di Roma* (Rome: Società Editrice, 1986), pp. 356–70; but the attribution of the fountain entirely to Pietro seems to be contradicted by the documentation presented in this chapter.

20. Concerning Finelli's career, Jennifer Montagu, "Bernini Sculptures Not by Bernini," in Irving Lavin, ed., *Gianlorenzo Bernini: New Aspects of his Art and Thought: A Commemorative Volume* (University Park: Penn State University Press, 1985), pp. 25–61, and Damian Dombrowski, *Giuliano Finelli: Bildhauer zwischen Neapel und Rom* (Frankfurt: Lang, 1997).

21. Angelo Davoli, *Bibliografia storica del poema piacevole "Lo scherno de gli Dei" di Francesco Bracciolini* (Reggio Emilia: Davoli, 1930); John Beldon Scott, *Images of Nepotism: The Painted Ceilings of Palazzo Barberini* (Princeton: Princeton University Press, 1991).

22. Carmine Jannaco, *Il Seicento* (Milan: F. Vallardi, 1963), p. 662.

23. *Selva di concetti scritturali* (Venice: 1617).

24. Donatella L. Sparti, *Le collezioni Dal Pozzo: storia di una famiglia e del suo museo nella Roma seicentesca* (Modena: Franco Cosimo Panini, 1992), as well as the contributions to Francesco Solinas, ed., *Cassiano Dal Pozzo. Atti del Seminario Internazionale di Studi* (Rome: De Luca, 1989). In addition, articles by Ingo Herklotz, David Freedberg, and Henrietta MacBurney in Elizabeth Cropper, Giovanna Perini, and Francesco Solinas, eds., *Documentary Culture: Florence and Rome from Grand-Duke Ferdinando I to Pope Alexander VII. Papers from a Colloquium held at the Villa Spelman, Florence, 1990* (Baltimore: Johns Hopkins University Press, 1992), pp. 81–126, 349–62.

25. *Novum organum*, aphorisms 2, 101–3.

26. On the more theatrical aspects of collecting, Paula Findlen, *Possessing Nature: Museums, Collecting and Scientific Culture in Early Modern Italy* (Berkeley: University of California Press, 1994); for other aspects, the article by Giuseppe Olmi in Oliver Impey and Arthur MacGregor, eds., *The Origins of Museums: The Cabinet of Curiosities in Sixteenth- and Seventeenth-Century Europe* (Oxford: Clarendon Press, 1985), as well as Olmi's *Ulisse Aldrovandi. Scienza e natura nel secondo Cinquecento* (Trent: Libera Università di Trento, 1976); not to mention Arnaldo Momigliano, "Ancient History and the Antiquarian," in his *Studies in Historiography* (London: Weidenfeld and Nicholson, 1966), pp. 1–39; and Francis Haskell, *History and Its Images: Art and the Interpretation of the Past* (New Haven: Yale University Press, 1993), chap. 5.

27. David Freedberg and Enrico Baldini, *The Paper Museum of Cassiano Dal Pozzo, Series B, Natural History; pt. 1: Citrus Fruit*, with contributions by Giovanni Continella, Eugenio Tribulato, and Eileen Kinghan (London: Harvey Miller, 1997).

28. On his career, there is an entry by Alberto Vecchi in *Dizionario critico della letteratura italiana* (Turin: UTET, 1986), 4:334–35; still useful is Christian Gottlieb Jöcher, *Ällgemeines Gelehrten-Lexikon* 4 (Leipzig, 1751), p. 156ff. The work in question was published as Alfonso Chacon, *Vitae et res gestae pontificorum*, 2 vols. (Rome: Typis Vaticanis, 1630).

CHAPTER SIX
THE WIDENING CIRCLE

1. Concerning the various editions, Sergio Bertelli and Piero Innocenti, *Bibliografia machiavelliana* (Verona: Edizioni Valdonega, 1979).

2. Giuseppe Chiecchi and Luciano Troisio, *Il Decamerone sequestrato. Le tre edizioni censurate nel Cinquecento* (Milan: UNICOPLI, 1984). The novels in question are 4:2, 1:6, and 3:7. Concerning Gennaro: Vincenzo Forcella, *Iscrizioni delle chiese e d'altri edificii di Roma dal secolo XI fino ai giorni nostri*, 14 vols. (Rome: Tip. delle scienze matematiche e fisiche, 1869–84), 9:538.

3. Castellani's identity is revealed in *Morandi Trial*, fol. 750r. On Trithemius, see Thomas Ernst, "Schwarzweisse Magie: Der Schlussel zum dritten Buch der Steganographia des Trithemius," *Daphnis* 25 (1996): 1–205.

4. Franz Heinrich Reusch, *Der Index der verbotenen Bucher. Ein Beitrag zur Kirchen- und Literaturgeschichte* (Bonn: Verlag von M. Cohen & Sohn, 1885), 2:183.

5. Lynn Thorndike, *History of Magic and Experimental Science* (New York: Columbia University Press, 1923), 2:280; also 2:813–21. In addition, David Pingree, *Picatrix: The Latin Version of the Ghayat Al-Hakim* (London: Warburg Institute, 1986).

6. Francesco Inghirami, *Storia della Toscana: Biografia* (Fiesole: Poligrafia Fiesolana, 1843), 1:32; and Giovan Maria Mazzuchelli, *Gli scrittori d'Italia*, 2 vols. (Brescia: Bossini, 1753–63), I:i:178.

7. Reusch, *Der Index*, 1:389. To be sure, a Latin translation containing the omitted passages had been printed as *Historiarum sui temporis libri viginti* (Basel: Perna, 1566).

8. Venice, Archivio di Stato, *Inquisitori di stato*, b. 472, Roman newsletter contained in the dispatch of Angelo Contarini, dated November 10, 1629.

9. In general, Niccolò Del Re, *La curia romana. Lineamenti storico-giuridici* (Rome: Edizioni di storia e letteratura, 1970).

10. Entry by G. Formichetti in *Dizionario biografico degli Italiani* 41 (1992): 167–70.

11. I found the Sixtus V bull in Vatican City, Archivio Segreto Vaticano, *Misc. IV-V*, 66, dated October 11, 1586. Pius V's is cited in Valerio Castronovo, "I primi sviluppi della stampa periodica fra Cinque e Seicento," in Castronovo et al., *La stampa italiana dal Cinquecento all'Ottocento* (Milan: Laterza, 1976), p. 12. Of the theorists, I have in mind Botero's *Della ragion di stato*, ed. Luigi Firpo (Turin: UTET, 1948), p. 442; and Ammirato's *Della segretezza* (Venice: Giunti, 1598), p. 26. On these questions, I refer the reader to my *Social History of Skepticism: Experience and Doubt in Early Modern Culture* (Baltimore: Johns Hopkins University Press, 1999), chap. 3.

12. *Morandi Trial*, fol. 144r.

13. The report is edited in Nicolò Barozzi and Guglielmo Berchet, *Relazioni degli stati europei lette al Senato dagli ambasciatori veneti*, ser. 3: Italia; Relazioni di Roma, vol. 1 (Venice: Naratovich, 1877). Concerning the circulation of these reports, Michele Fassina, ed., *Corrispondenze diplomatiche veneziane da Napoli: Dispacci* (Rome: Istituto Poligrafico e Zecca dello Stato, 1995), preface.

14. Reusch, *Der Index*, 2:281. The identities of Bertolli and Faliero are revealed in *Morandi Trial*, fols. 130r, 174r.

15. *Morandi Trial*, concerning V. Regii, fol. 144r.

16. See my *Social History of Skepticism*, chap. 1, as well as the articles by S. Baron, Mario Infelise, and Jean-Pierre Vittu in Brendan Dooley and Sabrina Baron, eds., *The Politics of Information in Early Modern Europe* (London: Routledge, 2000). Enrico Stumpo has recently published an entire year of a 1588 avviso: *La gazzetta de l'anno 1588* (Florence: Giunti-Barbera, 1988).

17. The identifications are from *Morandi Trial*, fols. 171r and 149r.

18. Jean Delumeau, *Vie economique et sociale de Rome dans la seconde moitié du XVIe siècle*, Bibliothèque des Écoles Françaises d'Athenes et de Rome, fasc. 184 (Paris: E. de Boccard, 1957), vol. 1, chap. 2.

19. Rome, Archivio di Stato, *Governatore*, *Curia Savelli*, b. 134, Cardinal Spada to Governor Cardinal Spinola, September 18, 1681.

20. The last item was *Pedaços de historia o Relaçiones* (London, 1593).

21. *Magnum bullarium*, vol. 4 pt. 4 (Rome: Mainardi, 1757), p. 179, no. 26. Concerning the astrology debates, Eugenio Garin, *Astrology in the Renaissance: The Zodiac of Life*, trans. Carolyn Jackson and June Allen, revised in conjunction with the author by Clare Robertson (New York: Arkana, 1990).

22. On which, see Franca Petrucci-Nardelli, "Il Cardinale Francesco Barberini senior e la stampa a Roma," *Archivio della Società Romana di Storia Patria* 108 (1985): 133–98; and V. Romani, "Notizie su Andrea Brogiotti libraio, editore e stampatore camerale," *Accademie e biblioteche d'Italia* n.s. 2 (1973): 72–75. On Platonism in general, James Hankins, *Plato in the Italian Renaissance*, 3rd. ed. (Leiden: E. J. Brill, 1994).

23. Eugenio Garin, *La cultura del Rinascimento* (Bari: Laterza, 1967), p. 150.

24. On this work, Thorndike, *History of Magic and Experimental Science*, 1:310–13.

25. *Morandi Trial*, fol. 199v.

26. See the entry by A. Lauro in *Dizionario biografico degli Italiani* 20 (1977): 13–16.

27. Armand De Gaetano, *Giambattista Gelli and the Florentine Academy*, Biblioteca dell' "Archivium Romanicum," ser. 1, vol. 119 (Florence: Olschki, 1976). On Bandiera, Girolamo Tiraboschi, *Biblioteca modenese*, 1 (Modena: Società tipografica, 1781), p. 280.

28. Christian Jöcher, *Allgemeines Gelehrten-Lexikon* 4 (1751): 156; Donald R. Kelley, "Johann Sleiden and the Origins of History as a Profession," *Journal of Modern History* 52 (1980): 573–98.

29. *Morandi Trial*, fols. 253r, 258r. Concerning the Roman book industry in this period, Francesco Barbieri, *Per una storia del libro. Profili, note, ricerche*

(Rome: Bulzoni, 1981), pp. 197–235; Franca Petrucci-Nardelli, "Torchi, famiglie, libri nella Roma del Seicento," *La Bibliofilia* 86 (1984): 159–72.

30. *Morandi Trial*, fol. 580r, letter dated June 9, 1629.

31. On whom, see Elio Durante and Anna Martellotti, *Don Angelo Grillo O.S.B. alias Livio Celiano: poeta per musica del secolo decimosesto* (Florence: Studio per edizioni scelte, 1989).

32. For what follows, F. W. Gravit, "The Accademia degli Umoristi and Its French Relationships," *Papers of the Michigan Academy of Science, Arts and Letters* 20 (1934): 505–21; Michele Maylender, *Storia delle accademie d'Italia* (Bologna: Cappelli, 1930), 5:370–81.

33. Andrea Argoli, *De diebus criticis et de aegrorum decubitu libri duo* (Padua: Paolo Frambotti, 1639); Andrea Argoli, *Ephemerides annorum 50 juxta Tychonis hypotheses et accurate e coelo deductas observationes ab anno 1630 ad annum 1680* (Padua: Paolo Frambotti, 1638).

34. For the cardinals' allegiances, I have followed Angelo Contarini's report in 1624, printed in Barozzi and Berchet, *Relazioni*, ser. 3: Italia; Relazioni di Roma, vol. 1, pp. 253–312.

35. Information here is from Konrad Eubel et al., *Hierarchia Catholica*,Vol. 3, ed. Patrick Gauchat (Regensburg: Libreria Regensbergiana, 1910); Vol. 4, ed. Konrad Eubel (Regensburg: Libreria Regensbergiana, 1935).

36. On whom, see R. P. Mortier, *Histoire des maîtres généraux de l'ordre des Frères Prêcheurs* (Paris: Picard, 1913), 6:282–492.

37. Reusch, *Der Index*, 2:192.

38. Sharon Kettering, "Gift-giving and Patronage in Early Modern France," *French History* 2 (1988): 133.

39. A. F. Orbaan, *Documenti sul barocco in Roma* (Rome: Società Romana di Storia Patria, 1920), 1:283, quoting from the avviso in Biblioteca Apostolica Vaticana, Urbinati latini, 1079, fol. 292.

40. *Morandi Trial*, fol. 572r.

41. *Edizione nazionale delle opere di Galileo Galilei* (Florence: Giunti-Barbera, 1967), 14:107, letter dated May 24, 1630.

42. *Morandi Trial*, fol. 667r.

CHAPTER SEVEN
HEAVENLY BODIES

1. *Morandi Trial*, fol. 746r.

2. There is no point in listing the entire literature here. Among the more specific of recent works, limited to Spain, is Stephen Haliczer, *Sexuality in the Confessional* (New York: Oxford University Press, 1996). Also note Oscar Di Simplicio, "Perpetuas: The Women Who Kept Priests, Siena, 1600–1800," trans. Mary M. Gallucci, in Edward Muir and Guido Ruggiero, eds., *History from Crime* (Baltimore: Johns Hopkins University Press, 1994), pp. 32–64. On the other hand, Jean Leclercq, *The Love of Learning and the Desire for God: A Study of Monastic Culture* (New York: Fordham University Press, 1982).

3. *Morandi Trial*, fol. 746v.

4. Ibid., fol. 740v. Letter to Maggi from Morandi, 12 June, 1626, reporting a communication from the general of the order.

5. Ibid., fol. 676r, letter dated March 1627.

6. Ibid., fol. 678r, letter dated April 6, 1629.

7. Marc Fumaroli, "Introduction," in Françoise Wacquet, *Rhétorique et poétique chrétiennes. Bernardo Perfetti et la poésie improvisée dans l'Italie du dixhuitième siècle* (Florence: Olschki, 1992), p. 22. The Blind Man of Forlì is mentioned in Traiano Boccalini, *Ragguagli di Parnaso*, vol. 2, ed. Luigi Firpo (Bari: Laterza, 1948), Centuria 2, no. 18.

8. *Morandi Trial*, fol. 685r.

9. To be sure, even the most adventurous clearly had nothing to do with the tradition of erotic poetry explored by Riccardo Reim and Antonio Veneziani, eds., *L'altra faccia della poesia italiana. Dal Poliziano al De Amicis* (Milan: Savelli, 1982), or Marisa Milani, ed., *Contro le puttane. Rime venete del XVI sec.* (Bassano: Tassotti, 1994).

10. *Morandi Trial*, fol. 682r.

11. On which, see Ugo Enrico, *Il Latino maccaronico* (Florence: Le Monnier, 1959); and an example: *Facetiae facetiarum* (Pathopoli [= Leyden]: "Gelastinum Severum," 1645).

12. Compare Lubin Eilhard, *Anacreontis . . . carmina* (Rostock: Mylander, 1597). Some pleasing verses of Horace in this meter are noted in William Ramsay, *A Manual of Latin Prosody* (London: Charles Griffin and Co., 1870), p. 201.

13. On this topic, Eva Cantarella, *Bisexuality in the Ancient World* (New Haven: Yale University Press, 1992).

14. Used by Michael Rocke as a frontispiece for his *Forbidden Friendships: Homosexuality and Male Culture in Renaissance Florence* (New York: Oxford University Press, 1966), but, oddly, not explained. Enlarging on a similar theme, Kent Gerard and Gert Hekema, eds., *The Pursuit of Sodomy: Male Homosexuality in Renaissance and Enlightenment Europe* (New York: Harrington Park Press, 1989).

15. Antonio Rocco, *Alcibiade fanciullo a scuola*, ed. Laura Coci (Rome: Salerno Editrice, 1988), p. 86. See also his *"Della bruttezza," e "Amore è puro interesse,"* ed. Walter Lupi (Pisa: ETS Editrice, 1990). On him, Giorgio Spini, *Ricerca dei libertini. La teoria dell'impostura delle religioni nel Seicento italiano* (Florence: La Nuova Italia, 1983), pp. 165–66.

16. *Voyage en Italie*, ed. Maurice Rat (Paris: Garnier, 1956), p. 120. For the repression of an alleged homosexual subculture among priests in Valencia, Rafael Carrasco, *Inquisición y represión sexual en Valencia: Historia de los sodomitas* (Barcelona: Laertes, 1985). In general, Nicholas Davidson, "Theology, Nature and the Law: Sexual Sin and Sexual Crime in Italy from the 14th to the 17th Century," in Trevor Dean and K.J.P. Lowe, eds., *Crime, Society and the Law in Renaissance Italy* (Cambridge: Cambridge University Press, 1994), pp. 74–98; Oscar Di Simplicio, "Sulla sessualità illecita in Antico Regime: secoli 17–18," in Luigi Berlinguer and F. Colao, eds., *Crimine, giustizia e società veneta in età moderna* (Milan: Giuffré, 1989), pp. 633–75.

17. Judith Brown, *Immodest Acts: The Life of a Lesbian Nun in Renaissance Italy* (Oxford: Oxford University Press, 1986).

18. Concerning libertinism, I consulted Sergio Zoli, *Europa libertina tra Controriforma e Illuminismo. L'oriente' dei libertini e le origini dell'Illuminismo* (Bologna: Cappelli, 1989); Tullio Gregory, *Etica e religione nella critica libertina* (Naples: Guida, 1986), pp. 54, 104, 108; as well as Tullio Gregory, ed., *Ricerche su letteratura libertina e letteratura clandestina nel Seicento. Atti del Convegno di Genova, 30 ottobre-1 novembre, 1980* (Florence: La Nuova Italia, 1981); Sergio Bertelli, ed., *Il libertinismo in Europa* (Milan-Naples: Ricciardi, 1980), chapters by Giuseppe Ricuperati, Anna Maria Battista, Cesare Vasoli, and Valerio Marchetti; René Pintard, *Le libertinage érudit dans la primière moitié du dix-septième siècle* (Paris, 1943; reprint, Geneva: Slatkine, 1983), esp. part 1, chap. 1: "L'impiété dans les moeurs"; Lucio Pala, *L'idea di "popolo" in Francia nel secolo XVII* (Milan: Editoriale Universitario, 1991); Lorenzo Bianchi, *Rinascimento e libertinismo. Studi su Gabriel Naudé* (Naples: Bibliopolis, 1996); and others mentioned below.

19. On him, see Spini, *Ricerca dei libertini*, pp. 139, 141. A somewhat eccentric interpretation is Luigi Corvaglia, *Le opere di Giulio Cesare Vanini e le loro fonti*, 4 vols. (Galatina: Congedo, 1994).

20. Consulted in the French version, *Les livres de Hierosme Cardanus . . . intitulez de la subtilité*, trans. Richard Le Blanc (Rouen: du Bosc, 1642), Book 13. On which, see Alfonso Ingegno, *Saggio sulla filosofia di Cardano* (Florence: Sansoni, 1980), pp. 209ff.

21. On which, Jean Toscan, *Le carnaval du langage. Le lexique erotique des poètes de l'équivoque de Burchiello à Marino, XVe-XVIIe siècles*, 4 vols. (Lille: Presses Universitaires de Lille, 1981).

22. I compared *La Murtoleide. Fischiate del Cavalier Marino* (Spira: Starck, 1629), fischiata xl.

23. *La Marineide. Risposta che fa'l Murtola al Cavalier Marino* (Spira: Starck, 1629), risata iii.

24. For what follows, Francesco Guardiani, ed., *Lectura Marini* (Ottowa: Dovehouse, 1989), especially the chapters on Canto 7 and Canto 8 by, respectively, Valeria Giannantonio and Marziano Guglielminetti at pp. 103–20 and 121–38; and Guardiani, *La meravigliosa retorica dell'Adone di Giambattista Marino* (Florence: Olschki, 1989).

25. Giambattista Marino, *Adone*, ed. Giovanni Pozzi (Milan: Mondadori, 1976), 6:15–16.

26. Ibid., 8:143.

27. Ibid., 8:148, ll. 1–2.

CHAPTER EIGHT
CLEAN TEETH, PURE SOULS

1. Robert Burton, *The Anatomy of Melancholy*, ed. Thomas C. Faulkner et al. (Oxford: Clarendon Press, 1989), vol. 1.

2. Keith Thomas, *Religion and the Decline of Magic* (New York: Scribners, 1971), chaps. 1–2.

3. Compare Roy Porter, *Health For Sale: Quackery in England, 1660–1850* (Manchester: Manchester University Press, 1989), chap. 2. In general, for what

follows, Gianna Pomata, *La promessa di guarigione. Malati e curatori in antico regime: Bologna, 16–18 sec.* (Bari: Laterza, 1994); as well as Leslie Clarkson, *Death, Disease and Famine in Pre-Industrial England* (New York: St. Martin's, 1975); Lucinda McCray Beier, *Sufferers and Healers: The Experience of Illness in Seventeenth-Century London* (London: Routledge, 1987); Roy Porter and W. F. Bynum, eds., *Living and Dying in London* (London: Wellcome Institute for the History of Medicine, 1991), especially the essays by Rosemary Weinstein and Andrew Wear; Marcel Sendrail et al., *Histoire culturelle de la maladie* (Toulouse: Editions Privat, 1980).

4. On which, see Norbert Elias, *The Court Society* (New York: Pantheon Books, 1983), chaps. 2, 4, 7; and on Renaissance moral philosophy in general, Eugenio Garin, *L'umanesimo italiano: filosofia e vita civile nel Rinascimento* (Bari: Laterza, 1952). Walter Ong's expression is in "The Shifting Sensorium," David Howes, ed., *The Varieties of Sensory Experience: A Sourcebook in the Anthropology of the Senses* (Toronto: University of Toronto Press, 1991).

5. Juan Luis Vives, *On Assistance to the Poor*, trans. Alice Tobriner (Toronto: University of Toronto Press, 1999), p. 55.

6. Apart from our manuscript, see the facial care recipes in Leonardo Fioravanti, *Del compendio de' secreti rationali, libri cinque* (Venice: Heredi Sessa, 1581), p. 133. On the whole tradition, there is William Eamon, *Science and the Secrets of Nature: Books of Secrets in Medieval and Modern Culture* (Princeton: Princeton University Press, 1994). Also, Fenja Gunn, *The Artificial Face: A History of Cosmetics* (New York: Hippocrene Books, 1973), as well as John Woodforde, *The History of Vanity* (New York: St. Martin's, 1992). Compare Neville Williams, *Powder and Paint: A History of the Englishwoman's Toilet, Elizabeth I to Elizabeth II* (New York: Longmans, 1957).

7. Johann Jacob Wecker, *De secretis libri xvii ex variis authoribus collecti* (Basel: Conrad Waldkirch, 1598), p. 135.

8. Ascaris lumbricoides or tapeworm was later described by Edward Tyson in the *Philosophical Transactions* of 1683, and in the early twentieth century cured by a liquid tract of felix mas, male fern, and a calomine purgative. So says the *Encyclopedia Britannica.*

9. Celsus, *De medicina* 1:437.

10. *Morandi Trial*, fol. 823v.

11. Ibid., fol. 888r.

12. Ibid., fol. 881r.

13. Ibid., fol. 881v.

14. Ibid., fol. 824r.

15. Ibid., fol. 834v.

16. Ibid.

17. Ibid., fol. 830v.

18. Patrick Brehal, ed., *Les admirables secrets d'Albert le Grand* (Paris: Nouvelle Office d'Edition, 1965), p. 248. Concerning Renaissance necromancy, Richard Kieckhefer, *Forbidden Rites: A Necromancer's Manual of the Fifteenth Century* (University Park: Penn State University Press, 1997).

19. *Morandi Trial*, fol. 821r; compare Wecker, *De secretis*, p. 110.

20. I saw the French version, *Le jardin medicinale enrichi de plusieurs et divers remèdes et secrets* (Geneva: Durant, 1578).

21. *Morandi Trial*, fol. 888r. I used Ruscelli, *De' secreti* (Venice: Biagio Maldura, 1683), p. 459.

22. Celsus, *De medicina*, 2:47.

23. *Morandi Trial*, fol. 827r. Cf. Celsus, *De medicina*, 1:308 and 2:6.

24. *Morandi Trial*, fol. 892v. Cf. Celsus, *De medicina*, 2:61, 65.

25. A partial bibliography could be misleading. Concerning the relation between learned and popular culture, the obligatory reference on this period is Carlo Ginzburg, *The Cheese and the Worms*, trans. John and Anne Tedeschi (Baltimore: Johns Hopkins University Press, 1975); but see the article by Paola Zambelli, "Uno, due, tre mille Menocchio," *Archivio storico italiano* 137 (1979): 51–90, to which Ginzburg replies in the introduction to this American edition of his work. In general, Peter Burke, *Popular Culture*, rev. ed. (Brookfield, Vt.: Ashgate, 1994). An interesting attempt to collect information about elite-popular correspondences is *Scienze credenze occulte. Livelli di cultura. Convegno internazionale di studio. Firenze 26–30 giugno 1980* (Florence: Olschki, 1982).

26. *Morandi Trial*, fol. 826v.

27. Ibid., fol. 838r.

28. J. G. Frazer, *The Golden Bough* (New York: Macmillan, 1917), vol. 1, chap. 3; and "Un segreto per far morire la persona del re," in Edward Muir and Guido Ruggiero, *History from Crime* (Baltimore: Johns Hopkins University Press, 1994). For modern equivalents, compare Ernesto De Martino, *Sud e magia* (Milan: Feltrinelli, 1959).

29. Joseph Bidez et al., eds., *Catalogue des manuscrits alchémiques grecs* (Bruxelles: Lamertin, 1928), vol. 6. The work is now known as the *Hieratic Art*. Here again, the bibliography is too vast to summarize. In general, M. L. Bianchi, *Signatura rerum. Segni, magia e conoscenza da Paracelso a Leibniz* (Rome: Edizioni dell'Ateneo, 1987); Ruth Hagengruber, *Tommaso Campanella: Eine Philosophie der Ähnlichkeit* (Sankt Augustin: Academic Verlag, 1994); and Michael Mönnich, *Tommaso Campanella. Sein Beitrag zur Medizin und Pharmazie in der Renaissance* (Stuttgart: Wissenschaftliche Verlagsgesellschaft, 1990), esp. chap. 5, "Naturphilosophische Grundlagen." In addition, the articles in Ingrid Merkel and Allen G. Debus, eds., *Hermeticism and the Renaissance: Intellectual History and the Occult in Early Modern Europe* (Washington, D.C.: Folger Books, 1988), and Cesare Vasoli, "Ermetismo e cabala nel tardo Rinascimento e primo Seicento," in Fabio Troncarelli, ed., *La città dei segreti* (Milan: Angeli, 1989), pp. 103–118. Our protagonists were of course of a far different sort than the one delineated by Marion Leathers Kuntz in *Guillaume Postel, Prophet of the Restitution of All Things: His Life and Thought* (Boston: Nijhoff, 1981).

30. *Morandi Trial*, fol. 840v.

31. On Paracelsus, I follow Walter Pagel, *Paracelsus: An Introduction to Philosophical Medicine in the Era of the Renaissance* (Basel: S. Karger, 1958), p. 146. In addition, Allen Debus, *The Chemical Philosophy* (New York: Science History Publications, 1975), 1:91ff.

32. *Magia naturalis libri XX* (Hannover: Wecker, 1619), Book 1, chap. 13.

33. Pagel, *Paracelsus*, p. 63.

34. Allen Debus, *Man and Nature in the Renaissance* (Cambridge: Cambridge University Press, 1979), p. 13. Concerning his system, the articles in *Giambattista Della Porta nell'Europa del suo tempo* (Naples: Guida, 1990), especially those by Gioacchino Papparelli and Helène Vedrine.

35. Hermes Trismegistus, *A Discourse of Mind to Hermes*, in *Hermetica* 1 (1924): 221, ed. Walter Scott, cited in Debus, *Man and Nature*, p. 33. Concerning the Hermes forgery, Anthony Grafton, *Forgers and Critics* (Princeton: Princeton University Press, 1990), chap. 3.

36. The Aristotelian reference is in *De Coelo*, 1:3.

37. *Opere* (Basel, 1576), III, i, pp. 532–33, *De vita coelitis comparanda*, Book 3. On which, see the introduction by Albano Biondi to Ficino, *De vita*, ed. Albano Biondi and Giuliano Pisani (Pordenone: Edizioni Biblioteca dell'Immagine, 1991).

38. Paracelsus, *Archidoxes*, trans. J. H. (London: Brewster, 1660), Book 4, p. 35.

39. Ibid., Book 4, p. 39.

40. Ibid., Book 4, p. 38.

41. Agrippa, *De occulta philosophia* (Cologne: Johann Soter, 1533), 1, chap. 14.

42. *Morandi Trial*, fol. 537r and ff. Letter from Agostino Lamponi dated January 27, 1629.

43. See for instance Agrippa, *De occulta philosophia*, 1, chap. 7.

44. Paracelsus's views on distillation are in the *Volumen paramirum*.

45. *Morandi Trial*, fol. 538r.

CHAPTER NINE
THE HARMONY OF THE UNIVERSE

1. Galileo's phrase is, of course, in *Il Saggiatore* (Rome: Mascardi, 1623), p. 25. Kepler's views are analyzed in Gérard Simon, *Kepler astronome astrologue* (Paris: Gallimard, 1979), pp. 44ff.; and Judith Veronica Field, *Kepler's Geometrical Cosmology* (Chicago: University of Chicago Press, 1988). A famous attempt to join numerology to theology was Francesco Giorgio, *De harmonia mundi totius cantica tria* (Venice: In aedibus Bernardini de Vitalibus, 1525).

2. Concerning the Christian cabala: Chaim Worszubski, *Pico della Mirandola's Encounter with Jewish Mysticism* (Cambridge, Mass.: Harvard University Press, 1989), especially chap. 4; Frances Yates, *Giordano Bruno and the Hermetic Tradition*, 5th ed. (Chicago: University of Chicago Press, 1991), chap. 5.

3. I found some useful remarks in E. A. Waite, *The Holy Kabbalah* (Secaucus, N.J.: University Books, 1960), pp. 98–99, 612ff. In addition, three works by Gershom Scholem: *Major Trends in Jewish Mysticism* (Jerusalem: Schocken Publishing Institute, 1941); *La Kabbale et sa symbolique* (Paris: Payot, 1966); and *Les origines de la Kabbale* (Paris: Aubier-Montagne, 1966). Concerning Jewish magic, Erich Bischoff, *Die Mystik und Magie der Zahlen (Arithmetische Kabbalah)* (Berlin: Barsdorf, 1920). Concerning the Jewish tradition in the sixteenth century, David B. Ruderman, *Kabbalah, Magic and Science: The Cultural Universe of a Sixteenth-Century Jewish Physician* (Cambridge, Mass.: Harvard University

Press, 1988); and, in Rome, Riccardo Di Segni, "La Qabbalah nella comunità ebraica romana," in Fabio Troncarelli, ed., *La città dei segreti: magia, astrologia e cultura esoterica a Roma (secoli XV-XVIII)* (Milan: F. Angeli, 1985), pp. 119–26.

4. Karl Anton Nowotny, "The Construction of Certain Seals and Characters in the Work of Agrippa von Nettesheim," *Journal of the Warburg and Courtauld Institutes* 12 (1949): 46–57; Wilhelm Ahrens, "Studien über die 'magischen Quadrate' der Araber," *Der Islam* 7 (1917): 186–250; Gotthelf Bergstrasser, "Zu den magischen Quadraten," *Der Islam* 13 (1923): 227–35; and in general, Wolf-Dieter Müller-Jahncke, *Magie als Wissenschaft im frühen 16 Jahrhundert. Die Beziehung zwischen Magie, Medizin und Pharmazie im Werk des Agrippa von Nettesheim* (Marburg: E. Symon, 1973). A useful compendium of numerological lore is Athanasius Kircher, *Arithmologia* (Rome: Baresio, 1665); another, John Heydon, *The Holy Guide* (London, 1662), 1:17. Both add considerable material to that already published by Johann Reuchlin, *De arte cabalistica* (Hagenau: Thomas Anshelm, 1517).

5. Agrippa, *De occulta philosophia*, 2, chap. 20. Also Wayne Shumaker, *The Occult Sciences in the Renaissance* (Berkeley: University of California Press, 1979), p. 143.

6. Catherine Swietlicki, *Spanish Christian Cabala: The Works of Luis de Leon, Santa Teresa de Jesus and San Juan de la Cruz* (Columbia: University of Missouri Press, 1986), p. 89.

7. Annibale Raimondi, *Opera dell'antica et honorata scientia de Nomandia, specchio d'infiniti beni e mali che sotto il cerchio della luna possono alli viventi intervenire* (Venice: Rapirio, 1549), p. 6.

8. Domenico has not yet been identified. Concerning Bronzini there is the entry by M. Capucci in *Dizionario biografico degli Italiani* 14 (1972): 463–64.

9. *Morandi Trial*, fol. 28v. Pythagorean roots are the subject of Matila C. Ghyka, *Le nombre d'or. Rites et rythmes pythagoriciens dans la développement de la civilisation occidentale*, 2 vols. (Paris: Gallimard, 1931). The medieval background is discussed by Vincent Foster Hopper, *Medieval Number Symbolism* (New York: Columbia University Press, 1938).

10. I borrow the game analogy from Brian Vickers, "On the Function of Analogy in the Occult," in Ingrid Merkel and Allen G. Debus, eds., *Hermeticism and the Renaissance: Intellectual History and the Occult in Early Modern Europe* (Washington, D.C.: Folger Books, 1988), pp. 265–92.

CHAPTER TEN
CHARTING THE FIRMAMENT

1. *Morandi Trial*, fol. 1250r.
2. Ibid., fol. 1313r.
3. Ibid., fol. 1280r.
4. Ibid., fol. 1313r.
5. The obligatory reference concerning experiences of childhood is Philippe Ariès, *Centuries of Childhood* (New York: Vintage, 1962); which traces a picture that has subsequently been modified in Giulia Calvi, *Il contratto morale. Madri e*

figli nella Toscana moderna (Bari: Laterza, 1994), and Marina D'Amelia, ed., *Storia della maternità* (Rome-Bari: Laterza, 1997).

6. Paola Zambelli, "Many Ends of the World: Luca Gaurico Instigator of the Debate in Italy and in Germany," in Paola Zambelli, ed., *"Astrologi Hallucinati": Stars and the End of the World in Luther's Time* (Berlin-New York: de Gruyter, 1986), pp. 239–63. In addition, Robin Bruce Barnes, *Prophecy and Gnosis: Apocalypticism in the Wake of the Lutheran Reformation* (Stanford: Stanford University Press, 1988); Paul Albert Russell, "Astrology as Popular Propaganda," in Antonio Rotondò, ed., *Forme e destinazione del messaggio religioso. Aspetti della propaganda religiosa nel Cinquecento* (Florence: Olschki, 1991), pp. 165–95. Concerning the structure of astrological belief, Franz Boll et al., *Sternglaube und Sterndeutung. Die Geschichte und das Wesen der Astrologie* (1918; reprint, Darmstadt: Wissenschaftliche Buchgesellschaft, 1977), esp. chaps. 4–6; but compare Eugenio Garin, *Astrology in the Renaissance: The Zodiac of Life* (London: Routledge, 1983), chap. 1.

7. Germana Ernst, "From the Watery Trigon to the Fiery Trigon: Celestial Signs, Prophecies and History," in Paola Zambelli, ed., *"Astrologi Hallucinati,"* pp. 265–80. In addition, Enrico De Mas, *L'attesa del secolo aureo, 1603–25. Saggio di storia delle idee del secolo XVII* (Florence: Olschki, 1982), esp. chap. 1; and Ilan Rachum, "'Revolution' in Seventeenth-Century Astrology," *History of European Ideas* 18 (1994): 869–83.

8. Text reproduced in Mario Pavone, *Introduzione al pensiero di Giambattista Hodierna* (Modica: Setim, 1981), 1:153.

9. Compare Peter Laslett, *The World We Have Lost* (London: Methuen, 1965), chap. 1. In general, Keith Thomas, *Religion and the Decline of Magic* (Oxford: Oxford University Press, 1997). For another context, Hilary M. Carey, *Courting Disaster: Astrology at the English Court and University in the Later Middle Ages* (London: Macmillan, 1992), introduction.

10. On popular fears in another part of Europe, Robert Muchembled, *Culture populaire et culture des élites dans la France moderne. XVe-XVIIIe siècles* (Paris: Flammarion, 1978), chap. 1. Of course, the violence wrought on the gentry by a ruler was sometimes far less than what the gentry wrought upon each other. See Gigi Corazzol, *Cineografo di banditi su sfondo di monti: Feltre, 1634–42* (Milan: Unicopli, 1997).

11. See my "Introduzione" to Giovanni Baldinucci, *Quaderno. Guerra, peste e società a Firenze nel Seicento*, ed. Brendan Dooley, with notes by Barbara Marti Dooley (Florence: Poligrafica, 2001).

12. Bartolomeo Maranta, *Lucullianarum quaestionum libri quinque* (Basel: Oporino, 1564), p. 125. On him and on the other theorists, Bernard Weinberg, *A History of Literary Criticism in the Italian Renaissance*, 2 vols. (Chicago: University of Chicago Press, 1961).

13. Giovanni Bonifacio, *Discorso academico . . . del modo di ben formar una Tragedia* (Padova: G. B. Martini, 1624), p. 13.

14. Here and below, Alessandro Piccolomini, *Annotazioni nel libro della poetica d'Aristotile, con la traduzione del medesimo libro in volgare* (Venice: Guarisci, 1575), pp. 101–2.

15. Also note the reflections of Mario Santoro, *Fortuna, ragione e prudenza nella civiltà letteraria del Cinquecento*, 2nd ed. (Naples: Liguori, 1978).

16. Some of the examples that illustrate this paragraph are *Relazione dell'empia scelleragine dei Bernesi, Zurigani e Grigioni Heretici nella loro passata in Valtellina* (Milan: alla Regio Ducale Corte, Malatesta, 1620); *Relazione degli ultimi progressi fatti da S. A. S. [Carlo Emanuele I] nello stato di Milano* (Turin: Pizzamigli, Stampatore Ducale, 1617); *Relazione del successo nell'acquisto della villa e castello di Ottaggio, fatto dall'Altezza Serenissima Carlo Emanuele duca di Savoia, li 9 aprile, 1625* (Turin: Pizzamigli, Stampatore Ducale, 1625); and *Relazione dell'arrivo et soggiorno dell'armata del signor Duca di Guisa nella campagna e contado di Nizza e del ritorno che ella fece in Provenza dalli 13 di marzo sino alli 10 di aprile 1629* (Turin: Pizzamigli, Stampatore Ducale, 1629). In general, Gino Benzoni, *I "frutti delle armi": Volti e risvolti delle guerre nel Seicento in Italia* (Rome: Edizioni dell'Enciclopedia italiana, 1980).

17. Secondo Lancellotti, *L'hoggidì. Ovvero, il mondo non peggiore né più calamitoso del passato* (Venice: Guerigli, 1623), p. 350; in addition, p. 92.

18. Rome, Archivio di Stato, *Governatore*, Atti di Cancelleria, b. 105.

19. *Raccolta di avvertimenti e raccordi per conoscere la peste* (Venice: Ciera, 1630). In addition, *Ragioni della Repubblica Veneziana contro gli Uscochi* (Dalmazaglio: Boron, 1617 [probably Venice, 1617]); *Relazione del negotiato delli Deputati di Savoia in Milano per l'accomodamento delle differenze con Mantova* (Turin: Pizzamigli, Stampatore Ducale, 1622).

20. The first, published by Malatesta of Milan, 1610; the second, by Regettini of Venice, 1610.

21. Macerata: Martinelli, 1614.

22. Published in Venice by the firm of Discepoli, 1605.

23. *Successo d'un carbonaro morto abruciato* (Venice, 1623).

24. On this topic there are useful remarks by Enrico Stumpo, Rodolfo Savelli, Marco Cattini, Dante E. Zanetti, and Giovanni Vigo in Amelio Tagliaferri, ed., *I ceti dirigenti in Italia in età moderna e contemporanea. Atti del convegno, Cividale del Friuli, 10–12 settembre, 1983* (Udine: Del Bianco Editore, 1984); not to mention Franco Angiolini and Paolo Malanima, "Problemi di mobilità sociale tra le metà del Cinquecento ed i primi decenni del Seicento," *Società e storia* 4 (1979): 17–48; and Sandra Gasparo, "Gerarchie economiche e gerarchie sociali," *Studi storici* 21 (1980): 865–75.

25. Serra's remarks were in "Breve trattato delle cause che possono far abbondare li regni d'oro e argento" (1613), now edited by Raffaele Colapietra in *Problemi monetari negli scrittori napoletani del Seicento* (Rome: Accademia dei Lincei, 1973), pp. 179–87. Contarini's remarks are in Domenico Sella, "The Rise and Fall of the Venetian Woollen Industry," in *Crisis and Change in the Venetian Economy in the Sixteenth and Seventeenth Centuries* (London: Methuen, 1968); see also Richard T. Rapp, *Industry and Economic Decline in Seventeenth Century Venice* (Cambridge, Mass.: Harvard University Press, 1976), and the review of the latter by John Marino in *Studi storici*, 19, no. 1 (1978): 79–107. There is no point here in pursuing the polemics surrounding the important thesis of Immanuel Wallerstein, *The Modern World Economy*, vol. 1, *Capitalist Agriculture and the Origins of the European World Economy in the Sixteenth Century*, and vol. 2,

Mercantilism and the Consolidation of the European World Economy (New York: Academic Press, 1974–80), for which I refer the reader to Peter Imbush, *Das moderne Weltsystem: eine Kritik der Weltsystemtheorie Immanuel Wallersteins* (Marburg: Verlag Arbeit und Gesellschaft, 1990). An excellent summary of the economic history of Italy in this whole period is in Domenico Sella, *Italy in the Seventeenth Century* (New York: Longmans, 1997). See also Eric Cochrane, *Italy, 1530–1630*, ed. Julius Kirshner (New York: Longmans, 1988), chap. 8.

26. Also, Rosario Villari, *The Revolution of Naples*, trans. James Newell (Cambridge: Polity Press, 1993), and Antonio Calabria, *The Costs of Empire: The Finances of the Kingdom of Naples in the Time of Spanish Rule* (Cambridge: Cambridge University Press, 1991). Enrico Stumpo, *Il capitale finanziario a Roma fra Cinque e Seicento: Contributo alla storia della fiscalità pontificia in età moderna (1570–1660)* (Milan: Giuffrè, 1985); also his *Finanza e stato moderno nel Piemonte del Seicento* (Rome: Istituto Storico Italiano per l'Età Moderna e Contemporanea, 1979).

27. Brian Pullan, "The Old Catholicism, the New Catholicism and the Poor," in Giorgio Politi et al., *Timore e carità. I poveri nell'età moderna* (Cremona: Biblioteca statale e libreria civica di Cremona, 1982), p. 13.

28. Edoardo Grendi, *La repubblica aristocratica dei Genovesi* (Bologna: Il Mulino, 1987), p. 295.

29. Aurelo Musi, "Pauperismo e pensiero giuridico a Napoli nella prima metà del secolo XVII," in Politi et al., *Timore e carità*, p. 264. In general, Brian Pullan, "Poveri mendicanti e vagabondi, secoli 14–17," in Ruggiero Romano and Corrado Vivante, eds., *Storia d'Italia: Annali 1: Dal Feudalismo al Capitalismo* (Turin: Einaudi, 1978), p. 987.

30. Nicolò Barozzi and Guglielmo Berchet, *Relazioni degli stati europei lette al Senato dagli ambasciatori veneti*, ser. 3: Italia; Relazioni di Roma, vol. 1 (Venice: Naratovich, 1877), p. 200, from the report by Pietro Contarini, Extraordinary Ambassador in 1623–27.

31. *Della limosina* (Rome: Mascardi, 1611), on which, see Luigi Fiorani, "Religione e povertà. Il dibattito sul pauperismo a Roma tra Cinque e Seicento," *Ricerche per la storia religiosa di Roma* 3 (1979): 98–99.

32. *La povertà contenta descritta e dedicata ai ricchi non mai contenti* (Rome: Manelfi, 1650). Cited in Fiorani, "Religione e povertà," p. 65.

33. Vincenzo Paglia, *La pietà dei carcerati. Confraternita e società a Roma nei secoli XVI e XVIII* (Rome: Edizioni di storia e letteratura, 1980), pp. 62–65.

34. Fiorani, "Religione e povertà," p. 98.

35. Nicolò Barozzi and Guglielmo Berchet, *Relazioni degli stati europei*, p. 118, from Girolamo Giustinian, Antonio Grimani, Francesco Contarini, and Girolamo Soranzo, writing in 1621. On this topic in general, Vincenzo Monachino, *La carità cristiana in Roma* (Bologna: Cappelli, 1968). In addition, Volker Reinhardt, *Überleben in der frühneuzeitlichen Stadt. Annona und Getreideversorgung in Rom, 1563–1797*, Bibliothek des Deutschen Historischen Instituts in Rom, Band 72 (Tübingen: Max Niemeyer, 1991), pp. 114ff.

36. Quoted in James Cushman Davis, *The Decline of the Venetian Nobility as a Ruling Class*, Studies in History and Political Science, ser. 80, vol. 2 (Baltimore: Johns Hopkins University Press, 1962), p. 45. Like Davis, I too am drawn to

Thorstein Veblen, *The Theory of the Leisure Class* (1899), in this connection. In addition, Domenico Sella, "L'economia," in Gaetano Cozzi e Paolo Prodi, *Storia di Venezia*, vol. 6, *Dal Rinascimento al Barocco* (Rome: Enciclopedia Italiana, 1994), pp. 651–712.

37. Giorgio Doria, "Investimenti della nobiltà genovese nell'edilizia di prestigio, 1530–1630," *Studi Storici* 27 (1986): 5–55.

38. Paola Scavizzi, "Considerazioni sull'attività edilizia a Roma nella prima metà del Seicento," *Studi storici* 9 (1968): 186; but see also Peter J.A.N. Rietbergen, "Pausen, Prelaten, Bureaucraten," Ph.D. dissertation, University of Nijmegen, 1983, p. 323.

39. Jean Delumeau, *Vie économique et sociale de Rome dans la seconde moitié du XVIe siècle*, Bibliothèque des Écoles Françaises d'Athenes et de Rome, fasc. 184 (Paris: E. de Boccard, 1957–59), 1:469–84.

40. For what follows, Claudio Donati, *L'idea della nobiltà in Italia: secoli XIV-XVIII* (Bari: Laterza, 1988); and Peter Burke, *The Fortunes of the Courtier* (University Park: Penn State Press, 1995); and my own research in Venice, Archivio di Stato, Petizion, Inventari, 356:21:67, 367:32:33, 366:30:90, and elsewhere.

41. Quoted in Fiorani, "Religione e povertà," p. 64.

42. Laurie Nussdorfer, *Civic Politics in the Rome of Urban VIII* (Princeton: Princeton University Press, 1992), chaps. 3, 6; Peter Partner, *The Pope's Men: The Papal Civil Service in the Renaissance* (Oxford: Oxford University Press, 1990); Renata Ago, *Carriere e clientele nella Roma barocca* (Rome: Laterza, 1990); Maria Antonietta Visceglia, "Burocrazia, mobilità sociale e 'patronage' alla corte di Roma tra 5 e 600: alcuni aspetti del recente dibattito storiografico e prospettive di ricerca," *Roma moderna e contemporanea* 3 (1995): 11–55; and Andreas Kraus, *Das päpstliche Staatssekretariat unter Urban VIII, 1623–44* (Rome: Herder, 1964).

43. Delumeau, *Vie économique et sociale de Rome,* 1:469–84. Interesting remarks on Machiavelli's cosmos are in Anthony J. Parel, *The Machiavellian Cosmos* (New Haven: Yale University Press, 1992).

44. Justus Lipsius, *De constantia*, trans. Nathaniel Wanley (London: J. Redmayne for James Allestry, 1670), chap. 16. Richard Tuck discusses the significance of Neostoicism in *Philosophy and Government, 1572–1651* (Cambridge: Cambridge University Press, 1993), chap. 2.

45. Lipsius, *De constantia,* chap. 6.

46. Ibid., chap. 13.

47. *Morandi Trial*, fol. 755r, letter dated July 29, 1627.

CHAPTER ELEVEN
THE SCIENCE OF THE STARS

1. In general, Mary Ellen Bowden, "The Scientific Revolution in Astrology: The English Reformers, 1558–1686," Ph.D. dissertation, Yale University, 1974.

2. Rudolf Goclenius, *Uranoscopiae, Chiroscopiae, Metoposcopiae, et Ophthalmoscopiae Contemplatio* (Frankfurt, 1608), p. 272. See Anthony Grafton, *Cardano's Cosmos: The Worlds and Works of a Renaissance Astrologer* (Cambridge, Mass.: Harvard University Press, 2000), chap. 3.

3. Kepler, in *Gesammelte Werke*, ed. Franz Hammer et al. (Münich: C. H. Bech, 1969), 10:36; although in his *Tertius interveniens*, *Gesammelte Werke*, 4:161, he calls astrology astronomy's "silly little daughter."

4. Carl B. Boyer, *A History of Mathematics* (New York: John Wiley, 1968), pp. 342–45; and especially Charles Naux, *Histoire des logarithmes de Neper à Euler*, 2 vols. (Paris: Blanchard, 1971).

5. Albert Van Helden, *The Invention of the Telescope*, Transactions of the American Philosophical Society, 67 (Philadelphia: American Philosophical Society, 1977). In addition, Alexandre Koyré, *The Astronomical Revolution*, tr. R.E.W. Maddison (Ithaca: Cornell University Press, 1973).

6. The quote is in *Morandi Trial*, fol. 758r. Concerning the various methods of calculation of astrological charts, see John David North, *Horoscopes and History*, Warburg Institute Surveys, vol. 13 (London: Warburg Institute, 1986).

7. See G. Stano and F. Balsinelli, "Un illustre scienziato francescano," *Miscellanea francescana* 43 (1943): 81–149; and the article by G. Odoardi in *Dizionario biografico degli Italiani* 2 (1960): 567–68. Altobelli's chief works were *Tabulae regiae divisionum dodecim partium coeli et syderum obviationum ad mentem Ptolemaei* (Macerata: Bonomi, 1628) and *Demonstratio ostendens artem dirigendi et domificandi Ioannis de Monteregio non concordare cum doctrinam Ptolomaei* (Foligno, 1629).

8. Francis Bacon, *Advancement of Learning*, ed. Edward Creighton (New York: Colonial Press, 1900), 3:4 (p. 90 in this edition). Not in the least Whiggish is Paolo Rossi, *Francesco Bacone: Dalla magia alla scienza*, 2nd ed. (Turin: Einaudi, 1974), and especially see D. P. Walker, "Spirits in Francis Bacon," in Marta Fattori, ed., *Francis Bacon: Terminologia e fortuna nel secolo XVII* (Rome: Edizioni dell'Ateneo, 1984), pp. 315–27. Of course, I am not confusing Bacon's empiricism with the "empirics" whom he condemns. See Didier Deleule, "Experientia-experimentum chez F. Bacon," in *Francis Bacon*, pp. 59–72. From a different perspective, Stephen Gaukroger, *Francis Bacon and the Transformation of Early Modern Philosophy* (Cambridge: Cambridge University Press, 2001).

9. *Morandi Trial*, fol. 108r, Morandi deposition, July 15, 1630.

10. Here and below, *Morandi Trial*, fols. 959r and ff.

11. See, for instance, Heikki Mikkeli, *An Aristotelian Response to Renaissance Humanism: Jacopo Zabarella on the Nature of the Arts and Sciences* (Helsinki: SHS, 1992), and Charles B. Schmitt, *The Aristotelian Tradition and Renaissance Universities* (London: Variorum Reprints, 1984).

12. Egidio's translation was first published as *Liber quadripartiti* (Venice: Ratdolt, 1484). Camerarius's translation of Books 1 and 2, with parts of Books 3 and 4, was published as *Libri quattuor* (Nuremberg: Petreius, 1535); Melanchthon's was published by Oporinus at Basel in 1553; Antonio Gogava's was *Operis quadripartiti in latinum sermonem* (Louvain: Batius, 1548). This was the version used by Cardano in his commentary.

13. Compare James Lattis, *Between Copernicus and Galileo: Christopher Clavius and the Collapse of Ptolemaic Cosmology* (Chicago: University of Chicago, 1994), chap. 1. The best analysis of Ptolemy's theories and their background is still Auguste Bouché-Leclercq, *L'astrologie grecque* (Paris, 1899; reprint, Aalen: Scientia Verlag, 1979).

14. Among other studies on the impact of heliocentrism there is Michel-Pierre Lerner, *Tre saggi sulla cosmologia alla fine del Cinquecento* (Naples: Istituto Italiano per gli Studi Filosofici, 1992).

15. Here and below, *Operis quadripartiti*, I, iv.

16. Nifo's work was *De diebus criticis* (Venice: Ponti, 1504). On Girolamo Cardano's contributions concerning critical days, Nancy G. Siraisi, *The Clock and the Mirror: Girolamo Cardano and Renaissance Medicine* (Princeton: Princeton University Press, 1997), chap. 6. Pseudo-Ptolemy's *Centum Ptolomaei sententiae* was published by Aldus Manutius in Venice (1519), among others. Concerning astrology and humoral theory see Fritz Saxl, Raymond Klibansky, and Erwin Panofsky, *Saturn and Melancholy* (London: Nelson, 1964), part 2, chap. 1.

17. Germana Ernst, "Aspetti dell'astrologia e della profezia in Galileo e Campanella," in Paolo Galluzzi, ed., *Novità celesti e crisi del sapere. Atti del convegno internazionale di studi galileiani, 1982* (Florence: Giunti-Barbéra, 1984), pp. 255–66.

18. Of Offusius, note his *De divina astrorum facultate* (Paris: Royer, 1570); and see Owen Gingerich and Jerzy Dobrzycki, "The Master of the 1550 Radices: Jofrancus Offusius," *Journal of the History of Astronomy* 24 (1993): 235–54. The work in question of Robert Fludd was *Utriusque Cosmi, maioris scilicet et minoris Metaphysica, Physica atque Tecnica Historia*, vol. 1 (Oppenheim: Galler, 1617), Treatise 1, Book 2, pp. 45ff., and Treatise 1, Book 5, chap. 10, pp. 146ff. A late example of astrological medicine, among many: Giovanni Antonio Magini, *De astrologica ratione ac usu dierum criticorum* (Venice: Zennari, 1607), present in the Santa Prassede library. For what precedes, Mary Ellen Bowden, "The Scientific Revolution in Astrology," chap. 2; Lynn Thorndike, *A History of Magic and Experimental Science* (New York: Columbia University Press, 1941, 1958), 6:113 and 7:98; on Fludd, Allen Debus, *The Chemical Philosophy: Paracelsian Science and Medicine in the Sixteenth and Seventeenth Centuries* (New York: Science History Publications, 1977); William H. Huffman, *Robert Fludd and the End of the Renaissance* (London: Routledge, 1988).

19. Modified from Kepler, *The Secret of the Universe*, trans. A. M. Duncan (New York: Abaris, 1981), pp. 115–16. In addition, Bowden, "The Scientific Revolution in Astrology," p. 112. In addition to Gérard Simon, *Kepler: Astronome, Astrologue* (Paris: Gallimard, 1979), there is Fernand Hallyn, *Structure poétique du monde: Copernic, Kepler* (Paris: Seuil, 1987); J. V. Field, "A Lutheran Astrologer: Johannes Kepler," *Archive for the History of the Exact Sciences* 31 (1984): 189–272; Bruce Stephenson, *Kepler's Physical Astronomy* (New York: Springer Verlag, 1987); and, especially, Owen Gingerich, "Johannes Kepler and the New Astronomy," *Quarterly Journal of the Royal Astronomical Society* 13 (1972): 346–73.

20. *De fundamentis astrologiae certioribus*, in *Gesammelte Werke*, 4:418–21, Thesis 4.

21. *Gesammelte Werke*, 6:264–86, quoted in Thorndike, *History of Magic and Experimental Science*, 7:22.

22. For the different chapter divisions in the various editions see Wolfgang Hübner's edition, more correctly entitled *Apotelesmatika*, of Ptolemy's *Tetrabiblos* (Stuttgart and Leipzig: B. G. Teubner, 1998), pp. vii–li. Numbers in pa-

rentheses in my translation from the manuscript indicate the order in which chapters were placed. There was no numeration in the original.

23. Compare Bouché-Leclercq, *L'astrologie grecque*, p. 177; for the preceding clause, p. 245.

24. Most probably, the book of Albumasar present in the library was the *Flores Astrologiae*, first printed by Sessa in Venice, 1488.

25. *Morandi Trial*, fol. 943r.

CHAPTER TWELVE
THE BUSINESS OF ASTROLOGY

1. *Morandi Trial*, fol. 183r, deposition of Marcantonio Conti, August 6, 1630. Concerning the astrological tradition in Rome, Germana Ernst, "Astrology, Religion and Politics in Counter Reformation Rome," in Stephen Pumfrey, Paolo L. Rossi, and Maurice Slawinski, eds., *Science, Culture and Popular Belief in Renaissance Europe* (Manchester: Manchester University Press, 1991).

2. The second witness was Francesco Modesti, who deposed on September 9, 1630, *Morandi Trial*, fol. 436v.

3. Ibid., fol. 504r, deposition of Agostino Lamponi, November 5, 1630.

4. Concerning the entrepreneurial aspects of astrology, apart from Anthony Grafton, *Cardano's Cosmos*, see Pierre Brind'Amour, *Nostradamus astrophile: les astres et l'astrologie dans la vie et l'oeuvre de Nostradamus* (Ottawa: Presses de l'Université d'Ottawa, 1993).

5. *Morandi Trial*, fol. 662r.

6. For what follows I rely much on Enrico Stumpo, *Il capitale finanziario a Roma fra Cinque e Seicento*, pp. 99ff.; and Delumeau, vol. 2, pt. 3, chap. 2, pp. 751ff.

7. Pascoli's early-eighteenth-century *Testamento politico* is analyzed by Nicola La Marca, *Tentativi di riforme economiche nel Settecento romano* (Roma: Bulzoni, 1969), pp. 55–56.

8. Enrico Stumpo, *Il capitale finanziario*, p. 60; also, Michele Monaco, *La situazione della R.C.A. nell'anno 1525* (Rome: Biblioteca dell'Arte Editrice, 1960), p. 47; and Claudio Rotelli, *La distribuzione della proprietà terriera e delle colture ad Imola nei XVII e XVIII secoli* (Milan: Giuffrè, 1966), chap. 3. I found particularly helpful the article "Censi" in Gaetano Moroni, *Dizionario di erudizione storico-ecclesiastica*, 11 (Venice: Tipografia Emiliana, 1841), pp. 80–82.

9. *Morandi Trial*, fol. 535r.

10. Ibid., fol. 919r, Francesco Lamponi's undated letter to his lawyer.

11. Ibid., fols. 860r-61v, 920r, including a list of Agostino's books.

12. The works in question were Pietro Andrea Mattioli, *Compendium de plantis omnibus* (Venice: Valgrisi, 1571), and Valerius Cordus, *Pharmacorum conficientorum ratio* (Nuremburg: Petreius, 1546).

13. *Morandi Trial*, fol. 1411v.

14. I learned this by studying Henrik Rantzau, *Tractatus astrologicus de genethliacorum thematum iudiciis pro singulis nati accidentibus* . . . (Frankfurt: Wechel, 1593), p. 104. Concerning the Arab astrologers, Edward S. Kennedy,

Astronomy and Astrology in the Medieval Islamic World (Aldergate: Variorum Reprints, 1998).

15. *Morandi Trial*, fol. 1427r.
16. Henrik Rantzau, *Tractatus astrologicus*, p. 50.
17. *Morandi Trial*, fol. 856r, prediction in Lamponi's possession.
18. Ibid., fol. 536r, letter dated March 21, 1628.

CHAPTER THIRTEEN
DE RE PUBLICA

1. On the Swedish empire, Michael Roberts, *Gustavus Adolfus and the Rise of Sweden* (London: English Universities Press, 1973); in addition, Geoffrey Parker et al., *The Thirty Years War* (London: Routledge, 1984), part 2, chap. 3 (E. Ladewig Petersen), part 4, chap. 1 (Bodo Nischan), part 4, chap. 4 (Richard J. Bonney); J. H. Elliott, *Olivares: The Statesman in an Age of Decline* (New Haven: Yale University Press, 1986), part 1, chap. 2; part 3, chap. 1; Jonathan I. Israel, *The Dutch Republic and the Hispanic World, 1606–1661* (Oxford: Clarendon Press, 1982), chaps. 3–6.
2. Angelika Geiger, *Wallensteins Astrologie. Eine kritische Überprüfung der Überlieferung nach dem gegenwärtigen Quellenbestand* (Graz: Akademische Druck- und Verlagsanstalt, 1983). In general, B. Bauer, "Die Rolle des Hofastrologen und Hofmathematikus als fürstlicher Berater," in August Buck, ed., *Höfischer Humanismus* (Weinheim: VCH, 1989), pp. 93–117.
3. *Morandi Trial*, fol. 93v. Concerning political satire, *Pasquinate del Cinque e Seicento*, a cura di Valerio Marucci (Rome: Salerno Editrice, 1988).
4. For what follows, R. A. Stradling, *Spain's Struggle for Europe, 1598–1668* (London: Hambledon Press, 1994); for the political situation in Italy, still useful is Romolo Quazza, *Preponderanza spagnuola, 1559–1700* (Milan: Vallardi, 1950), part 2, chap. 2.
5. Concerning this commerce, Sandro Bulgarelli, *Il giornalismo a Roma nel Seicento* (Rome: Bulzoni, 1988); Mario Infelise, "Gli avvisi di Roma. Informazione e politica nel secolo XVII," in Gianvittorio Signorotto and Maria Antonietta Visceglia, eds., *La Corte di Roma tra Cinque e Seicento. "Teatro" della politica europea* (Rome: Bulzoni, 1998), pp. 189–205; Infelise, "Professione reportista. Copisti e gazzettieri nella Venezia del Seicento," in Sandro Gasparri, Giovanni Levi, and P. Moro, eds., *Itinerari per Venezia* (Bologna: Il Mulino, 1997), pp. 183–209; as well as my *Social History of Skepticism* (Baltimore: Johns Hopkins University Press, 1999), chaps. 1–2.
6. For what follows, *Morandi Trial*, fols. 146r, 151v, 172r, 174v.
7. Ibid., fol. 176v.
8. Ibid., fol. 680r, letter from Diego de Franchi in Bergamo, March 13, 1630.
9. Ibid., fol. 191r, deposition of August 9, 1630.
10. Ibid., fol. 576r.
11. Particulars can be found in J. H. Elliott, "Spain and the War," in Geoffrey Parker et al., *The Thirty Years War*, part 3, chap. 4. See especially David Parrott, "The Mantuan Succession, 1627–31: A Sovereignty Dispute in Early Modern Europe," *English Historical Review* 112, no. 445 (1995): 20–65.

12. Concerning factionalism within Rome, Riccardo Bassani and Fiora Bellini, *Caravaggio assassino. La carriera di un "valenthuomo" fazioso nella Roma della Controriforma* (Rome: Donzelli, 1994), pp. 137ff. For a slightly earlier period, A. Enzo Baldini, *Puntigli spagnoleschi e intrighi politici nella Roma di Clemente VIII* (Milan: Angeli, 1981).

13. The engraving is reproduced in Mario Caravale and Alberto Caracciolo, *Lo stato pontificio da Martino V a Pio IX* (Turin: UTET, 1978), facing p. 417; and explained in more detail in J. A. F. Orbaan, *Rome ouder Clemens VIII (Aldobrandini), 1592–1605* ('s Gravenhage: Martinus Nijhoff, 1920), p. 54.

14. *Morandi Trial*, fol. 149r, deposition of Matteo Vincenteschi, August 28, 1630.

15. Ibid., fol. 143r, deposition of Constantino Amati, July 27, 1630.

16. Rome's absolutism is analyzed in Paolo Prodi, *The Papal Prince: One Body and Two Souls: The Papal Monarchy in Early Modern Europe*, trans. Susan Haskins (Cambridge: Cambridge University Press, 1987); but see Pierangelo Schiera, "Legittimità, disciplina, istituzioni: tre presupposti per la nascita dello stato moderno," in Giorgio Chittolini, Anthony Molho, and Pierangelo Schiera, eds., *Origini dello stato. Processi di formazione statale in Italia fra medioevo ed età moderna* (Bologna: Il Mulino, 1994), and the English translation by Barbara Marti Dooley et al., *The Origins of the State in Italy, 14th–16th Centuries*, ed. Julius Kirshner (Chicago: University of Chicago Press, 1995).

17. Concerning the cardinalate as an international aristocracy, G. Fragnito, "Le corti cardinalizie nella Roma del Cinquecento," *Rivista storica italiana* 106 (1994): 5–41; and C. Weber, *"Senatus divinus." Verbogene Strukturen im Kardinalskollegium des frühen Neuzeit (1500–1800)* (Frankfurt am Main: Peter Lang, 1996). A particularly interesting bibliographical study is Maria Antonietta Visceglia, "'La giusta statera de' porporati.' Sulla composizione e rappresentazione del sacro collegio nella prima metà del Seicento," *Roma moderna e contemporanea* 4 (1996): 167–211.

18. Geoffrey Parker, *The Military Revolution: Military Innovation and the Rise of the West* (Cambridge: Cambridge University Press, 1988), chap. 1; Paul Kennedy, *The Rise and Fall of the Great Powers* (New York: Random House, 1987), chap. 2. On incipient national consciousness, Liah Greenfeld, *Nationalism: Five Paths to Modernity* (Cambridge, Mass.: Harvard University Press, 1992), introduction.

19. *Morandi Trial*, fol. 442r, deposition of Francesco Ripa, September 10, 1630, concerning Morandi's activities.

20. Ibid., fol. 263v, deposition dated August 18, 1630.

21. Nicolò Barozzi and Guglielmo Berchet, *Relazioni degli stati europei lette al Senato dagli ambasciatori veneti*, ser. 3: Italia; Relazioni di Roma (Venice: Naratovich, 1877), 1:170ff.

22. Ibid., 1:271.

23. Ibid., 1:273.

24. Ibid., 1:268.

25. Ibid., 1:281.

26. *Morandi Trial*, fols. 147r, 229r.

27. *Discorsi ai principi ed altri scritti filo-ispanici*, ed. Luigi Firpo (Turin: Chiantore, 1945), pp. 38, 159. Also note *City of the Sun*, ed. Romano Amerio, in *Opere di Giordano Bruno e Tommaso Campanella* (Milano-Napoli: Ricciardi, 1956), p. 1115. In general, Enrico De Mas, *L'attesa del secolo aureo, 1603–25. Saggio di storia delle idee del secolo XVII* (Florence: Olschki, 1982).

28. Interesting reflections on this theme in René Taylor, "Architecture and Magic: Considerations on the Idea of the Escorial," in Douglas Fraser et al., eds., *Essays on the History of Architecture Presented to Rudolf Wittkower* (London: Phaidon, 1967), pp. 81–109; as well as Janet Cox-Rearick, *Dynasty and Destiny in Medici Art: Pontormo, Leo X and the Two Cosimos* (Princeton: Princeton University Press, 1984), chaps. 7–9; and Mario Biagioli, *Galileo Courtier* (Berkeley: University of California Press, 1993), chaps. 1–2.

29. Domenico's text appears in two versions, one in his own hand in *Morandi Trial*, fol. 15r-v; one in Morandi's hand at fol. 17r-v. For what follows, see also Warren Kenton, *The Anatomy of Fate: Kabbalistic Astrology* (London: Rider, 1978).

30. Domenico's analysis is in *Morandi Trial*, fols. 18r-19v.

31. The same conspiracy, planned in 1618, dramatized by Thomas Otway in *Venice Preserv'd* (London, 1685), and analyzed by Giorgio Spini in "La congiura degli Spagnoli contro Venezia del 1618," *Archivio storico italiano* 107 (1949): 16–53; 108 (1950): 159–74. Concerning the myth, Paolo Preto, "Le 'paure' della società veneziana," Gaetano Cozzi e Paolo Prodi, eds., *Storia di Venezia*, vol. 6, *Dal Rinascimento al Barocco* (Rome: Enciclopedia Italiana, 1994), pp. 228–33; Richard Mackenney, "'A Plot Discover'd'? Myth, Legend and the 'Spanish' Conspiracy against Venice in 1618," in John Martin and Dennis Romano, eds., *Venice Reconsidered: The History and Civilization of an Italian City-State, 1297–1797* (Baltimore: Johns Hopkins University Press, 2000), pp. 185–216.

32. Morandi's explanations appear in *Morandi Trial*, fol. 16r. Compare Lorenzo Del Panta, *Le epidemie nella storia demografica italiana, secoli 16–18* (Turin: Loescher, 1980), chap. 4.

CHAPTER FOURTEEN
OCCULT POLITICS

1. *Morandi Trial*, fol. 750r, letter dated May 15, 1629. Compare Lorraine Daston and Katherine Park, *Wonders and the Order of Nature, 1150–1750* (New York: Zone Books, 1998), chaps. 5–6.

2. *Morandi Trial*, fol. 575r.

3. Michele Mercati, *De gli obelischi di Roma* (Rome: Domenico Basa, 1589); Piero Valeriano, *Hieroglifici: ovvero commentari delle occulte significationi degli Egittiani* (Venice: Franceschi, 1602), Book 9, chap. 1; Book 20, chaps. 28, 30, 43. In general, Leslie Greener, *The Discovery of Egypt* (London: Cassell, 1966); Giovanni Cipriani, *Gli obelischi egizi. Politica e cultura nella Roma barocca* (Florence: Olschki, 1993); Michel Dewachter and Alain Fouchard, eds., *L'égyptologie et les Champollion* (Grenoble: Presses universitaires de Grenoble, 1994). For the uses of hieroglyphs in the Renaissance, Ludwig Volkmann, *Bilderschriften der*

Renaissance. Hieroglyphik und Emblematik in ihren Beziehungen und Fortwirkungen (Leipzig: Hiersemann, 1923).

4. The two versions are mentioned by Secondo Lancellotti, *L'Hoggidì* (Venice: Guerigli, 1623), p. 92. A reproduction is in Paolo Arrigoni and Achille Bertarelli, *Le stampe storiche conservate nella raccolta del Castello Sforzesco* (Milan: Tipografia del "Popolo d'Italia," 1932), facing p. 8.

5. *Morandi Trial*, fol. 258r. The work occurs in a list of books belonging to Fra Alberto from Santa Maria sopra Minerva at fol. 476r.

6. *Profetie dell'abate Gioacchino et di Anselmo Vescovo di Marisco, con l'imagine in dissegno intorno a' pontefici passati, e ch'hanno a venire* (Padova: Tozzi, 1625), no. 5. I compared *Vaticinia sive prophetiae abbatis Joachimi, et Anselmi Episcopi Mariscani, cum imaginibus aere incisis, correctione et pulchritudine plurium manuscriptorum exemplarium opere et variarum imaginibus aliis ante hoc impressis* (Venice: Porri, 1589). The latter edition has copper engravings rather than the usual woodcuts. Concerning the manuscript record, Marjorie Reeves, *The Influence of Prophecy in the Middle Ages: A Study of Joachimism* (Oxford: Clarendon Press, 1969), p. 523. In general, Giorgio Cracco, *Gioacchino da Fiore e il gioacchinismo* (Naples: Liguori, 1976).

7. *Morandi Trial*, fol. 258r.

8. *Profetie dell'abate Gioacchino*, no. 9.

9. Ibid., no. 10.

10. Ibid., no. 2.

11. Lodovico Dolce, *Imprese nobili et ingegnose di diversi principi et d'altri personaggi illustri nell'armi e nelle lettere* (Venice: Girolamo Porro, 1578), n.p.; Claudio Donati, *L'idea di nobiltà in Italia: secoli XIV–XVIII* (Rome: Laterza, 1988); Robert Klein, "La théorie de l'expression figurée dans les traités italiens sur les 'imprese,' 1555–1612," *Bibliothèque d'humanisme et Renaissance* 19 (1957): 320–42; Lina Bolzoni, *La stanza della memoria. Modelli letterari e iconografici nell'età della stampa* (Turin: Einaudi, 1995), chap. 5.

12. Alessandro Farra, *Settenario dell'humana riduttione* (Casal Maggiore: Farra di Bartoli, 1571), chap. 7.

13. *Morandi Trial*, fols. 230ff. contain a draft copy of the writing in Morandi's hand and a fine copy in another hand.

14. In episodes best recounted by William J. Bouwsma, *Venice and the Defense of Republican Liberty* (Berkeley: University of California Press, 1968).

15. *Morandi Trial*, fol. 442r.

16. Ibid., fol. 147r.

17. Ibid., fol. 229r, deposition dated August 2, 1630.

CHAPTER FIFTEEN
THE LAST PROPHECY

1. Nicolò Barozzi and Guglielmo Berchet, *Relazioni degli stati europei lette al Senato dagli ambasciatori veneti* (Venice: Naratovich, 1877), ser. 3: Italia; Relazioni di Roma, 1:211, from the report of Pietro Contarini in 1627.

2. Cases mentioned in this paragraph are documented in Mary Ellen Bowden, "The Scientific Revolution in Astrology: The English Reformers, 1558–1686,"

Ph.D. dissertation, Yale University, 1974, p. 110; Anthony Grafton, *Cardano's Cosmos: The Worlds and Works of a Renaissance Astrologer* (Cambridge, Mass.: Harvard University Press, 1999), chaps. 2, 6.

3. Luigi Amabile, *Tommaso Campanella ne' castelli di Napoli, in Roma ed in Parigi* (Naples: Morano, 1887), 2:153, 172ff.

4. Described by Campanella in his *De siderali fato vitando*, a pirate version, published in 1629 without his knowledge, as Book 7 of his *Astrologicorum* (Leyden: Prost, 1629 [actually, Rome: Brogiotti, 1629]). See Germana Ernst, *Religione, ragione e natura. Ricerche su Tommaso Campanella e il tardo Rinascimento* (Milan: Angeli, 1991), chap. 1.

5. On this subject, Auguste Bouché-Leclercq, *L'astrologie grecque* (Paris, 1899; reprint, Aalen: Scientia Verlag, 1979), pp. 416–28. Ptolemy describes his method in Wolfgang Hübner's edition, more correctly entitled *Apotelesmatika*, of Ptolemy's *Tetrabiblos* (Stuttgart and Leipzig: B. G. Teubner, 1998), 3, 11.

6. Several versions of Urban VIII's horoscope can be found in *Morandi Trial*, with slight differences, at fols. 13r, 1050r, and 1264r.

7. No copy of Morandi's document remains. What follows is a reconstruction based on second-hand information presented in *Morandi Trial*.

8. On this topic, see my "The Ptolemaic Astrological Tradition in the Seventeenth Century: An Example from Rome," *International Journal of the Classical Tradition* 5 (1999): 546 and note.

9. Two copies of the document dated "Lyons, January 21, 1630" containing the prophecies regarding Urban VIII exist in *Morandi Trial*, both in Morandi's hand: a rough draft at fols. 90r and following; and a fine copy at fols. 486rff. Internal references demonstrate authorship by Visconti.

10. Ibid., fol. 110r, Morandi deposition, July 15, 1630.

11. Ibid., fol. 536r, letter dated March 21, 1628.

12. Ibid., fol. 110r, Morandi deposition, July 15, 1630.

13. Luigi Amabile, *Tommaso Campanella*, 2:149, quoting a report in the files of the Este secretary of state, dated May 4, 1630.

14. Galileo Galilei, *Edizione nazionale delle opere*, ed. Antonio Favaro (Florence: G. Barbera, 1967), 14:103, newsletter dated May 18, 1630.

15. Tommaso Campanella, *Lettere*, ed. Vincenzo Spampanato, Scrittori d'Italia, no. 103 (Bari: Laterza, 1927), p. 288, letter to Urban VIII dated April 9, 1630.

16. Tommaso Campanella, *Lettere*, pp. 287–88. Cited in Germana Ernst, "Scienza, astrologia e politica nella Roma barocca," in Eugenio Canone, ed., *Bibliothecae Selectae, da Cusano a Leopardi* (Florence: Olschki, 1993), p. 221.

17. Luigi Amabile, *Tommaso Campanella*, 2:150, from a report in the files of the Este secretary of state, dated May 18, 1630.

18. As later recalled by Theodore Ameyden in his manuscript *Elogia*, cited by Alexandro Bastiaanse, *Teodoro Ameyden (1586–1656). Un Neerlandese alla corte di Roma* ('s Gravenhage: Staatsdrukkerij, 1968), p. 51.

19. Tommaso Campanella, *Disputatio an bullae SS. Pontificum Sixti V et Urbani VIII contra iudiciarios calumniam in aliquo patiantur*, in his *Atheismus triumphatus* (Paris: Dubray, 1636), pp. 267–68.

20. Two references are irresistible here: first, to Clifford Geertz, *The Interpretation of Cultures* (New York: Basic Books, 1973), chap. 11; second, to Norbert Elias, *The Court Society*, trans. Edmund Jephcott (New York: Pantheon, 1983).

CHAPTER SIXTEEN
THE VENDETTA

1. *Morandi Trial*, fol. xviii. The work in question was *Oratione delle lodi di S. Cecilia, vergine e martire* (Milan: Trudate, 1599).

2. The letter to Don Carlo Scaglia is in *Morandi Trial*, 569v, dated March 15, 1630. The information about the manuscript on the conclave is in fol. 421v, deposition of Benigno Bracciolini.

3. F. Grillo, "Questioni campanelliane: la stampa fraudolenta e clandestina degli *Astrologicorum liber*," *Calabria nobilissima* 14 (1961): 69–102. According to Grillo, responding to Luigi Firpo, *Ricerche Campanelliane* (Florence: Sansoni, 1947), chap. 5, the edition was published in Rome by Brogiotti, with the false indication that it was published in Leyden by Prost in 1629.

4. Luigi Amabile, *Tommaso Campanella ne' castelli di Napoli, in Roma ed in Parigi* (Naples: Morano, 1887), 2:149, quoting a newsletter from May 4, 1630.

5. Vallombrosa, Archivio dell'Abbazia, cod. 6 II 5, fol. 73r: "Litteris saecularium relatum fuit quendam Patrem Domicanum hanc charitatem in Abbatem effecisse."

6. *Morandi Trial*, fol. 752r, letter from Valerio Lancellotto dated April 20, 1629.

7. Ibid., fol. 669r. Letter from Alberto Del Vivaio, dated June 9, 1629.

8. Ibid., c. 753r. Concerning Vivaio, Giulio Negri, *Istoria degli scrittori fiorentini* (Ferrara: Pomatelli, 1722), p. 11.

9. Concerning Pico's arguments and their significance, Paola Zambelli, *L'apprendista stregone: Astrologia, cabala e arte lulliana in Pico della Mirandola e seguaci* (Venice: Marsilio, 1995). In addition, Eugenio Garin, *Astrology in the Renaissance. The Zodiac of Life* (London: Routledge, 1983), chaps. 3–4; also S. J. Tester, *A History of Western Astrology* (Woodbridge, Suffolk: Boydell Press, 1987), pp. 207–17. Still useful concerning later debates is Lynn Thorndike, *A History of Magic and Experimental Science* (New York: Columbia University Press, 1958), 7:89–152. Concerning the free will problem, Hans Baron, "Willensfreiheit und Astrologia bei Marsilio Ficino und Pico della Mirandola," in *Kultur und Universalgeschichte: Festschrift für Walter Goetz zu seinem 60 Geburtstage* (Leipzig-Berlin: G. Teubner, 1927). Concerning the wider issues, interesting reflections may be found in Paul Choisnard, *Les preuves de l'influence astrale sur l'homme* (Paris: F. Alcan, 1927).

10. On him, Christian Gottlieb Jöcher, *Allgemeine Gelehrten-Lexikon* (Hildesheim: Olms, 1961), 4:199.

11. Domenico Scevolini, *Discorso nel quale . . . si dimostra l'astrologia giudiziaria esser verissima et utilissima* (Venice: Zirletti, 1565), fols. 4r, 10r, 12r-v, 13r, 15r, 19v and 27v. The necessity of the science was particularly insisted upon in medical circles. Compare Rudolph Goclenius's defense in *Uraniae divinatricis* (Frankfurt: Schönwetter, 1608), "Turpe est igitur, ea reprehendere, quae quis ig-

norat; turpius est fundamenta artis convellere, quae quis non intelligit." A similar argument occurs in Giovanni Antonio Magini, *De astrologica ratione ac usu dierum criticorum* (Venice: Zenari, 1607).

12. *Della fisonomia dell'uomo*, ed. Mario Cicognani (Milan: Longanesi, 1971), pp. 210–12. Concerning Della Porta's theory, in addition to the articles in *Giambattista Della Porta nell'Europa del suo tempo* (Naples: Guida, 1990), see Cosimo Caputo, "La struttura del segno fisiognomico (Giambattista Della Porta e l'universo culturale del Cinquecento)," *Il Protagora* 22 (1982): 63–102.

13. *Coelestis physiognomonia*, ed. Alfonso Paolella (Naples: Edizioni scientifiche, 1996), Book 2, chap. 1.

14. *Morandi Trial*, fol. 6r bis.

15. See Alexandro Bastiaanse, *Teodoro Ameyden (1586–1656). Un Neerlandese alla corte di Roma* ('s Gravenhage: Staatsdrukkerij, 1968), p. 56.

16. *Morandi Trial*, fol. 3r.

CHAPTER SEVENTEEN
THE BODY OF THE ACCUSED

1. *Morandi Trial*, fol. 364v.

2. Prospero Farinacci, *Praxis et theorica criminales, pars 1 et 2* (Frankfurt: Endter, 1622), p. 598. In addition, Paulus Grillandus, *De quaestionibus et tortura* (Venice: Ziletti, 1584); Piero Fiorelli, *La tortura giudiziaria nel diritto comune*, 2 vols. (Milan: Giuffré, 1953–54); John H. Langbein, *Torture and the Law of Proof: Europe and England in the Ancien Regime* (Chicago: University of Chicago Press, 1977).

3. Farinacci, *Praxis et theorica criminales*, quaest. 36, no. 143.

4. Ibid., p. 598.

5. *Morandi Trial*, fol. 133r.

6. Ibid., fol. 146r.

7. Ibid., fol. 228r, report dated August 13, 1630.

8. Ibid., fol. 7r. Concerning early modern statehood as disciplining, see Paolo Prodi, ed., *Disciplina dell'anima, disciplina del corpo e disciplina della società tra Medioevo ed età moderna* (Bologna: Mulino, 1994).

9. Ibid., fol. 527v. The report was filed on November 13, 1630.

10. Vallombrosa, Archivio dell'Abbazia, cod. 6 II 5, fol. 80r.

11. *Bullarum, diplomatum et privilegiorum*, vol. 14, ed. Francisco Gaude (Turin: Dalmazzo, 1868), p. 211, dated April 1, 1631.

12. *Disputatio an bullae SS. Pontificum Sixti V et Urbani VIII contra iudiciarios, calumniam in aliquo patiantur*, in his *Atheismus triumphatus* (Paris: Dubray, 1636), p. 255.

13. Of the *Astrologicorum libri VII*, I consulted the edition of Frankfurt (Tampach, 1630), where the passages in question are in the unpaginated Praefatio. In addition, Didaco Pritto Pelusiensi [= Placido Titi], *Quaestionum physiomathematicarum libri tres* (Milan: Malatesta, 1647), chaps. 5–6.

14. This and the next quote are in *Astrologicorum libri VII*, p. 255. Other places mentioned are at pp. 256, 259–62, and 269.

15. Ibid., p. 272.

EPILOGUE

1. *Edizione nazionale delle opere* 14:236, dated March 29, 1631.

2. Here, and for what follows, the bibliography is immense and cannot be summarized. Apart from Mario Biagioli, *Galileo Courtier* (Berkeley: University of California Press, 1993), see, for the decision-making process at this time, as well as some of the issues involved, Pietro Redondi, *Galileo Heretic* (Princeton: Princeton University Press, 1987); taking account, however, of the comments in Vincenzo Ferrone and Massimo Firpo, "Galileo tra inquisitori e microstorici," *Rivista storica italiana* 97 (1985): 177–238, translated in *Journal of Modern History* 58 (1986): 485–524; and Redondi's reply, in *Rivista storica italiana* 97 (1985): 934–56. Concerning the Florentine context, Eric Cochrane, *Florence in the Forgotten Centuries* (Chicago: University of Chicago Press, 1973), Book 3. In addition, Leonida Rosino, "Il *Dialogo* come occasione per il processo e la condanna di Galileo," in *Giornate Lincee indette in occasione del 350° anniversario della pubblicazione del "Dialogo sopra i massimi sistemi" di Galileo Galilei, Roma, 6–7 maggio 1982* (Rome: Accademia Nazionale dei Lincei, 1983); articles in *Novità celesti e crisi del sapere. Atti del convegno internazionale di studi galileiani, 1982*, ed. Paolo Galluzzi (Florence: Giunti-Barbéra, 1984); Mario D'Addio, *Considerazioni sui processi a Galileo* (Rome: Herder, 1985); Eugenio Garin, "Gli scandali della nuova 'filosofia,'" *Nuncius* 8, n. 2 (1993): 417–31; Paolo Simoncelli, "Galileo e la curia: un problema," *Belfagor* 48 (1993): 29–42; as well as my *Science and the Marketplace in Early Modern Italy* (New York: Lexington Books, 2001), chap. 1.

3. On literacy and philosophy, Paola Zambelli, "From the *Quaestiones* to the *Essais*: On the Autonomy and Methods of the History of Philosophy," in G. Gavroglu et al., eds., *Science, Politics and Social Practice* (Dordrecht: Kluwer Academic Publishers, 1995), pp. 373–90.

4. Tommaso Garzoni, *Piazza universale di tutte le professioni del mondo* (Venice: Olivier Alberti, 1616), discourse no. 39, p. 161.

5. Antonio Bertolotti, "Giornalisti astrologi e negromanti in Roma nel secolo XVII," *Rivista europea* 5 (1878): 466–514.

6. Alexandro Bastiaanse, *Teodoro Ameyden (1586–1656). Un neerlandese alla corte di Roma* ('s Gravenhage: Staatsdrukkerij, 1968), chap. 4.

7. Luigi Fiorani, "Astrologi, superstiziosi e devoti nella società romana del Seicento," *Ricerche per la storia religiosa di Roma* 2 (1978): 97–162.

8. Germana Ernst, "Scienza, astrologia e politica nella Roma barocca. La biblioteca di don Orazio Morandi," ed. Eugenio Canone, *Bibliothecae selectae, da Cusano a Leopardi* (Florence: Olschki, 1993), pp. 217–32.

9. Starting with G. Campori, *Carteggio galileiano inedito con note ed appendici* (Modena, 1881), pp. 595–97.

10. Paul Poupard, "Introduzione," in Poupard, ed., *Galileo Galilei: 350 anni di storia (1633–1983)* (Rome: Edizioni Piemme, 1984).

11. Guido Morpurgo-Tagliabue, *I processi di Galileo e l'epistemologia* (Rome: Armando, 1981).

12. Giorgio De Santillana, *The Crime of Galileo* (Chicago: University of Chicago Press, 1955).

13. Concerning this theme, see John M. Headley, *Tommaso Campanella and the Transformation of the World* (Princeton: Princeton University Press, 1997), epilogue.

14. On this theme, Richard S. Westfall, *Science and Religion in Seventeenth-Century England* (New Haven: Yale University Press, 1958); Margaret J. Osler and Paul Lawrence Farber, eds., *Religion, Science, and Worldview: Essays in Honor of Richard S. Westfall* (Cambridge: Cambridge University Press, 1985); Paul Feyerabend and Christian Thomas, eds., *Wissenschaft und Tradition* (Zurich: Verlag der Fachvereine, 1983).

INDEX